VOLUME 27   NUMBER 1   2021

Queer Political Theologies

Edited by Ricky Varghese, David K. Seitz, and Fan Wu

Introduction: Queer Political Theologies

THEOSOPHY OF THE QUEER UNSEEN

Ricky Varghese

Two years ago, when this special issue was first conceived by David, Fan, and me, I would have never thought that I would be writing this introduction in the midst of a global pandemic. The world feels like a very different place now than it did then. A psychoanalyst I know (I am a practicing psychotherapist and am currently training to become a psychoanalyst myself at the Toronto Institute of Psychoanalysis) recently wrote to me in an email, "We are living history, I think" (pers. comm., April 3, 2020). And in a way, I would have to agree with her. There is definitely something quite historic about what feels like a cataclysm in the history of humanity, a period in which life as we know it may be changed forever.

But queers have already lived through a historic event involving a viral contagion, not too long ago. There are many critical differences between the HIV/AIDS epidemic and the current pandemic, but I also find myself thinking of the many similarities. Then, as well, there was a near-invisible, impossible-to-fathom object to reckon with. It reckoned with us, too. It reorganized how we lived, how we fucked, how we encountered each other, and how we communed with one another in both the intimacy we have come to expect in our private lives and the sociality on which our public worlds depended. Coronavirus will do the same. The coordinates of its reach and the scale of its magnitude may differ, but these "unseeable, undead, unliving blobs dotted with suction pads waiting to fasten themselves to our lungs," as writer Arundhati Roy (2020) referred to them, will irrevocably and in an almost obstinate manner reconstitute human life in ways that have yet to become clear to us. Clarity—in all senses of the word—evades us in this moment, be it with respect to what the future may look like for us locally and globally or even in regard to our ever-evolving knowledge about this new virus.

Garden-variety philosophical punditry aside—punditry that is as much a byproduct of the helplessness many of us might presently be feeling as of knowl-

GLQ 27:1

DOI 10.1215/10642684-8776820

edge production, of having the first say or the final word on the topic; a kind of punditry that can ostensibly find fertile ground amid the ruins of a crisis—I have been taken in by the need to reexamine the course and nature of doing the work of producing theory in this very instance. What can queer theory, or the theological impulses within social and political life, possibly teach us about the present? How might we engage theoretical work in the foreground of a crisis-ridden eschatological background? On what object or objects of inquiry might the shadow of our thought and thinking, our very queer way of thinking and living, fall? What, even, might knowledge production mean in this version of what appears to be a kind of end times?

There might not be any easily arrived-at answers to these concerns. However, when we consider how life might be reorganized and reconstituted at a scale that may be unimaginable or inconceivable, for which we are not prepared in the least, one thing may indeed be certain: what we are reckoning with right now is an experience with loss. And along with that experience of loss, an experience with grief and grieving. On one hand, there is the very real potential loss of life of those most vulnerable to the illness at hand, the precarious tether on which our lives and the lives of our loved ones may be hanging ever so gently. In another register, there is also the loss of the ways of living to which we may have arguably become accustomed or that we have come to take for granted, like sitting on a park bench, going for a walk, picking up groceries, gathering at a club, at a community event, a bathhouse, or even a religious assembly. Even the gestures of conviviality and sociality have changed for the foreseeable future. A handshake now feels as risky as barebacking might have to some. Even the ways in which we seek and offer support have shifted, as in the case of my own therapeutic practice, which has moved entirely to working with my patients over the phone.

Psychoanalysis replicates something of the theological sensibility that is a particular mainstay of the Judeo-Islamo-Christian faith trifecta. These Abrahamic traditions are well-known for their prohibition against images when it comes to conceptualizing the figure of God. Unrepresentable, God may variously be experienced as a spirit or force or unseen figure in, an invisible host to, or a guest within the life of a believer. Similarly, in the therapeutic scene of psychoanalysis, the encounter between analyst and analysand (or patient, as they are more colloquially known) appears to have an element of the unseen that is implicit to this dyadic relationship. The patient walks into the analyst's office and is led to the couch, on which the former lies down to engage in the emotional work that therapy demands. The analyst sits, listening, some short distance behind and away from the couch. What is enacted is an exchange in which the analyst is never in the line of the patient's vision and remains unseen as such for the duration of the session. This allows the patient, in a relaxed manner and free from the presumption of judgment, to speak freely and free-associatively about their emotional world. The immediately perceivable difference between the experience of a believer's communion with the invisible figure of God and that of an analysand in a session with their analyst is that, in the latter scenario, the analyst is ostensibly present in the room with the analysand, and the latter is aware of this corporeal presence in a very immediately responsive manner. It is not that the analyst is God, in this instance, or even God-like, but that there is a theological and theosophical edge to the belief that an analysand might place in the analyst, a belief in the sense that the analyst is truly and earnestly listening to their worries and concerns, not dissimilar to the way a believer ardently believes their prayers are being heard.

Moving our work from the space of my office to the phone in the wake of the pandemic—a requirement that was put in place taking to heart the public health advisory regarding social distancing that was announced in various jurisdictions—has added another layer of disembodiment to the dyadic experience of analytic work, in one sense perhaps bringing it closer to the dynamic between a believer and a truly unseen version of God. Phone sessions require an altogether different kind of psychic energy, it feels, to work from within. I miss the ritual of having my patients come in physically for their sessions. My patients have admitted to feelings of profound loss tied to this ritual as well. If an aspect of psychoanalytic work requires the development of an acute and highly attuned capacity on the part of the analyst to listen, then listening to one's patient's disembodied voice—or their listening to your own disembodied voice—requires a finer sort of attunement and tests the very nature of listening itself. In the absence of both my patients' and my physical yet unseen presence in the same space, the virus has come to reconstitute the very ways by which therapy has taken place thus far. There is a sort of grief and mourning at play here in what has transpired over the last few weeks, a grief and mourning related to the things we have lost.

Furthermore, while both the scene of psychoanalysis and the Abrahamic version of God require a structure of belief in an unseen figure, the ontological nature of the virus is determined by an affect altogether seemingly different: fear in the unseen. We know the virus exists. Microscopic imaging has made it possible to visually represent it. We also feel its effects in the varied symptoms it presents us with. However, rendered invisible to the naked eye and wildly contagious, it feels omnipresent. Every surface should be presumed to be a host to the microbial matter, every person should be understood to be an unwitting carrier, according to the logics of social distancing protocols that have been put in place the world over. Tanya Goel, a visual artist based in Delhi, India, created a series of sound-based videos archiving the silence that has enveloped quotidian life in the country under a national lockdown. The series of images on Instagram, titled "'The Virus in the Air, Is Abstract,' Spring in Curfew, Sounds in Spring" (2020), records the silence in the air as the virus makes its way even more quietly through the nation of 1.3 billion. The virus in the air might be an abstraction, borne of both a belief in its pervasiveness and a fear of its indiscernible reach, which translates to a fear of the other. The material losses incurred, the ravage it leaves behind in its wake, however, may not be so abstract.

It is with these thoughts in mind that I pushed forth in compiling this special issue with my collaborators on the interplay between the queer and the theological in the scene and space of the political. We attempted, to the best of our abilities and for the time being, to organize an issue that made room for a diversity of voices, disciplinary approaches, and ethical and sociopolitical investments. This compilation is not, in the least bit, exhaustive. We hope that it is but a mere yet potentially worthwhile contribution and provocation to what is an ongoing set of debates. I would like to take this opportunity as well to express thanks to our various contributors for their richly incisive essays, to the peer reviewers whose comments and insights only further strengthened this issue, and to Umair Abdul Qadir, whose critical eye and acumen facilitated the copyediting and proofreading of the issue's manuscript in its entirety. I hope that you find the texts here a worthwhile read demanding of close engagement, whichever end of the queer political theological debate you find yourself on.

References

Goel, Tanya (@tanyagoel01). 2020. "'The Virus in the Air, Is Abstract,' Spring in Curfew, Sounds in Spring, 2020." Instagram photo, April 15. instagram.com/p/B _AO3WDpMN-lFP_AKGdozrsRKwcmmiKYNjNBXk0.

Roy, Arundhati. 2020. "The Pandemic Is a Portal." *Financial Times*, April 3. ft.com /content/10d8f5e8-74eb-11ea-95fe-fcd274e920ca.

HOME FOR NEITHER BIRD NOR HOLINESS

Fan Wu

*T*he world in which we live is too dire to call foolish and too funny to forsake.
Stained glass learns to begin to rust.
The gay pain of your early twenties shoots like a spine through your bum hip:
      round these
parts we wander approximating power or mistaking talk for it.
The name is holy, socketed by chains to keep it not carried away by whatever
      passing wind.

There's a sheathe of frost that lines your pockets.
The stars above Gabriola are cut at part-dawn
by a hawk whose windtrail blurs those stars' light.
I am waiting to be removed by love.
Those who are closest to knowing
what they don't know are halfway dwellers, who unite the more rigid masses by
      dint of the liminal.
The view from up top seems impossible, cloud and sea speckle into each other.

We sit and compose a human knot.
Now we are holding hands and forming a parameter around the divine.
Now we are vividly lost to ourselves and transfixed to breath.
Now family's a loop de loop fountain
of ceaseless blood in chromakey cycle.
Now we swallow pandemic fears and speak not in tongues of revelation.
Now we risk only the Identity that stands next to death.
Now there's lichen in our eyes obscuring our view of the kingdom.

Now a chewy fog of dissolution settles at the base of the lung.
Fables deform us; the same stars we'd used to chart our course lay stunned at the
      bag's
bottom, smelling of sheep's knuckle and whalebone.
What gnaws at our lives as we gather in silos, drinking water and listening to
      music?

A paralytic power gestates:
Nor Lord nor state but the haze of hope and how slow its speed,
encratered in the hurry of
the litheness of a line that would divide East from waste.
The worried talk to God goes on.

THE BERN: A QUEER POLITICAL THEOLOGICAL FEELING

David K. Seitz

"Both the notion of having a rupture with your self *and* the notion of
narrated personal coherence are Protestant conventions, heightened
in all the American variants of Protestantism."
—Michael Warner, "Tongues Untied: Memories of a Pentecostal
Boyhood"

$\mathcal{I}$'ll never forget my mother's words to me when I came out to her again, this time
as a democratic socialist: "Is this going to go on your permanent record?"

Her query recalls brutal and ongoing histories of state surveillance and
repression of leftists and queers, as well as more banal practices of disciplinary
infantilization well known to a wide range of historically subordinated persons.
But beyond this expression of concern, my mother was unfazed, not particularly
surprised by my "news."

Chantal Mouffe (2000: 102, original emphasis) writes that "to accept the
view of the [political] adversary is to undergo a radical change in political identity.
It is more a sort of *conversion* than a process of rational persuasion." History is
littered with dramatic socialist conversion stories with heavy religious overtones
(Debs 1908) as well as apocalyptic, racist, and erotophobic right-wing warnings of
socialist "recruitment" (Bérubé 2011). Many such conversions are precipitated by
galvanizing historical events—in my case, a graduate teaching assistant strike in
Toronto and Bernie Sanders's historic US presidential campaigns. But the actual
event of conversion often follows years of rumination and experimentation—for me,

a gradual drift away from the neoliberal, white suburban Democratic party politics of my childhood, nurtured by independent media and queer activism. Indeed, as Michael Warner (2004) reminds us, political-theological conversions are rarely total ruptures. Both my Lutheran upbringing and my training in queer theory have in fact nurtured my socialist sensibilities.

These affinities are in part intellectual. For all its faults (and they are considerable), Lutheran theology's emphasis on God's capacious, loving grace, rather than individual good works, as the path to salvation informs and shapes my appreciation for the radical ethical potential of universal social programs like single-payer healthcare. I am accordingly skeptical of neoliberal, means-tested approaches to social welfare reliant upon essentialized hierarchies of deservingness (Hagan 2019), approaches against which socialist, feminist, queer, Black, and other racialized activists and scholars have long militated (Cohen 1997; Day 2018). And although I was a middling student of the Lutheran catechism in high school, the central place of writers ranging from the Combahee River Collective (1983) to Lisa Duggan (2003) to Jasbir K. Puar (2007) in my undergraduate and graduate training formatively introduced me to critiques of racial capitalism and empire as the indispensable contexts for understanding gender and sexual politics (Taylor 2012).

But my attachment to democratic socialism, an affinity that shows up in the mundane work of organizing, is also profoundly, queerly visceral. For one thing, I have never teared up so regularly as at political organizing meetings or rallies, as complete strangers open up to me about the horror that the US healthcare or criminal justice system has wrought in their lives, or as long-repressed socialist and anti-imperialist convictions belatedly and provisionally (re)enter into politically admissible speech in the United States. I have also been surprised by the ways in which my banal, anxious habitus cultivated on queer Internet hookup and dating apps—mustering the openness required for fleeting, alienating, potentially thrilling, disappointing, boring, life-changing, or even life-threatening encounters with strangers every weekend—has prepared me for the improvisatory, cross-race, cross-class intimacies of door-to-door canvassing for a political organizing campaign (Delany 1999). And although I have never knocked on doors as a (formally) religious evangelist, I would imagine proselytizers experience similar surprises in these strange conversations, listening intently, going off-script, giving voice to their training and convictions in unpredictable, sometimes inchoate ways, as the moment might seem suddenly to require.

My previous scholarly work examines the radical political potential of affective moments when normatively white, queer, Protestant formations are dis-rupted, moved beyond liberal identitarian states of injury (Brown 1995) toward more coalitional and capacious forms of solidarity. "What are the *affective* con-ditions," I ask, "under which differently marginalized people might engage in meaningful solidarity and reciprocal intimacy with one another?" (Seitz 2017: 227, original emphasis). There are many answers to this question. But I hear the begin-nings of one answer in Sanders's own question (2019), which became something of a religious refrain for campaign volunteers: "Are you willing to fight for a person you don't know as much as you're willing to fight for yourself?" Julia Kristeva would have a field day.

Our aim in this special issue is to build on scholarly accounts of this strange, visceral *queerness* already immanent to political-theological life and to efforts to transform it. Reflecting on the relationship between his Pentecostal upbringing and his latter-day secular queer theorizing, Warner (2004) notes affinities between Pen-tecostal and queer ethical and textual practices—a profoundly suspicious herme-neutic tradition and a visceral, pleasurable investment in the cancellation of the world in its present form.

But narrative and subjectivity are not the only game in town here. In his consideration of what he amalgamates as "Blackpentecostalism" for Black study and Black queer studies, Ashon T. Crawley (2017: 4, original emphasis) privileges the transformative work of flesh, vibration, movement, aesthetics, and performance, arguing that "the tradition of [Blackpentecostal] performances is an *a*theological-*a*philosophical project, produced against the grain of liberal logics of subjectivity." Crawley's approach reverberates with the work of psychoanalytic critic Eric L. Sant-ner (2011: 60), for whom the sovereign subject is also "fundamentally precarious," because it is "subject, in a singular fashion, to a radical ontological vulnerability whereby a form of life can become horribly *informe* [shapeless]." But where the sov-ereign, for Santner, fears the "formlessness" that the liminal space between forms of creaturely life entails, Crawley (2017: 2), working in the abolitionist tradition of Black studies, sees liberation, transformation, "otherwise possibilities."

Each of the contributions to our special issue examines precisely this site of jointure, the place where people's nonnormative erotic, affective, and psychic invest-ments exceed or depart from secular, (neo)liberal forms of political-theological life. Such excesses offer glimmers of otherwise possibilities—possibilities that Crawley is quick to point out are not necessarily new but remain immanent in potentially emancipatory ways. Such visceral attachments to otherwise possibility, because they are irreducible to philosophy or theology, will always elide capture—whether, to return to my mother's query, by the disciplinary form of a "permanent record" or even by the more pleasantly subjectivizing form of my Democratic Socialists of America membership card. Our collective project in this special issue, then, is not one of capture, but one of thinking with and through *some* otherwise possibilities of *some* queer political theologies, with the knowledge that no academic journal article or issue could ever come close to exhausting them.

References

Bérubé, Allan. 2011. *My Desire for Queer History: Essays in Gay Community and Labor History*. Chapel Hill: University of North Carolina Press.

Brown, Wendy. 1995. *States of Injury: Power and Freedom in Late Modernity*. Princeton, NJ: Princeton University Press.

Cohen, Cathy J. 1997. "Punks, Bulldaggers, and Welfare Queens: The Radical Potential of Queer Politics?" *GLQ* 3, no. 4: 437–65.

Combahee River Collective. 1983. "The Combahee River Collective Statement." In *Home Girls: A Black Feminist Anthology*, edited by Barbara Smith, 264–74. New York: Kitchen Table: Women of Color Press.

Crawley, Ashon T. 2017. *Blackpentecostal Breath: The Aesthetics of Possibility*. New York: Fordham University Press.

Day, Meagan. 2018. "Targeted Programs Make Easy Targets." *Jacobin*, January 14. jacobinmag.com/2018/01/targeted-social-programs-make-easy-targets.

Debs, Eugene V. 1908. "How I Became a Socialist." In *Debs: His Life Writings and Speeches*, 79–84. Girard, KS: Appeal to Reason.

Delany, Samuel R. 1999. *Times Square Red, Times Square Blue*. New York: New York University Press.

Duggan, Lisa. 2003. *The Twilight of Equality? Neoliberalism, Cultural Politics, and the Attack on Democracy*. Boston: Beacon.

Hagan, Ampson. 2019. "How Medicare For All Challenges our Ideas of Black Deservingness." *Somatosphere*, May 27. somatosphere.net/2019/how-medicare-for-all-challenges-our-ideas-of-black-deservingness.

Mouffe, Chantal. 2000. *The Democratic Paradox*. London: Verso.

Puar, Jasbir K. 2007. *Terrorist Assemblages: Homonationalism in Queer Times*. Durham, NC: Duke University Press.

Sanders, Bernie (@BernieSanders). 2019. "Are you willing to fight for a person you don't know as much as you're willing to fight for yourself?" Twitter, December 8. twitter.com/berniesanders/status/1203783495748849664

Santner, Eric L. 2011. *The Royal Remains: The People's Two Bodies and the Endgames of Sovereignty*. Chicago: University of Chicago Press.

Seitz, David K. 2017. *A House of Prayer for All People: Contesting Citizenship in a Queer Church*. Minneapolis: University of Minnesota Press.

Taylor, Keeanga-Yamahtta. 2012. *How We Get Free: Black Feminism and the Combahee River Collective*. Chicago: Haymarket.

Warner, Michael. 2004. "Tongues Untied, Memoirs of a Pentecostal Boyhood." In *Curiouser: On the Queerness of Children*, edited by Steven Bruhm and Natasha Hurley, 215–24. Minneapolis: University of Minnesota Press.

SUSCEPTIBILITY

Ashon Crawley

0

*A*nd black life is circum-sacred, it is a kind of life that is antagonistic to the division between sacred and secular, holy and profane, and is enacted when such a distinction is not allowed to be believed. Circum-sacred names the fact of the centrifugal-centripetal—which, together, is the centrifugitive—movement as constituting a way of life. Black life is about relation, about sociality, in orbit. Because of the circum-sacred, what is marked is the deep and complex relationship between that which is considered to be black religiosity and that which is considered to be, on the other side and categorically distinct, black sociality. This division, I argue, is illusory and unnecessary, impossible to order, impossible to enclose, impossible to maintain. And, I also argue, the circum-sacred performance staged in the space of Blackpentecostalism—the fleshliness, the speaking in tongues, the use of breath, the commenting on and critique of language as speaking in tongues, the shouting and euphoria—the Black Church, in general, is imagined in popular culture as Blackpentecostal.

That is, what Blackpentecostals are known to do, what they are known to have cultivated, is how the Black Church as a historical institution is imagined in the social imagination. This does not mean that every church is or does what Blackpentecostals are or do, but that the imagined relation to popular culture is one of this particular performance. This also does not mean, importantly, that Blackpentecostals own or are the originators of the practices they engage. It just means that they cultivated, tended to, and allowed to flourish a particular mode of refusal.[1] Blackpentecostalism is *exemplary* of otherwise possibility, not the normative space from which possibility emerges, because it does not emerge from any space as a kind of pure object. The sacred does not belong to particular religious traditions or to the zone and category and enclosure called the religious itself. This

GLQ 27:1
DOI 10.1215/10642684-8776834
© 2021 by Duke University Press

epistemological shifting, the search for otherwise possibility of religion and the social as nondivisional, is the gift of friendship and the interruption to political theology.

Further, yet, and still, I argue that all black performance is imagined to have the capacity to produce circum-sacred possibility reached for in Blackpentecostalism. Because of the illusory division between black religiosity and black sociality, what black popular culture, in general, reaches and strives for is the affective mood and movement (but not, it must be said and maintained, the doctrinal and theological thought) of Blackpentecostal energy, fervor, and verve. Blackpentecostalism is *an* example—not the only one, of course—of what black life performs, practices, produces in terms of joy, love, relation. The spirit, the movement, and verve desired in religious Blackpentecostal performance is reached for and desired for all black performance. And so, we speculate on characters and characterizations in black popular culture that announce black religiosity to learn something about black gender and sexuality, and to learn about and contend against the interruption to political theology simultaneously. Black performance is complex and complexity, it is complicated and it complicates. This is a speculative writing, attempting to reach for energy and spirit and verve in the cause of love.

The (assumed to be cisgender) male choir director and male church pianist and organist have, in circum-sacred performance, been made to carry the content of queerness as objects of desire as well as carry queer desire and queerness *as* desirous.[2] Because they are friends. And because friendship can serve as a way of life (Foucault 1997). As such, the male choir director and male musician, imagined as Blackpentecostal, are meant to stand in for a range of queer possibilities in black social life in general (and I think black men singing non-gospel music also have to contend with the imagined queerness of black singing because of these characters). Notions of black masculinity are often antithetical to spirituality precisely because of the worry over porosity and vulnerability that spirituality seems to require.

This article is an attempt to put into relation various modes of black performance: the vibration emanating from a Hammond organ; the practice of friendship of Black American Muslim women; what I call the *an*epistemology of feeling; the sound of Islam; the problem blackness poses to the concepts *political* and *theology*. This writing jumps and leaps and moves like chord changes, the thread that binds together being the *key signature*, and resolving in the tonic, of black performance, the idea that anything can be put in relation if we attend to performance of possibility. This article contends that characters in black popular culture might give us a way to think the generativity and spirit of black life. And the hope is that this article will prompt the imaginations of readers to consider characters and characterizations in ways that augment and enliven what is here, what is here but not fleshed out, what is here but remains hidden.

I

And we have to figure out a way to be together. To begin here with the word *and* is to begin with the joint, with the connection, with the hinge. But then and also, to begin with the word *and* is to imply with intense force that there was something before that could be connected, that there was a mode of operation that is announced by a kind of absence, an absence that is present in the word, in the concept, in the beginning, such that beginning is *not*. And . . .

There is a presence that pervades black life, a presence that Western constructions for rationality and instrumentality have renounced. But this presence remains in and as blackness—blackness as the refusal of renunciation of the flesh, of the social—a presence found in what I call circum-sacred performance, a presence that is about marking relation, existence, or being *with*, a presence that is about sociality as the ground of irreducibly plural existence. This circum-sacred is that which black life is gathered around but is, like vibration detected as sound and song of music some might call nothing,[3] there but barely raised to the level of detection though it is sensed, felt, known. Like blackqueerness, the fact of the presence of "nothing" does not necessarily occasion the celebration of it, and for some produces relinquishment, the giving up of it, though—like blackqueerness—that which is considered by some to be "nothing" is what makes life worth living. What can the vibration-as-sound-and-song emanating from the Blackpentecostal worship space tell us about life and love as queer horizon and thrust?

In his argument about words and things, about knowledge and how it is ordered, Michel Foucault turns to the enunciative power of the breath, of the word, of the spoken, which is another way to say, he turns to the performance of relation made through sound. He says (1990: 27), "There is no binary division to be made between what one says and what one does not say; we must try to determine the different ways of not saying such things. . . . There is not one but many silences, and they are an integral part of the strategies that underlie and permeate discourses." Silence is the surround, it is the wraparound, the turnaround chord, it is the inventive space of possibility because one must hear into the silence, feel its vibration, understand something of what such silence—before and after words, a kind of stylizing of momentary quietude—is attempting to say. Silence is like, and is, nothing. Can you feel it?

The Hammond B-3 organist in the Blackpentecostal tradition helps me think about silence, saying, and the relation between. The Hammond B-3 organist also lets me think about the power of the flesh that produces protest through praise. With the Hammond musician, I think about the ways—and investigate the fact—that there is no binary division between what the instrument says and plays and what it does not say and play, such that attending to relation between what is and is not sounded out is raised to the level of existential concern and, perhaps even, an attempt to wrestle with an, if not *the*, existential crisis: what does it mean to be, to be in relation, to be otherwise than Man?[4] The musician stages and performs—which, stated plainly, heightens the awareness of listeners to the ongoing presence of—the intersensual and the intersonical, which tells us something about how life emerges against binary logics of thought, performance, practice, breath. The fact of intersensuality and intersonicality cannot go unremarked.

The intersensual is here defined as the production of feeling and feel as a communal practice and process, feeling and feel as a collective, improvisational intellectual practice. The intersensual names the fact that feeling and feel is always *between things*: whether the mechanical instrument and the musician, the musician's chording and the congregation, the congregation and preacher, between congregants, or—most likely—between all these various objects in varied intensities. The intersensual names the fact of sense as communal and always in-process. What can attending to these mutually constitutive, and at times overlapping, at times contentious, relations reveal about blackness, the sacred, and the practice of social life? And what when such social life is practiced by way of rumor, gossip, and categories that attempt to contain and denounce the very fact of its existence? The intersensual announced that fact of feeling and feel always being in relation, only ever being about and belonging to the social.

And I define *intersonicality*, here, as the space between instrumentalists; it is about the relationality that is played out—that emerges—in the vibrations of sound and song, that is supposed to mark the difference of the same, a difference that is about relation and sociality. Intersonicality is one practice of the intersensual, though there are certainly others. The intersensual and intersonical index the fact of openness and availability as the way knowledge is produced through feeling, through what the musicians play, through which the music is felt. What is carried, what is the content released, from such performance? The sounding out of the instrument is about what is not played and what is played and the relation, complex and ongoing, between the two. But there is no easy division between what is and is not; it is a relation of intensity and dynamism. It is the practice of everyday blackqueer life.

One thing unsaid but certainly felt and told is the blackqueerness of black sacred music. One way the unsaid is felt and told is through rumor and gossip that circulate about the density and potentiality of blackqueer relationality (Crawley 2013). Alisha Lola Jones (2017: 216), for example, notes, "When I share with African American gospel enthusiasts that I research Black men's performance of gender and sexuality in gospel music, the most frequent responses I receive are: 'Why are there so many "effeminate" men in music ministries? And why are so many choir directors gay?'" I want to linger with the question, not of gayness and effeminacy as forms of identity per se, but with the idea that with the very contemplation, with the very thinking about, with the practice of sound and song, a space is opened up for us to think about blackness and queer possibility as emerging from an intensely and intentionally sacred desire and relation to worlds.

I agree with Eve Kosofsky Sedgwick (2008: 24): "There is a large family of things *we know* and need to know about ourselves and each other with which we have, as far as I can see, so far created for ourselves almost no theoretical room to deal." I inflect this to consider the ways blackqueerness as circum-sacred is known but also how this knowing can only emerge by way of rumor and gossip, and how rumor and gossip can be the theoretical space of operation, how rumor and gossip can be the theoretical room in which thought can occur, flourish, be argued over, contended with and against. Listening to the Hammond and considering circum-sacred sound and song of black popular culture is of vital importance and urgency because we must continue to sense and feel and contend against the effects of ongoing misogynoir, homophobia, transphobia, and a general antagonism against blackqueer life and flourishing. There is a presence of blackqueerness, like the sound and song of nothing music, with which there is no theoretical room to deal and which creates the occasion for the violence against blackqueer life.

Yet the presence of blackqueerness makes possible the very practice of praise and worship. A strong claim, to be sure, but one I am willing to wager in the hopes of a liberatory practice, a liberatory form of life. Often considered to be the sissy in the sanctuary,[5] the category of this character is a kind of containment that simultaneously announces and denounces the presence of blackqueerness. To quote from Sedgwick (2008: 27), again, I seek "to ask how certain categorizations work, what enactments they are performing and what relations they are creating, rather than what they essentially *mean*." What does placing blackqueerness in the music *do* in terms of a full range of affectional possibility, without ever reducing such possibility to the Western constructs of intimacy and delimitation? What do the characters of the sissies—whether choir director or Hammond musician—*do* to the life of a doctrinal position and theological inclination that demean queerness as a way of life? What does the categorization of the music—as the space from which queerness emerges and returns for the circum-sacred performance of blackness to occur—produce in terms of relational possibility, even if such possibility is denounced after having been put online?

But I also agree with later, post-*Epistemology*, Sedgwick (Sedgwick and Frank 2003: 124): when speaking about whether research about HIV/AIDS was a racialized, sexualized, militaristic conspiracy, she said, "Whether or not to undertake this highly compelling tracing-and-exposure project represents a strategic and local decision, not necessarily a categorical imperative." She continued by stating that it is important "to open a space for moving from the rather fixated question Is a particular piece of knowledge true, and how can we know? to the further questions: What does knowledge *do*—the pursuit of it, having and exposing of it, the receiving again of knowledge of what one already knows? *How*, in short, is knowledge performative, and how best does one move among its causes and effects?" This means, for me, that I must ask the question, why the concern about tracing the blackqueerness of this music: what does it allow us to do, to make, to think, to be?

My search for the rumor and gossip, and what this mode makes available for thought, for imagination, in black popular culture as uniquely situated to bespeak something about blackqueerness, is not a reading of and with paranoia as object, as Sedgwick describes. Mine is a descriptive project, an attempt to think relation and not suppression. I am interested in the many ways—after Foucault—relation happens through what is veiled suppression, veiled repression; we have to seek relation otherwise, sociality like and as feeling the spirit in the dark. This is a blackqueer sensing (I am resisting the word *reading* here for the moment) of possibility that goes in multiple directions simultaneously. It is not a search for symmetry that Sedgwick posits paranoia does as method, it is not a search for equilibrium and balance; this is a search for the affective excesses that are blackqueerness, a mode of living and relation that is previous to situation—philosophical, theological, political or, here even, psychoanalytic. I am not attempting to for the last time uncover "the truth" of blackqueerness as some kind of coherent object that can be known in fullness, that can be fully exhausted. I am searching for the practice of blackqueerness as the undergrounded destabilizing force that allows the flourishing of the question of black life itself, the question of nothingness, the playing of existential concerns.

And I think post-*Epistemology* Sedgwick is correct to argue that visibility and *exposure* of the "truth" will not itself change the epistemology of violence and violation that makes the doctrinal and theological practices that shame blackqueerness. She asks (Sedgwick and Frank 2003: 141), "The paranoid trust in exposure seemingly depends . . . on an infinite reservoir of naïveté in those who make up the audience for these unveilings. What is the basis for assuming that it will surprise or disturb, never mind motivate, anyone to learn that a given social manifestation is artificial, self-contradictory, imitative, phantasmatic, or even violent?" What is necessary, and what this article attempts, is a sensing of vibration as sound not to replace sight but to say the visibility of exposure as the possibility for correction is itself part of ocularcentric epistemology of Western thought with its very modern liberal subjects. Sound occasions an epistemological ordering that allows for the full range of sense experience to be the grounds, not a hierarchy, of fleshed feeling.

I am attempting to think with the Black Church's production of music and musicality to think about the construction of gendered and sexed flesh, and I argue that a sound-studies analysis of music making makes vulnerability and openness not possible but noticeable, not possible but detectable. What the vibration-as-sound-and-song announces, underscores, and undergrounds is the anoriginal vulnerability and openness as a fleshly, unbounded way of life. There is a complex relation between musicality and race when thinking about masculinity, when thinking about the aspiration for manhood, straightness. Music making is a place that opens up and breaks down such possibility for aspiration. I want to ask what we can know from the musicality of black religiosity, what the *an*epistemology of black sacred sound making is. This is explicitly a project drawing on black feminist, womanist, blackqueer critiques of ethics, of epistemology, of Man, ethics, worldviews, and a moral center based on exclusion and renunciation of the flesh, which is to say blackness and the feminine and queerness.

II

And it's all about friendship, right? It's all about the possibility for establishing, and, after having established, maintaining relationship. But what would it mean to say that it—life, the worlds we inhabit, the zones from which we have been excluded or in which we have been included—is itself about the practice of friendship? It is, for me at least, to go where I always go, to Foucault and his interview "Friendship as a Way of Life" (1997); it is to underscore the fact that what we are is ephemeral and inventional, that ours is a way of life we have to commit to fashioning, as Foucault might say, to invent from *A* to *Z* a practice of relation that is formless in its inception. But more, I think about the "joyful militancy" of friendship:

>Can friendship be revalued as a radical, transformative form of kinship? . . .
>Under neoliberalism, friendship is a banal affair of private preferences:
>we hang out, we share hobbies, we make small talk. We become friends
>with those who are already like us, and we keep each other comfortable,
>rather than becoming different and more capable together. . . . . This neolib-
>eral friend is the alternative to hetero- and homonormative coupling: "just
>friends" implies a much weaker and insignificant bond than a lover could
>ever be. Under neoliberal friendship, we don't have each other's backs,
>and our lives aren't tangled up together. But these insipid tendencies do
>not mean that friendships are pointless; only that friendship is a terrain of
>struggle. (Bergman and Montgomery 2017: 93)

Friendship is a site of struggle. It is not a thing we know, it is not an object we
can hold. It is only a practice in which we share, a practice that has the capacity to unmake us over and over again. It is formless. And to make a claim for
the formlessness of the initial, of the previous to form and constitution, is to say
that incoherence, dissidence, or what my friend Sylvia Chan-Malik (2018) might
call *againstness*, is what we have as our right of birth and breath. Friendship is not
just theoretical, it is about a practice of being in the world with others, practicing
difference as dissidence, practicing difference as the very possibility for care. To
say that friendship is formless at its inception is to say that something could be
connected, could be joined, could be hinged such that friendship would be the
result, that—like the word *and*—there was something that could be connected,
that could be joined, that could be hinged. I am after that thing, that thing that
precedes form that makes available and possible connection, I am interested in
what kind of thought practice is necessary, what do we think we are and have to be,
in order for there to be possibility?

Chan-Malik's *Being Muslim: A Cultural History of Women of Color in
American Islam* makes me think about friendship, friendship between women,
which is another modality of the possibility of connecting and joining and hing-
ing the same with difference. I think about the way she discusses Toni Morrison's
Sula, how "they were neither white nor male, and that all freedom and triumph was
forbidden to them" such that they had to "set about creating something else to be"
(Chan-Malik 2018: 33), which meant a kind of reckless abandon against what the
world would tell them they should be and do and how they should behave, a reckless abandon as a kind of social ecstatics, an outpouring and being beside oneself
in the service and cause of the one that is different, the one that could be joined,
as friendship. What Chan-Malik's rumination on friendship of two women in *Sula*

poses for me is the question: can this be a model for how we can be together, can it help us figure out how to practice with one another?

What Chan-Malik demonstrates, especially in the chapter "Four American Moslem Women," is that it takes courage and wisdom—as Stevphen Shukaitis (2011) might say—to make worlds, and theirs was a courageous intellectual practice of wisdom precisely because there was no model by which they could detect black women as Muslim except by what they imagined, what they constituted together with texture and verve. What they were, what they'd become, was through what Chan-Malik (2018: 44) calls their visionariness—"women who came to look at, inhabit, and experience the world as Black American Muslim women during a time when there was no such thing. To see the world as Muslim women required their continual vigilance and labor, not only in terms of Islamic practices, like praying or fasting, but also by navigating how they as Black women could enact and embody Islamic practices in the racialized and gendered environments in which they lived." This is a visionariness that I would augment and describe as their audiovisual imagination, a choreosonic way of life.

What I mean by *choreosonic* for the four Black American Muslim women in the photograph with which Chan-Malik produces a speculative ahistoriographic way for us to understand the day-to-day operations, particularly of Sister Zeineb, is that they had to choreograph and sound out continually together as mutually constitutive practice, a way that was formless, a way that utilized their inventional and creative impulses, the practice of a collective improvisational imagination. The photograph Chan-Malik thinks about displays women who are utilizing the technologies they have in order to practice piety that desired to inculcate, Saba Mahmood might argue,[6] their sartorial style as unique to the individual but in the service of a collective practice of difference.

But to dress as they did—and one wonders what the result of such dress would be on Wabash Avenue in 1920s and 1930s Chicago—in the time that they did, to call attention to themselves as such dressing must have done, is to say that there was a kind of courage and fortitude, a kind of joyful militancy, to use the language of Carla Bergman and Nick Montgomery, and delight and pleasure from marking out difference, a kind of practice of exuberance and seriousness. They practice what Chan-Malik (2018: 15) describes as *affective insurgency*, "the multiscalar, diffuse, and ever-shifting forms of againstness" that life takes when one lives as difference, whether desired or forced or some combination thereof. Againstness, the affective insurgency, Chan-Malik says, "is not, nor has never been directed at a single target; instead it is a set of affective responses that emerge out of the ways Islam is consistently lived insurgently by women, responses that arise out of the ways US Muslim women engage, navigate, and encounter the ways Islam is imagined as an unruly and insurgent political presence at various moments in history" (16).

Friendship is on my mind because of the urgency of our times, by which I mean this long historical moment called modernity with its thought-philosophical, thought-theological, thought-political, thought-ethical, thought-epistemological that was inaugurated before 1492 and that remains with us. Perhaps Cedric J. Robinson would say the gestating moment of racial capitalism as a thought practice was deployed on and against Europeans first, and finds its *perfection* with its encounter with Amerindians and Africans stolen and transported to the so-called New World. We are still in the *thenthere* of that *whenwhere*. This political economy is about perfectibility grounded in Christian doctrine that considers itself the perfectible, or even supersessionist, form of Greek thought. And if we are still living the *thenthere* of that *whenwhere*, then perfectibility seeks to devour still.

This to say that perfectibility might be a problem for thought, a problem against the flourishing of life, a problem thwarting friendship. The perfectibility problem in Western thought is continual and is the grounds for various forms of violence. New modes of violence—Islamophobia, for example—with regard to perfectibility do not come to replace settler colonial genocide as ongoing or anti-black violence as perpetual but come to augment with otherwise modalities of the same, targeted toward same old new populations.

Robinson, in his *Black Marxism: The Making of the Black Radical Tradition* ([1983] 2000), sharpens for readers the idea that racial capitalism is a mode of organization that is internal to European thought, that racialization is not universal but is an ethnocentrism that has taken on global force and magnitude. The encounter with African and New World labor was a *making perfectible* the racialization logic; thus I focus on perfectibility as a problem for thought, a problem of interrogation. Robinson says,

> Europe was God's world, the focus of divine attention; the rest of mankind belonged for the moment to Satan. For perhaps a thousand years or more, western European world historical consciousness was transformed into theosophy, demonology, and mythology. And, indeed, in a most profound sense European notions of history, both theological and pseudo-theological, negated the possibility of the true existence of earlier civilizations. The perfectibility of mankind, the eschatological vision, precluded the possibility of pre-Christian civilization having achieved any remarkable development in moral law, social organization, or natural history (science). (86)

Perfection would then not just be a problem of thought but also a problem thwarting thought and the flourishing of possibility. Other resonances of this problem are sensed in the Greek concept of the ideal and the Christian and monotheistic religions' concept of salvation. This, perfectibility, is what apophatic and cataphatic thought presupposes, a perfectibility that leads to silence standing in the presence of the divine, the perfect one. But what if we did not organize ourselves around the desire for the perfect or perfectible? What if we gave up our need for perfectibility?

What we have to have is a preferential option for the practice of ongoing imperfectability. The forgetfulness of *alternative modes of sociality* is because of the concept of perfectibility, supersession, and dialectics, that what is "originary" needs to be worked in order to be perfected. We have to get over our obsession with perfection. Perfection and perfectibility are produced in Western thought by the ideas that it is a goal worth aspiring toward and that it is attainable. And its modern strain finds one strand of its genesis in Newtonian conceptualizations for space-time as linear and self-corrective over temporal measures.

And it is because of Wabash Avenue. Florence Watts, who would eventually become Sister Zeineb, lived blocks away and eventually joined the Al-Sadiq mosque at 4448 Wabash Avenue. This would be and still is the oldest mosque in the United States and would serve as a site of interracial spiritual community. And as Chan-Malik shows, Mufti Muhammad Sadiq sought black women in the *Chicago Defender*, advertising in the Women's Page about the Sunday meetings. The mosque was commissioned in 1923. But it is Wabash Avenue that intrigues me. Years later in 1929, the First Church of Deliverance would organize in the home of Father Clarence Cobb's grandmother in the Bronzeville section of Chicago at 3363 South Indiana Avenue. The first building they acquired was at 4155 South State Street. And, important for me in this writing, they held their first meeting on June 8, 1933, at what is now their present location, 4315 South Wabash Avenue.

These places of worship are between 43rd and 45th Streets on Wabash, so they are quite literally across the street from each other and one-minute's walking distance from one another. It is not that I think the church and mosque have the same theologies and doctrines but that by focusing on Sister Zeineb and others walking down the street, we can speculate how they would have encountered various kinds of people who would have had to work together in order to live peaceably. But I don't just want to focus on the coincidence of these two worship spaces on the same street, I want to think about the exchange between that the street allows me to imagine. Is there the possibility of interreligious friendship? Is there the possibility for relationality? What can the sound of the Hammond organ incite in our imaginations toward formless and always-on-the-move sociality?

To tell the story differently is to begin otherwise, to produce a version of the same that inflects. So a return, like in the coda of *Blackpentecostal Breath: The Aesthetics of Possibility*, to First Church of Deliverance in Chicago and the musicianship of Kenneth Morris. Credited for introducing the Hammond organ to black gospel music, Morris had a sonic imagination charged by and cultivated within a centrifugitive, choreosonic mode of sociality. The mode of sociality in which Morris engages and extends takes as instrument any tool, any technology, and this in the service of praise and worship.

The centrifugitive, choreosonic force of the black sonic commons is about the making instrument of various forms, various technologies. And it is a sonic imagination that cannot ever be private property but is a critique of the proper. What Morris was able to imagine with the sound of the Hammond organ was because of what had made him possible, the mode of sociality, the black sonic commons. The sound of the Hammond organ, its electricity and vibration and hum and buzz and—eventually, with the Leslie speaker—its spin and breath, will have been an emphatic demonstration of Morris's participation in such a commons. But more, it was the kind of church that First Church of Deliverance was, a black-queer space of vitality, that perhaps gives a cue and clue into the relationality I investigate.

First Church of Deliverance was a major stop on the blackqueer night-life circuit in the mid-twentieth century. "Former members of the First Church of Deliverance on Wabash Avenue remembered it as a major stop on the gay nightlife circuit in the 1930s and 1940s. The church welcomed gay people and Reverend Clarence Cobbs, along with many of his staff, was rumored to be gay," and "after attending the live broadcast at the church, which ran from 11:00 pm to midnight, club goers would simply walk from First Church of Deliverance to one of the area nightspots, usually the Kitty Kat Club, the Parkside, or the 430" (Best 2005: 188). In this particular work, I am seeking to intentionally think about the blackqueer-ness of the vibrations felt as sound and song, emanating from the relationships created by vibrations being made instrument in the service of praise and worship for congregants. The sound of the Hammond organ emerging from First Church of Deliverance for me is a way to think blackqueerness and the sacred in intentional and intense ways. This space was a place of gathering, the practice of friendship in the flesh. The sound of the instrument emerges and becomes felt and known through a blackqueer space of potentiality that perhaps we might consider the practice of circum-sacred performance.

And I am informed about circum-sacred performance that Langston Hughes fictionally narrates and that provides cues and clues. In his short story

"Blessed Assurance" (2002: 374–75), the character Delmar, the young son of the main character John and wife Arletta, was "turning out to be a queer." More, "Delmar sang in the Junior Choir," and they "even went so far as to want to render a jazz recessional—Delly's idea—which was vetoed." In the story, the Minister of Music, Dr. Manley Jaxon, wrote a song based on the story of Ruth:

> 'Entreat me to not leave thee,
> Neither to go far from thee.
> Whither thou goeth, I will go.
> Always will I be near thee. . . .'

> The work was dedicated to Delmar who received the first handwritten copy as a tribute from Dr. Jackson. In spite of its dedication, one might have thought that in performance the solo lead—Ruth's part—would be assigned to a woman. Perversely enough, the composer allotted it to Delmar. . . . So without respect for gender, on the Sunday afternoon of the program, Delmar sang the female lead. Dr. Jaxon, saffron robed, was at the organ. (376)

The story continues,

> As the organ wept and Delmar's voice soared about the choir . . . backwards off the organ stool in a dead faint fell Dr. Manley Jaxon. Not only did Dr. Jaxon fall from the stool, but he rolled limply down the steps from the organ loft like a bag of meal and tumbled prone onto the rostrum, robes an all. *Amens* and *Hallelujahs* drowned in the throats of various elderly sisters who were on the verge of shouting. (377)

What this story marks out is a way to think about the queerness of circum-sacred performance, a performance that is never about the one but about the plural, never about the individual but about the social from which the individual emerges. What is marked are the various intensities of relationality not that the music makes possible but that the vibration gathered as sound and song makes evident as always already happening, the otherwise possibility in the flesh. Hughes gives us a cue and clue regarding the allowed to flourish in and as nothing, ceaseless noise as sensed and felt through temporal shifting, imagined and rumored of, which is to say the practice that, queering, queers the vibration of blackness. These relationships and feelings of intensity and emotion emerge from anti-institutional practices of affection, love, joy, heartbreak. They are practices of friendship as a way of life.

C. Riley Snorton (2017: 11) asks, "What does it mean to have a body that has been made into a grammar for whole worlds of meaning?" I expand upon this question to ask how Blackpentecostal intersensual and intersonical performance allows the feeling and flourishing of blackqueer possibility to transform the performance of vibration-as-sound-and-song into the possibility for an entire range of affectional directional movements. Hughes's story gives at least one example of a blackqueer relationality that is a kind of friendship that has all kinds of affect dripping out of its pores and enclosures and impossibilities. James Baldwin, too, gets at this through his various depictions: whether of John Grimes's longing for the pianist and friendship with Elisha; or Arthur's relationship with Crunch made possible by singing. This happens through friendship. Friendship, *through sound and song*, is a generative staging ground through which to think about intimacy, desire, blackqueer possibility.

The vibration emanating as sound and song from within Blackpentecostal life is a grammar of blackqueerness as a vital and vitalizing force: it lives and causes life. This to argue, then, that we all have the capacity for queerness insofar as we have the potential for relationality. It is just that some of us live into, rather than practice renunciation against, this idea. I am interested in how blackqueerness is the ante-Man, a prior form not in a linear temporality but in terms of anepistemological possibility. Blackqueerness is life as *and*. We are trained into the epistemological delimitations of Western thought regarding Man, the human, the person, the subject, the citizen, and varied intensities for pleasures and relationalities are possible, and this is the grounds for existence. This is not to say that everyone is gay, but that the queer potentialities are anoriginal, are originary displacement, are marks for the very possibility for relationality of any sort. I am seeking to figure out why the musicking in the Blackpentecostal anaesthetic field I investigate has been made to carry these potentialities; why is it the song, the sound, and its necessary sensorium? It is all about feeling and feel.

III

And what I'm trying to say, in other words, is that the *an*epistemology through and in which the vibration of sound and song is played, through and in which the Instrument—the musician and the mechanical object of the Hammond organ *together*—is made, is an anepistemology of feeling, a critique of Man's epistemological possibility. Listen to Elbernita "Twinkie" Clark (TheClarkSistersTV 2008).

Nina Sun Eidsheim (2015: 18) says, "A given epistemic framework developed through a cultural system enables us to recognize and name, say, a G#. In other words, G# is historically situated within a chromatic, tempered scalar system that is culturally bound to the Western tonal system." What does it mean to recognize the vibration-as-sound-and-song emanating from the Blackpentecostal space as the potential for blackqueer life? It means that there is an epistemology in operation—which is also the critique of Man and *his* epistemological possibility, here called the *an*epistemology—that has blackness, queerness, and the sacred together as co-constitutive. It means that we have to investigate the epistemology of operation—the *an*epistemology of feel—to get at what is there, what is there for us to learn, what is there for us to utilize to disrupt the practice of racial capitalism and its violence.

Listening to the soft chording and pad music of Jason St. Clair (marshall1517 2010)—what I describe in *Blackpentecostal Breath* (Crawley 2016) as "nothing music"—allows us to think about the way flesh inhabits space-time within the context from which emerges the imagination of blackqueer life. What I hear in Jason St. Clair's playing is the joy of nothing, the pleasure in the vibration of sound and song called nothing music. The changing tonic center to me highlights the fact that there is no center of the universe such that the very concept of centering needs to be played with, another way to say the instrument—through arpeggio and chord resolve—interrogates. We land in centers but also steal away because, as the spiritual says, we ain't got long to stay anywhere called here. St. Clair's playing of nothing music is an existential claim played out in the vibration of sound and song, enunciated through the chording of nothing that is music.

Soft chording as nothing music lets me ponder softness, the feminine, the maternal, the reproductive, and nothing/lack from which emerges life that we should not escape out of but retreat into. These terms, these concepts, are renounced in the service of becoming-normal, becoming-normative. But instead of escaping from them, what if we had a preferential option for secreting into the interior? To make a claim for feeling as the *an*epistemological ordering through which the Instrument makes vibrations of sound and song on the Hammond is to make a claim for blackqueerness as celebratory and worthy of protection and care. And to make a claim for blackqueerness is to threaten the normative striving, the desired assumption into aspirations for inclusion in white supremacist practices of exclusion and violence.

Though song selection may occur previous to the church service—of course, these performances do not *lack* form or organization—musicians do not coordinate or schedule or consult with pastors or other musicians regarding when and how to respond to various modes and moods of intensity during the church service. Rather, they feel their way into it: they feel the congregation, they feel for the preacher, they feel for the Spirit and reach for spirit in the way they play. It is the intellectual practice of the collective ensemble. The congregation and preacher respond to the instrument, and the instrument responds likewise to them. They are continually pushing each other and also pulling on one another. What we are after, what we detect in the Blackpentecostal instrument, is the enfleshment of a nonproprietary and improper (improper insofar as it is the refusal of the making of private property and thus the making of the proper) relation to sound, the enunciation of a relation to sound making that is about the gathering of vibration in the service of connecting with the congregation.

Fumi Okiji (2018: 2) states:

> A musical work, through the way it comes together in composition and unfolds in performance, points to a way for us to be together in the world, against the world's tendency to reduce us, qualitatively. On various levels of structuration a composition is formed through a productive tension between particularity and communion. The composer wrestles with an active pool of found musical material; chords, intervals, feel, and generic sensibility may all pull in divergent directions. The single note similarly stakes its claim to significance against the phrase or chord in which it falls.

The work of sound making in the Blackpentecostal circum-sacred performance is always the labor, courage, and, yes, wisdom, to make worlds otherwise, to make worlds alternate, to make worlds plural. The vibration—whether sound or song—is the practice of composition, of architecture, of fashioning and bringing together through particularity, through the possibilities enfleshed by being in the space with others, through the practice of friendship. The composer is always more than the individual, the composer is the plural possibility of the event; the Hammond musician with mechanical object—as instrument—is the coming together of forces social, mechanical, ecological. This *coming together*, however, is a misnomer. What I should have said, rather, is the *letting happen* of the social, mechanical, and ecological, the plural event of existence, the practice of *and*.

The harmonic structure of the Instrument typically accommodates a tritone song, and this—tritonality—is the primary thrust of music from within this space. This marks difference from other choral musics and thus from the accompaniment of such music. As such, even the nothing music is the would-be evidence of this general organizational thrust, the arpeggio and riff, the chromaticism and chronoticism—what I consider to be the breaking with temporality through arrangement, organization, and capacity overflow. Both play with and at the relation to the tritone as its sonic form. Such that focus on the Hammond musician as Instrument—as mechanical flesh, as always in dialogue with other musicians, as always in concert with the congregation, as, in other words, an irreducibly social object and socially produced possibility—helps to avoid "the term *individual*, which in its most common usage leads us to the image of the defunct bourgeois subject of earlier and less malignant permutations of capitalism," to avoid "an abstraction that leads to the fetishization of the solo as the essence," not only of jazz but of gospel musicianship as well (Okiji 2018: 7).

Blackqueerness, like nothing music, is the zone from which emerges the normative but also, importantly, the infinite range of possibility otherwise than the normative. The infinite range of otherwise possibility, the infinite range of plurality, is the space of the social, the space of the common and commons, the space of the popular and criminal. Circum-sacred possibility is enacted from within such a zone of plurality, and it is the renunciation of this anoriginal, primordial fleshliness, openness, dissidence from which the normative, with violent force, is produced. The point is the practice against the normative in the service of life's flourishing.

The problem with the confrontation with the terrible triteness and violence of homophobia, transphobia, and the general antagonism against the feminine, the maternal, and queerness that exists within and emerges from the same space that produces the vibrations gathered as sound and song is not only that it causes folks marginalized by this rhetoric to flee after having been excluded then considered by those who remain to be unsensed nonsense, transformed into cogs that do not feel. The problem is also, and more fundamentally, about the ordinary and quotidian and the practice of the everyday, that because of the general *an*epistemology of feeling that grounds the circum-sacred life of blackness, the terribleness, triteness, and violence is felt *along with and inside* the same social, cultural, religious space that produces pleasure, joy, delight. It's not that we don't feel but that we feel too much. How to continue on in the practice of openness and vulnerability to feeling while protecting with care from harm those exposed to the violence such openness and vulnerability make happen?

Blackqueer folks ask, in varied registers because of theologies and doctrines of our supposed sinfulness and shame: *Am I broken? Am I beyond repair? Who will love me? Who will touch me?* This is a question of the *letting be* of the social, the mechanical and the ecological, a question of the Instrument. This is, following Sedgwick (2007), an attempt at reparation, a reparative *sensing*, a reparative (more than) reading. She said, "What one already is puts its inevitable spin on what one says, does, and perceives—and vice versa" (641). I am not interested in the rumor and gossip that circulate queerness in order to tattle-tell, in order to expose the risqué subjects. I am attempting to figure out what we already *is*, and how this is heard through the Hammond, through the relationship the musicking allows folks to notice.

What perhaps is heard on the Hammond, announced and enunciated for and with and in congregation with others, is the possibility for putting to question doctrine, theology, politics. What perhaps is heard on the Hammond, announced and enunciated in the practice of nothing music, is the question of existence. What is experiential for blackqueer people—through normative theology-philosophy—spills over into the existential. It's not that some of us do not have relations—many of us do—but it's that the relations themselves are repulsive for many, that they are that which cause family and friends to recoil in horror. At times, we recoil from our very selves. We are made to feel, because of the fact of our existence, that we are supposed to endure and carry shame others project onto us. The problem of disavowal, of a general renunciation of what we all have the potential for being, is that it produces hierarchies of persons and sustains hierarchies with violent force.

Lawrence Lyles feels it (Lyles music 2012). At the end of the song, when the congregation sings repetitiously, "saith the lord," he plays certain chord changes that the congregation responds to by changing *their* harmonic structures within the same song. The lyrics are repeated with sonic material difference such that the song and the musician are constantly in flux and flow, the practice of improvisation, song as unalterably open to change. What if the congregation took the organist's play as a demand to live in the world differently, a demand to respond to the life and verve and force of blackqueer possibility by changing the harmonic structure within the same space of articulation? What would it mean to feel into one another using the vibration-as-sound-and-song as our guide? What the Instrument must do is practice openness and vulnerability in order for their being made instrument to happen, for their being made instrument to occur. To be made instrument, to be made implement, to be hollowed out such that wind and breath and vibration can happen through and to the flesh, is to make oneself available, splayed.

I am not fundamentally asking about doctrine and theology, because doctrines create hierarchies of persons based on who follows, does not follow, does not adhere, so this is not an argument for the augmentation of doctrine. Rather, this is an attempt to interrogate why—with doctrines of the human and theologies of original sin—these figures continue to show up and become conduits, instruments, for praise and worship. This is an *a*theology of the flesh, asking how it can remain undone, porous, open, vulnerable while simultaneously protecting from harm those who would exploit this undone, porous, open, vulnerable way of life. On one hand, we have to recognize that seeking the antitheses of these intensities does not, in fact, protect or produce care even though there is group differentiated vulnerability to the violence of not being protected. On the other hand, we have to contend with the idea that perhaps everything we have been taught to want is itself a problem.

I have so far been discussing the concept of renunciation of the blackqueerness that makes the Blackpentecostal instrument—the gathering of vibration-as-sound-and-song—possible. This renunciation is similar to what Neil Roberts (2015: 29) calls *disavowal*, as "a simultaneous *double movement*: an acknowledgment *and* a denial. By simultaneously acknowledging and denying an event, one does not silence its existence. Rather, one strategically locates an event and then rejects its relevance, knowing full well that it occurred. The double movement produces negative traumatic effects more damaging than silence." The rumor and gossip of blackqueerness as occupying the space of vibration-as-sound-and-song is both the acknowledgment and the denial. I use the concept of renunciation precisely because this disavowal with its double movement is always more than double (Chandler 2000). It is plural, it is irreducible in the ones aspiring toward ascendance, aspiring toward normativity, it is a double gesture without end because one can never reach ascendance nor normativity. But there is still violence done in such reaching, in such striving.

To renounce what we have been, to escape the noise of the social in the desire for purity, normativity, is the process of making Western Man, the person who is created by possessive individualism. Some of us cannot renounce because of the imposition of racial capitalism such that any aspirational move or desired perfectibility toward the Ideal is a failed project, because racial capitalism is predicated on exclusion and its attendant violence. But what if you don't want what was not offered in the first place? What is the *an*epistemology of such a not-wanting? What does it mean to feel something and to privilege feeling as the *an*epistemology of operation? Or, more precisely, not to privilege but to allow to unfold and refuse to renounce feeling as the ground for existence.

It means to think otherwise than normative function and form, to listen into the vibrations of sound and song as the emergence for relations of plentitude and possibility. It means to think that we might become what we have already been. But we have to have the verve and nerve for such an otherwise way of life. It would be an *an*epistemology of openness, of a sacred commons that announces availability and openness against enclosure, a commons from which to draw resources to tell the world about the joy of life and beauty and breath.

IV

And a gesture. The poem "In Lovely Blue," written by Friedrich Hölderin (1984: 249), begins:

> In lovely blue blooms the steeple blossoms
> With its metal roof. Around which
> Drift swallows cries around which
> Lies most loving blue . . .

Blue allows for the blossom, blue against the roof, the roof swirls and song is heard against loving blue. It's like the phrase says what it says twice, that the content of the idea—that blue is lovely, and that one can be in it—is repeated with difference. It is a minuscule moment, a quick happening, in a very long poem. The way the phrase ends "by most touching blue" is a turnaround; like a Hammond musician, it is inventional. The turnaround in the chord structure that Hammond musicians employ is how they end a phrase between lines, between choruses and verses, between verses. The turnaround is the place for invention, but the practice does not belong to the one but to the plural, what is marked is the relation between musicians. This turnaround, like Hammond musicianship in general, reminds me of the fact that dance and play are in the turnaround, the choreosonic space of improvisational drive and verve, it marks the same with difference.

What was originally titled *Les Mots et Les Choses* (*Words and Things*) was rendered in English as *The Order of Things*, written by Foucault (1994), and *The Order of Things* was chosen precisely because the publisher wanted to avoid confusion. But what was avoided is for me the occasion to think about the interpretation of thought as opposed to translation, about the movement of thought with the attempt to maintain the *quality* of the anoriginal phrase, a search for something that is quite literally the same with difference.

In two versions of the same, Fred Moten in "Preface for a solo by Miles Davis" (2007: 217) opens with:

> To speak from the position of the not supposed to speak is to submit to an even more fundamental disqualification: that in speaking from that position one relinquishes the possibility of thought or of being thought insofar as one (merely) provides the material conditions (in speech that is, as it were, beneath speech; speech borne in a soma-sonority that refuses to disavow itself) for another's thought and for another's being thought.

And in *Black and Blur* (2017: 66):

> To speak when and where one is not supposed to speak is to resist an even
> more fundamental disqualification: that such spatiotemporally disruptive
> enunciation relinquishes the possibility of thought or of being thought inso-
> far as one (merely) provides the material conditions (in speech that is, as
> it were, beneath speech; speech born in a phonocarnality that refuses to
> disavow itself) for another's thought and for another's being thought.

Further, again, Moten's two versions of the same:

> Jacobs cannot give the consent that, nevertheless, she can withhold. (2007:
> 218)

And

> Insofar as Jacobs cannot give consent that, nevertheless, she can withhold,
> she consents not to be a single being. (2017: 67)

These are the same lines with difference, attempting to capture something
of the same. They are the flatted fifths of one another, the blue notes, the turnaround that is the same with intentioned difference to produce surprise, delight,
deeper investigation, a digging in, a reaching back. The colloquial understanding
of Negro spirituals and black gospel to come is that they can be played with only
the black notes, what Western musicology and notation call the pentatonic scale.
In jazz and the blues, the blue note is supposedly lower than an expected tone, and
is the alternation of a quarter tone for a semitone. The blue note is about registering difference, but difference is anoriginal.

The blues retains a relationship to, and thus a mode of collective consciousness of, Islam. Sylviane Diouf (n.d.) offers the following:

> About 24 percent of the 400,000 Africans who landed in this country
> came from that West African area also known as Senegambia. Among them
> were a large percentage of Muslims. Peoples of the Western Sahel had been
> in contact with the Arab-Berber Islamic world since the eighth century
> and Islam had spread in a consistent manner since the first decades of the
> eleventh century.
>
> Among the cultural exchanges that took place between North Africa
> and the Middle East on the one hand and the Sahel on the other—through
> trade, migrations, and pilgrimages—was music. The Arab/Islamic musi-

cal style was adapted and transformed by West Africans into something entirely theirs that was at the same time very close but different. Similarly, West Africans deported through the trans-Saharan trade brought their music and rhythms (including those that had already been changed by the Arab/Islamic contact) North to the Maghreb. There was much cross-fertilization on both sides of the desert and it is this complex heritage that West African Muslim captives brought to the United States where it found a fertile ground.

She continues,

Two American specificities can thus explain the emergence of the blues. Of all the countries in the Western hemisphere, the United States received the highest proportion of men and women from Senegal, Gambia, Mali, and Guinea; and it is also the only place where drumming was forbidden. So it is not by chance that the blues evolved only there. What makes this music so different from Caribbean and Afro-South American music is specifically the presence of Sahelian/Arabic/Islamic stylistic elements. They can be found in the instrument playing techniques, the melodies, and the singing style.

To attend to the Muslimness of the blues is to think about style and the production of sound. What Diouf and others demonstrate are the ways the Black Muslim inventiveness was produced in the Americas as a sonic device. This sonic device is a gesture. This gesture is memory. And I want to consider the relationship that the blues has to gospel music and to think about this relationship as a kind of hiddenness that carries the content of black mysticism, a refusal of the individual subject as a mystic, a kind of individuation that is about the production of an identity to be claimed or renounced, but a mysticism that is about the practice of the plural, of the many, hidden in plainsong and sound. Listen, for example, to the relation between, on one hand, a Senegalese practice of the Adhan (Rahman TV 2019) or this bluesy version (Yahia Hegazy 2016) and, on the other, the Alan Lomax recording of the Levee Camp Holler (Grammercy Records 2012). Listening to these sonic events, there is a consistency that stretches beyond Islam and the blues. For example, "A Charge to Keep I Have" (Meeting Place Church 2014) in the Black Christian tradition shares in sonic relationship to the Adhan and the Levee Camp Holler.

The audiovisual, spatiotemporal incoherence enunciates itself as the melismatic rupture on the note, the ornamentation heard with each breath of each prayer or song, the melodic structure the prayer takes, the increase in antiphony between prayer leader and congregation, the elongation of notes, the worrying the note and line. This is all heard in the Islamic recitation, and the relationship of sound to song and breath is maintained across space, time, and, importantly, religious tradition. What is heard in the relation of black gospel to the blues to Islamic call and convocation is perhaps best described as *feeling the spirit in the dark*, where darkness is the enfolding of spirit as a practice of protection and care; where darkness enfolds to practice a kind of hiddenness in the service of ongoing encounter with the otherwise than this.

In other words, what is played out in black gospel music is the hiddenness of the blues, which would then be the hiddenness of the social and spiritual relation the blues enunciates and announces with every taken breath. Such hiddenness includes the blackqueer priority of life, previous to situation. Such a hiddenness is given and is withheld in sound and song, and the sonic manifestation of hiddenness is grounded in the ongoing play and dance of blackness and nothingness. What is carried is the relationship to augmentation; or, as the four Black American Muslim women demonstrate (and as Chan-Malik reminds us), what is carried is the relationship to invention, to the impulse to make worlds.

What is heard in black gospel music is the undercommon sound and song that infuses the circum-sacred practice of Islam. And it's about renunciation, the ongoingness of the sound means we have to make an inquiry into the ways blackness and Muslimness have been forgotten (and this rather than hidden), and how this forgottenness of what makes the tradition possible is one we must interrogate in order to more fully understand the black radical tradition as a spiritual striving, condition and *an*epistemological ordering. This means the refusal to think the gospel sound as the perfectibility and supersession of the Islamic call and convoking of the divine is one task, to attend to the undercommon sensuality is to refuse logics of overcoming, conquering, and settler colonial theft and exploitation. Like Robinson, I do not necessarily want to exhaust the subject of the possibility for interrelation, I want to merely point to what is there, and in the service of causing a reckoning—in the hope of thinking the possibility of a refusal to submit to doctrine and theology that separates—and, rather, think the possibility of friendship.

V

And I want to practice friendship. Political theology is an articulation of racial categorization and pure distinction. Robinson reminds us that racial capitalism, that capitalism is itself a racialized concept, was used first to distinguish peoples in Europe for a project of labor exploitation by theft of labor power transformed into profit for the capitalist class. To build with Robinson is to assert that there is racial theologism, that theology is itself and likewise a racialized concept that is itself used to distinguish peoples as available for and vulnerable to the violence of exploitation in the forms of land theft, forced labor, and physical displacement.

To make a claim for racial theologism is to consider the ways political theology is an articulation of Western constructions of purity and categorical difference, taking language and its conceptual delimitation from the theological; taking, in other words, the racialization fundamental to capitalism and theology as organizing principles for now, what Denise Ferreira da Silva (2007) calls a global idea of race. To think against racial capitalism and racial theologism is to think with the *a*theological-*a*philosophical. The negation of capitalism-theologism, which must be more than simple negation, is the *a*philosophical-*a*theological-*a*historical-*an*ethical-*an*epistemological; it is the more-than negation. One articulation of this more-than negation is found in the sounding out as sensual plea and pleasure of prayer, a mysticism of connection that negates the formation of the modern liberal subject and of its being a useful tool in the projects of capitalist political organizing and the political theologism that is the displacement of language for that organizing project.

If both the political and the theological were defined for and by what Sylvia Wynter (2003) calls the overrepresentation of Man—whether 1, 2, which I think includes a kind of biotechnological Man that overrepresents Technology as the cyber and digital—these categories together, as political theology, do not augment and widen the possibility for inclusion but sharpen for us the fact of exclusion. What sounding out of the Instrument and listening to the sound and song of Blackpentecostal vibration on the Hammond organ might gift us is a way to interrogate current conceptions of the Human and post-Human with their reliance on self-correction, evolution into the digital while also not having an aversion for using objects. Katherine McKittrick is useful here in her reading of Sylvia Wynter and her engagement with Jimi Hendrix. For example, she says she is interested in "how improvisational music and music making might be acts that are creatively scripted outside governing codes, and thus evidence of unbounded or ungoverned brain activity," and that "this attention to the scientific contours of the arts—which takes very seriously the physiological and neurological—challenges us, as intellectuals, to rethink how we take up racial-sexual justice precisely because it located knowledge making as connective to flesh, blood, bones, muscles, and brain matter while also forcing us to notice new forms of scientific life in the arts" (2014: 156).

She offers another way to understand human creaturely existence with art that does not submit itself to the ideas of technology as the answer of the goal or the end of who we are, have been, or could be. I argue that with Hammond musicians and their engagement with the mechanical object, we find other examples of this motive and practice. Relation exists. Can a speculative relationality—the relation of the musician to the mechanical object, a friendship along the lines of social, mechanical, and ecological flesh—produce the occasion of the whenwhere of a liberatory possibility?

Political theology is fundamentally concerned with sovereignty as a problem for thought (see, e.g., Schmitt 2010, 2015). In this way, political theology mines and is adjacent to minoritized knowledges, but these minoritize knowledges are not only or even primarily *about* the articulation of this problem, these knowledges are not in a dialectical relationship to political theology in any simple sense. And this because these knowledges are an attempt to articulate, as a fundamental anoriginal question and concern, what it means to live, to have life, to be in the world with others. That is, minoritized knowledges—and here I am thinking of black and blackqueer and black feminist and indigenous strains of knowledge production, strains that are otherwise possibilities of the normative, the practice of alternatives without ever making a claim that the alternative reached is "the" "one" that should be valorized; otherwise possibility does not negate the practice of interrogation or criticism but allows it to flourish—are not only or even primarily about an articulation of difference as much as they are about their lifeworlds. They articulate difference because they must, but they are more, Robinson might say.

In "Friendship as a Way of Life," Foucault (1997: 137) argues that friendship, as he detects it in gay life (which I expand to be blackqueer life), is a kind of relation that makes one *infinitely more susceptible to pleasure.* He notes, "What we must work on, it seems to me, is not so much to liberate our desires but to make ourselves infinitely more susceptible to pleasure [*plaisirs*]. We must escape and help others to escape the two readymade formulas of the pure sexual encounter and the lovers' fusion of identities." He does not say that one has infinite pleasure or that desire must be liberated—though it certainly should not be incarcerated or held in repression—but that one becomes more susceptible, more open, more vulnerable, which is to say the possibility for pleasure intensifies, increases. This susceptibility emerges through the practice of escape: of oneself and of others, together, as a social practice, escape of the normative world, normative striving.

One becomes *susceptible to*, and this is a gift of relation; one can begin to sense possibility for otherwise modalities for existence, alternatives to the normative, when one engages queer life. This is a question of, and against, political theology because it is not about the concern over the sovereign but about a practice that is against the very constitution of sovereignty. Becoming *susceptible to* is labor, is work, must continually be unsettled and practiced, is never reached as a complete, and is never an object of property to own. Being *susceptible to* is the practice of a general openness and zest for life, joy, and breath.

Notes

This research was completed while I was a Yale Institute of Sacred Music fellow, 2018–19.

1. For an extended argument about Blackpentecostal practice as an iteration and practice of blackness, see Crawley 2016.
2. Another character that must be explored but is very much beyond the scope of this article is the black woman preacher in twentieth-century black popular culture. Often called or thought to be "mannish," or occupying the "role" of the male pastor, black women too in black religiosity carry queer content, carry the possibility for thinking and conceiving blackqueer life.
3. See the "Coda" in Crawley 2016 for an extended discussion of "nothing music."
4. I am using *Man* informed by Wynter 2003.
5. For extended discussions about the character of the sissy in the Black Christian imagination, see Johnson 2008, Johnson 1998, and Crawley 2013.
6. For a discussion of inculcation, see Mahmood 2011.

References

Bergman, Carla, and Nick Montgomery. 2017. *Joyful Militancy: Building Thriving Resistance in Toxic Times*. Oakland, CA: AK Press.

Best, Wallace D. 2005. *Passionately Human, No Less Divine: Religion and Culture in Black Chicago, 1915–1952*. Princeton, NJ: Princeton University Press.

Chandler, Nahum. 2000. "Originary Displacement." *Boundary 2* 27, no. 3: 249–86.

Chan-Malik, Sylvia. 2018. *Being Muslim: A Cultural History of Women of Color in American Islam*. New York: New York University Press.

Crawley, Ashon T. 2013. "Blackqueer Aesthesis: Sexuality and the Rumor and Gossip of Black Gospel." In *Race and Displacement: Nation, Migration, and Identity in the Twenty-First Century*, edited by Maha Marouan and Merinda Simmons, 27–42. Tuscaloosa: University of Alabama Press.

Crawley, Ashon T. 2016. *Blackpentecostal Breath: The Aesthetics of Possibility*. New York: Fordham University Press.

da Silva, Denise Ferreira. 2007. *Toward a Global Idea of Race*. Minneapolis: University of Minnesota Press.

Diouf, Sylviane A. n.d. "African Muslims and American Blues." Muslim Voices: Arts and Ideas. www.muslimvoicesfestival.org/resources/african-muslims-and-american-blues.

Eidsheim, Nina Sun. 2015. *Sensing Sound: Singing and Listening as Vibrational Practice*. Durham, NC: Duke University Press.

Foucault, Michel. 1990. *The History of Sexuality, Vol 1: An Introduction*, translated by Robert Hurley. New York: Vintage.

Foucault, Michel. 1994. *The Order of Things: An Archaeology of the Human Sciences*. New York: Vintage.

Foucault, Michel. 1997. "Friendship as a Way of Life." In *Ethics: Subjectivity and Truth*, edited by Paul Rabinow, 135–40. New York: New Press.

Grammercy Records. 2012. "Bama—Levee Camp Holler." YouTube video, 2:52, October 31. youtu.be/KzxTfPmNTQE.

Hölderin, Friedrich. 1984. *Hymns and Fragments*, translated by Richard Sieburth. Princeton, NJ: Princeton University Press.

Hughes, Langston. 2002. "Blessed Assurance." In *The Short Stories*. Vol. 15 of *The Collected Works of Langston Hughes*, edited by R. Baxter Miller, 374–82. Columbia: University of Missouri Press.

Johnson, E. Patrick. 1998. "Feeling the Spirit in the Dark: Expanding Notions of the Sacred in the African-American Gay Community." *Callaloo* 21, no. 2: 399–416.

Johnson, E. Patrick. 2008. *Sweet Tea: Black Gay Men of the South*. Chapel Hill: University of North Carolina Press.

Jones, Alisha Lola. 2017. "'Are All the Choir Directors Gay?' Black Men's Sexuality and Identity in Gospel Performance." In *Issues in African American Music: Power, Gender, Race, Representation*, edited by Portia K. Maultsby and Mellonee V. Burnim, 216–35. New York: Routledge.

Lyles music. 2012. "Lawrence Lyles." YouTube video, 6:35, June 10. youtu.be/0x-es5TKzAg.

Mahmood, Saba. 2011. *Politics of Piety: The Islamic Revival and the Feminist Subject*. Princeton, NJ: Princeton University Press.

marshall1517. 2010. "Jason St.Clair (MUST SEE!!!)." YouTube video, 9:27, August 16. youtu.be/6o-NdSyItrg.

McKittrick, Katherine. 2014. *Sylvia Wynter: On Being Human as Praxis*. Durham, NC: Duke University Press.

The Meeting Place Church of Greater Columbia. 2014. "'A Charge to Keep I Have'—Hymn 'Lined' by Candace Heggs." YouTube video, 4:35, July 29. youtu.be/0XrS5i6gMdk.

Moten, Fred. 2007. "Preface for a Solo by Miles Davis." *Women and Performance* 17, no. 2: 217–46.

Moten, Fred. 2017. *Black and Blur*. Durham, NC: Duke University Press.

Okiji, Fumi. 2018. *Jazz as Critique: Adorno and Black Expression Revisited*. Stanford, CA: Stanford University Press.

Rahman TV. 2019. "The Most Beautiful Adhan, All the Way from Senegal." YouTube video, 3:47, February 13. youtu.be/YVOYLhiubDM.

Roberts, Neil. 2015. *Freedom as Marronage.* Chicago: University of Chicago Press.

Robinson, Cedric J. (1983) 2000. *Black Marxism: The Making of the Black Radical Tradition.* Chapel Hill: University of North Carolina Press.

Schmitt, Carl. 2010. *Political Theology: Four Chapters on the Concept of Sovereignty.* Chicago: University of Chicago Press.

Schmitt, Carl. 2015. *Political Theology II: The Myth of the Closure of Any Political Theology.* Hoboken, NJ: Wiley.

Sedgwick, Eve Kosofsky. 2007. "Melanie Klein and the Difference Affect Makes." *South Atlantic Quarterly* 106, no. 3: 625–42.

Sedgwick, Eve Kosofsky. 2008. *Epistemology of the Closet.* 2nd ed. Berkeley: University of California Press.

Sedgwick, Eve Kosofsky, and Adam Frank. 2003. *Touching Feeling: Affect, Pedagogy, Performativity.* Durham, NC: Duke University Press.

Shukaitis, Stevphen. 2011. "The Wisdom to Make Worlds: Strategic Reality and the Art of the Undercommons." *Transversal,* February. transversal.at/transversal/0311/shukaitis/en.

Snorton, C. Riley. 2017. *Black on Both Sides: A Racial History of Trans Identity.* Minneapolis: University of Minnesota Press.

TheClarkSistersTV. 2008. "Twinkie Clark and Richard White Clean—Accept What God Allows." YouTube video, 10:01, June 20. youtu.be/sceCHxTroLs.

Wynter, Sylvia. 2003. "Unsettling the Coloniality of Being/Power/Truth/Freedom: Towards the Human, after Man, Its Overrepresentation—An Argument." *New Centennial Review* 3, no. 3: 257–337.

Yahia Hegazy. 2016. "Adhan/Athan in the Blues Key." YouTube video, 3:00, January 17. youtu.be/6siV82N06Sg.

LIVING WITH THE NORM

The Nirvanam Ritual in South Indian Transfeminine Narratives of Self and Transition

Liza Tom and Shilpa Menon

The *thirunangais* of Tamil Nadu are one among several South Asian subcultures formed by people perceived as male at birth who prefer to adopt a feminine identity and appearance to various degrees. They may or may not invest in genital and other forms of body modification. Similar to the more visible *hijras* in other regions of India, they often live together in nonprocreative kinship units called *jamaaths* and share cultural and ritual practices of worship and labor, and a distinct language.[1] Colonial legal mechanisms and ensuing social stigma framed their work as criminal, disruptive, and premodern such that these communities have come to be seen as violating not just gender and sexual norms but those of respectable labor, religion, and sociality (Hinchy 2019). More recently, thirunangais have been rendered visible in public as subjects of government welfare schemes, as rights-seeking minority groups, and as targets for nongovernmental organization (NGO) intervention services. Increasingly, such venues also read them as transgender women, a label with which not all thirunangais identify. Unlike those who identify exclusively with the category transgender, thirunangai narratives of self and subjecthood draw not only from modern and secularized discourses for minorities, such as human rights and identity politics, but also from faith-based traditions and practices.

We focus on one such faith-based practice: the *nirvanam*. The nirvanam is a rite of passage that is not mandatory for membership within the community but is a marker of status and respect and therefore a valued goal for many thirunangais. The rite comprises the act of genital modification that was once performed by the *dayamma*, a thirunangai herself, but it now largely involves medicalized processes like sex reassignment surgery (SRS). Traditionally, the nirvanam is followed by ritu-

GLQ 27:1
DOI 10.1215/10642684-8776848
© 2021 by Duke University Press

als aimed at securing the blessings of Santhoshi Matha, the community's patron goddess.[2] Following a period of confinement with ritual proscriptions, the thirunangai is formally welcomed into the community through a final celebration (commonly called the *paal function*, or "milk ceremony") in which she pays her respects to the goddess. The nirvanam is a charged social event that is deeply embedded in exoticizing or pathologizing narratives of transfeminine communities from India that portray these communities variously as essentially different or criminal.[3]

In this article, we examine how mainstream narratives of rights-based citizenship and genital modification characterize thirunangais primarily as objects of reform, and we propose instead a recuperation of the nirvanam that is based on thirunangai understandings of the ritual. Our focus on the nirvanam is not to turn a cisheteronormative anthropological gaze onto an exotic practice but to look into what it does and the meanings with which it is invested, both within lived thirunangai experience and in dominant discourses. Here, we keep in mind Talal Asad's 1993 critique of anthropological constructions that frame the ritual as a bounded symbolic event that can be interpreted by the "expert" ethnographer to yield definitive truths about a monolithic community. When translated into a secular/medical frame of understanding as SRS, the ritual aspects of nirvanam appear as religious dross that scaffolds the "real" act of transition, serving as proof of thirunangais' inability to become modern, rights-bearing, agentive citizens. Here, we rely on thirunangais' narratives to explore the ideological underpinnings of such a framing and instead propose an understanding of the nirvanam as an assemblage of discourses, practices, and affinities that allow thirunangais to negotiate legible subjecthood within the intersecting logics of both the secular state and the goddess.

In the following sections, we begin by examining sets of interviews we conducted, drawing upon our interlocutors' understanding of nirvanam and the "worlding" it does. In the next section, we lay out the ways in which state-centric modernization narratives produce the transgender subject precisely by abjecting these nonsecular aspects of thirunangai lived experience. We look at how these discourses interpellate transgender subjects as objects of reform and how they also frame genital modification through the discourses of "castration" and SRS. We then turn to what it means to recuperate thirunangais as political theological subjects through an understanding of nirvanam. In conclusion, we make explicit our investment in political theology and in the ways in which the nirvanam pushes political theology beyond its Judeo-Christian moorings.

Methodology

We want to begin by acknowledging that the ease with which we wield queer politi-cal theology as a frame for thirunangai experiences is a product of our complicity in systems of knowledge and faith that abject them. Rather than attempting to make thirunangai practices palatable within domains of expertise from which they are excluded, we would like to see this as an act of translation (Arondekar and Patel 2016; Nagar 2014)—an attempt, however undercut by structural inequal-ity, to translate the value of practices from one world of meanings (those that the thirunangai inhabit) to another (that of academic knowledge production). By fram-ing this study as an inevitable act of translation, we hope to take into account the biases inherent to this act of sense making between ultimately incommensurable ways of knowing that can nevertheless exist in dialogue.

Given this epistemological orientation, we are attentive to the ways in which thirunangais—and others, such as *mangalamukhi*s, *jogappa*s, and *khwaja siras*— have been rendered legible in popular and academic discourse: as "local variants" of either transgender women or hijras. Thirunangais are usually elided within the discursive mechanisms that locate the "transgender native" in various regions of the global south (Towle and Morgan 2002). By this logic, hijras are reified as both essentially South Asian and essentially transgender, and this typology is material-ized through the flow of global capital as channeled through NGOs and community-based organizations (CBOs) (Dutta and Roy 2014). This conflation of transgender, hijra, and thirunangai has two effects: first, the experiences of variously located transfeminine subcultures become commensurable; and second, the figure of the transgender person in South Asia is typified as that of the exoticized figure of the hijra, erasing the diversity of subjectivities that identify as transgender— those who may not live in culturally cohesive communities and/or transmasculine persons.

In adopting a queer analytic, we stay away simply from proliferating an ethnocartographic impulse (Weston 1993) that portrays the thirunangais as the "transgender natives" of the region of south India or the state of Tamil Nadu. However, our strategy is not to delve into the networks of mobility and migration that shape transfeminine subcultures across South Asia, though that is a valuable undertaking (Hossain 2018). Rather, we pay close attention to the rubrics of dif-ference, equivalence, and similarity with these categories (hijra and transgender) that thirunangais themselves variously deploy to render themselves legible as sub-jects in various contexts, often by invoking religiosity and regional culture. On one hand, our interlocutors would differentiate themselves from hijras, saying that hijras were from "the north" and that hijras were celibate ritual performers unlike themselves, who were more modern. On the other, they explained their traditions of worship and their kinship systems by telling us that they were the same as those of hijras.

We draw on a set of twenty-two interviews we conducted with people from two prominent CBOs in Chennai, a major city in Tamil Nadu, for our discussion on the place of the nirvanam in thirunangais' lives. These CBOs define their beneficiary groups as thirunangais, transgender persons, men who have sex with men, and *kothis*.[4] They employed peer educators to provide sexual health services within these fluidly defined groups. We conducted two sets of interviews; the first set was done in 2015 and the next in 2019. Some interviews were unstructured conversations in which our interlocutors participated as a group, while others were individual interviews. All of them lasted between twenty minutes and an hour and were conducted in Tamil or English. Most of our interviews were conducted at the CBO offices and some at hospitals, thirunangai family residences, or individually owned living spaces.

Of the people with whom we spoke about the nirvanam, fourteen were either employed at or closely affiliated with CBOs or government undertakings for transfeminine communities. One of the CBOs largely served kothis and the other served thirunangais. As agencies operating in the same area, the two were closely associated and shared members. Among our thirunangai interlocutors too, some had identified as kothi before they adopted thirunangai traditions and culture. At the CBOs, we met a mix of staff members who worked as peer educators, and we met thirunangais and kothis who used the space to informally socialize with community members. Most of them held jamaath affiliations along with CBO affiliations; they were related to one another not just as colleagues but as sisters, daughters, aunts, and so on. Those who were in CBO supervisory roles were often mothers to many of the peer educators they supervised.

Most of our interlocutors relied on paid CBO jobs, sex work, or both to earn a living and were variously affiliated with the CBO, jamaaths, and their natal families. Those who lived with their natal families, as men or as women, spoke of the compromises they made to be able to do so—they could not acknowledge other jamaath members in public or speak freely of their gender identity. Some were college educated, and all the others had school-level education. Two were practicing Muslims, two were practicing Christians, and the others identified as Hindus. None of them saw their worship of Santhoshi Matha as irreconcilable with their natal religions.

Nikki, Sneha, Satya, and Navya[5] stood somewhat apart in being less closely affiliated to the jamaath. Nikki, a twenty-five-year-old trans woman who was a board member at a Chennai-based NGO for LGBTQ people, had a group of close transgender relations whom she considered her mother and sisters. She loosely followed nirvanam rituals but did not see herself as part of the jamaath as a whole. As a self-employed professional (she was a fashion designer), Nikki was relatively well-off and had the social and financial capital to live independently. Navya, who worked as a model and took part in CBO events, was similarly positioned—she had a guru and loosely followed ritual practices but did not affiliate herself further. Sneha, a trans woman from Chennai who worked in a bank, had no jamaath connections and lived with her natal family as a trans woman. She told us that she variously identified as a thirunangai, as someone of the third gender, or as a woman, depending on the context. Though Sneha was aware of nirvanam customs, she felt no need to follow them.

As we introduced ourselves as researchers interested in the nirvanam, and because our ignorance about thirunangai customs was immediately evident, our interlocutors spoke at length to us about community traditions, sometimes more than they did about themselves. Our positionalities—as students and community outsiders—informed their narration of nirvanam traditions. We also note the politically circumscribed space of the urban nonprofit organization and its imbrication in discourses of neoliberalism, development, and nation making (Bernal and Grewal 2014). Our interlocutors' self-presentation as thirunangais drew not only from their roles as community members but also from their interpellation within the CBO as reform providers or reform seekers who either offered or sought support in the form of capacity building, state benefits, counseling, or sexual health services. This positionality operated alongside their roles as jamaath members and informed their narratives of viable lives and political futures.

The Nirvanam in Thirunangai Narratives of Self

In our interviews, we began by asking our interlocutors what *nirvanam* meant. Sanjana, a twenty-nine-year-old jamaath member who had availed herself of the free SRS offered at a government hospital, said, "Nirvanam is the same as operation."[6] We then asked her why it had different names. "I don't know," she said. She paused, momentarily confused. Then she said, "Nirvanam is in the thirunangai language." Sneha, who was preparing for surgery and did not associate with the jamaath, said, "I have heard the term [*nirvanam*] being used generally, but I say SRS or sex affirmation surgery." Ramani, who was a member of Tamil Nadu's Transgender Welfare Board, clarified for us, "Nirvanam is operation. It is an operation that changes the sex of thirunangais. There are those who call it SRS, but nirvanam is the jamaath language. I won't go home and tell my parents, 'I did nirvanam.' At home, in public when I speak to the press, I say SRS or operation. Within the transgender jamaath, when we speak to other transgenders [*sic*], we use nirvanam in our language."

From these descriptions and our conversations, two things were apparent. First, the nirvanam did not itself refer to rituals but to the act of genital modification, which was usually a medical procedure ("doctor nirvanam") and, more rarely, a procedure carried out by the dayamma, who performed the excision in a ritual rather than medical context. Second, though we were told that nirvanam was the same as "operation," the former had a range of connotations that were closely tied to other arrangements in thirunangai communal life that existed outside state-sanctioned systems of kinship (the heteronormative family) and recognition (in public, legal, and policy discourse). In other words, though "operation" and "nirvanam" both served to indicate "corporeal markers" of identity (Reddy 2006: 98), the choice to use one term or the other was not without significance. In this section, we present some of our interlocutors' views and perspectives of the nirvanam, noting how their diverse positionalities influence their relationship with the jamaath and the authority of Santhoshi Matha and highlighting the common values that are articulated in their narratives of self.

Communality, Care, and Coercion

Forty-seven-year-old Ramani and fifty-eight-year-old Kaveri were the most senior thirunangais we interviewed, in terms of their ages and the positions they held both in advocacy organizations and in the jamaath. For both of them, the jamaath held a lot of importance; all their work was for the community, which they primarily saw as comprising the jamaath (though both mentioned that trans men as well as cisgender lesbian, gay, and bisexual persons, were also part of their broader community). When we asked whether thirunangais still invested in the rituals around nirvanam, even with the medicalization of nirvanam, Ramani said:

> Ninety-nine percent of them still do it. Because though the government offers free surgery today, thirunangais still never do it on their own, they do it as a group. They become members of jamaath. You will have a mother, a mother-in-law [*maamiyaar*], and they will be the ones who facilitate your operation. So you will have to do the necessary rituals . . . it lets everyone know that your nirvanam has happened. After this, nobody will tease me

saying, "You have male organs, you have a penis." Everyone accepts that I am a woman.

Kaveri, who continued to present as male, had a more egalitarian view of whether thirunangais had to undergo nirvanam and associated rituals to have respect in the jamaath: "Society will say one thing one day, and something else another day, it is fickle—and I mean transgender society. Ignore all that, you must take care of your own life." But she agreed that a majority of thirunangais chose to celebrate their nirvanam communally because of jamaath affiliations: "There are those who don't even tell others that they have done castration [*sic*]. They go to the doctor, get the operation done, and come home. That is because they are not strongly affiliated with the community."

Ramani's and Kaveri's words indicate that the world of nirvanam is one where communality, care, and coercion coexist. Specifically, the act of nirvanam, the ritual paal function (which is the celebration of a thirunangai's nirvanam), and jamaath relationships were often invoked together, even when those we spoke to had varying opinions on these practices and varying degrees of affiliation with the jamaath. For those who lived with their jamaath kin and therefore depended on the jamaath for support, the failure to undergo communally legible nirvanam (in terms of undertaking the required ritual observances) invited the risks not just of being left without care and respect but also of incurring the ill-will of the goddess in terms of bodily affliction. Sanjana, who worked as lower management in a restaurant and lived in a house with her sisters (*gurubais*) and her mother (*guru*), explained to us the nature of this impurity (*thittu*):

> The rituals of paal function are meant to remove impurity from within yourself. It is like how you take a bath after you come from a family where a death has taken place. The nirvanam is like death, and the paal function is like purification. So it is bad if you don't do it—you will not become beautiful after castration [*sic*]. . . . If you are in a jamaath, yes [it is mandated]. *Thittu* is not individual, it falls upon the house as a whole. If you do not do the paal function, you will face a lot of health problems, you will not look good. Others will also shame you for not looking feminine enough if you do not do it, they will say that there is *thittu*. If you do it, nobody will say anything.

There was a clear correlation between the extent to which our interlocutors were dependent on the jamaath—for employment, postoperative care, support networks, and so on—and the extent to which they observed a ritually framed nirvanam.

Nevertheless, Santhoshi Matha's authority influenced the choices made by even those who were independent or more dependent on their natal families. Nikki said that she loosely observed the ritual injunctions of the nirvanam because her friends cautioned her against rejecting the rituals. She wanted to risk neither bad luck nor the disapproval of her many jamaath-affiliated peers. Kamala, a postgraduate in her thirties who supervised peer educators and lived with her natal family, told us that belief in Santhoshi Matha was "superstition," but she also mentioned cases where the refusal to observe rituals had resulted in surgical complications.

Satya, who had an engineering degree from the US and a short-lived, though popular, career as a TV show host, also told us that she performed the rituals. She, however, did not use the language of faith but that of coercion:

> Despite me doing my own surgery, despite me deciding how I want my surgery done, despite me choosing where, and who to do the surgery . . . they somehow suck you back into their system. . . . Sickening it was. . . . I was actually beaten, kicked by members of the community. I was attacked for not sticking to their strict codes of conduct. . . . But I still stuck to my own policies of how I want to live my life . . . just because in this loose, adoptive social structure you're somehow higher than me in hierarchy, doesn't mean I have to somehow prostrate myself before you.

This view was echoed by Sneha. She noted the "tribal" nature of jamaaths and indicated that she faced consequences for her choice to remain independent:

> When I was starting transition, I wanted to know where to do surgery, how to start the process, but some people were unwilling to share that information. They do not share it in the community, so we [Sneha and her friends] struggled a bit in terms of where to get information. We were working people, not jamaath people . . . they did not give the information because we didn't show our interest to become their *chela* [daughter].

Understanding the Work that Nirvanam Does

From these accounts, it began to become clear to us that a thirunangai's contention with the authority of the jamaath and faith in Santhoshi Matha is simultaneously a negotiation with the very material conditions of care and coercion within communal networks. This negotiation allows thirunangais to strive for livable lives and legible subjecthood beyond the individuating logics of the state. What is at stake here is also the acquisition of legible gender—of appropriate and authentic levels of femininity—and of legible subjecthood in general. Satya's and Sneha's narratives reveal the jamaath as a system of subjectivation where care and protection are articulated within hierarchies of power that are often maintained violently. However, we argue that it is insufficient to see the world of nirvanam as one where notions of tradition simply constrain thirunangais' ability to avail themselves of individual freedoms.

By attending to the world of nirvanam and how it mediates the livability of thirunangai lives, we draw from a body of anthropological work in South Asia that challenges the complicity of academic analyses with the modernization project inherent in secular models of state recognition. We focus on the acts of worlding that the nirvanam engenders, building upon the works of Gayatri Reddy (2006) and Lucinda Ramberg (2014), which center religiosity and kinship among subjects—namely, hijras and women dedicated to goddesses—who have been incorporated into the secular nation-state as objects of reform. We follow Saba Mahmood's (2011) injunction to more closely interrogate liberal political rejections of religious norms as antithetical to freedom. Mahmood notes that "[religious] norms are not simply a social imposition on the subject but constitute the very substance of her intimate, valorized interiority" (23). Our aim here is to unpack the diverse ways in which thirunangais live with the norm of the nirvanam. We therefore see our engagement with nirvanam as a means to "listen to the obviousness and necessity of sexual identities and embodiments, and not to drain the corporeality of embodied experience by forcing it to stand for difference and difference alone" (Cohen 1995: 295). The thirunangai practice of nirvanam speaks directly to our interlocutors' desire for respect, independence, womanhood, and legibility, within both the community and the state.

South Asian Transfeminine Communities as Political Subjects

"I live in my parents' house. I don't like this *chela-naati* [daughter and granddaughter] stuff. Because I can't take them [jamaath relatives] home, you know? Because I'm at my parents' house. . . . After my work, I just leave. I won't even go where they all are. They won't let me go from home." Navya's words indicate that the nirvanam and its world are not just illegible to natal families, but disreputable. How has this come about?

Having foregrounded the complex practices of self-making indicated by the discourse and debate on nirvanam within thirunangai circles, we will now examine how the secular nation-state has shaped the language and mechanisms that have historically been available for thirunangais and other South Asian transfeminine subcultures to claim legible selfhood. The field of interaction between thirunangais demanding livability through and against the state and its neoliberal affiliates—such as NGOs and CBOs—has been shaped by postcolonial logics of purification and uplift that position them as individuated subjects of reform, "[producing] reasonable bodies shorn of magic, backwardness, and contagion, and thus eligible for inclusion in the national body" (Ramberg 2014: 102). By relying on existing literature, we note two broad discourses through which this has occurred: first, through the "naming" of transfeminine subcultures by state recognition at both the national and subnational regional scales; and second, by the framing of body modification by gender-variant persons through the medicolegal terminology of "castration" and "SRS."

Regimes of Recognition: Transgender, Aravani, Thirunangai

The term *transgender* as an encompassing medicolegal category, while being a term of self-determination and a rallying point for mobilization, has also been complicit in enforcing the teleology of modernization in a postcolony like India (Dutta 2013; Govindan and Vasudevan 2011). State recognition of transgender identity in India has depended on a model of inclusion that requires subjects to shed nonmodern ways of being in becoming full citizens. Informed by discourses on gender pathology and deviance, the category makes subcultures like that of the thirunangais legible within urban Indian centers saturated with LGBTQ identitarian models of activism and recognition (Shah 2014). However, even in academic critiques of government policies and the limits of contemporary rights-based frameworks, the roles of nonsecular actors like gods and goddesses appear as footnotes or spectacular ethnographic details that are peripheral or incidental to the more central question, in this case, of the thirunangais' precarity, which is seen as primarily born of their sexual/gender difference. Even though they criticize the assimilationist approach undertaken by the state, they fail to directly address the elision of religion and sociality that it also enacts.

Within the state of Tamil Nadu, the invitation to transfeminine communities to perform secular and modern subjecthood can be traced through the names given to such communities in the political context of Dravidian subnationalism.[7] While transfeminine persons were known in public only by various derogatory terms, this changed in the 1990s with the popularization of the term *aravani* and, later, through the term *thirunangai*. Examining these shifts—from derogatory terms to *aravani* and then to *thirunangai*—helps set up a genealogy of state recognition of gender variance in Tamil Nadu. What we foreground are the ways in which each of these naming acts invoked or erased religiosity and communality in the process of recognizing gender variance.

The earliest of these terms, *aravani*, is closely tied to a particular Hindu festival, celebrated annually by the people of the Koovagam village in northern Tamil Nadu. As part of the festival, the men of the village and thirunangais assume the role of the brides of Aravan, a character in the Mahabharata epic. At least since the 1980s, this festival has seen massive participation by transfeminine people (Hiltebeitel 1995). With the emergence of the development sector and the HIV/AIDS surveillance regime in India in the 1980s and 1990s, the festival also began to be characterized as a space for "risky" sexual behavior. The consequent influx of funding and events organized by NGOs provided transfeminine communities the opportunity to organize themselves as a distinct, rights-seeking social group united by common traditions at the festival—as "aravanis" (Samuel 2015; Saveri 2013). In 2008, aravanis succeeded in petitioning the government for the first comprehensive institutional setup for transgender welfare in Tamil Nadu—and in India itself—the Aravani/Transgender Welfare Board. Through the board, aravani activists, often jamaath leaders themselves, instituted special ID cards, state-sponsored housing, food, and eventually, free SRS. However, as Padma Govindan and Aniruddhan Vasudevan (2011: 96–97) note, such welfare measures assumed "a paternalistic mode of protection that imagines the aravani body and selfhood as one of psychic disorder and sordid lifestyle choices." In popular narratives, fetishized representations of thirunangais participating in the Koovagam festival serve to suspend transfeminine communities in mythic time and space, marking them as objects of developmentalist reform. It also erases the syncretism of quotidian thirunangai religiosity, which is a mix of Hindu and Islamic practices.

A more recent term to enter the vocabulary of transgender rights in Tamil Nadu is *thirunangai*. The term, possibly coined by a well-known dancer in the community, Narthaki Nataraj, was formally adopted by the Tamil Nadu government in the late 2000s as part of a wave of policy moves for minority welfare (Nadja 2018).[8] As a neologism, *thirunangai* combines "thiru," a Tamil prefix indicating respect, usually gendered masculine, with "nangai," meaning "woman." Located within the larger Dravidian ideology of self-respect, this was a move toward recognizing transfeminine subcultures as part of the Tamil subnationalist vision of society. It also distanced transfeminine identity from the label of *aravani*, which, with its religious connotations, was considered backward and harmful, particularly within Dravidian nationalist narratives that envisioned progress in opposition to traditions of Brahmanical Hinduism. Although *thirunangai* still evoked communality and was not as individuating as the term *transgender*, it was secularized, further increasing the legibility of thirunangai as a progressive label. It also enabled transfeminine communities in Tamil Nadu to fashion a regional identity that was distinct from the "Indianized" term *hijra*, associated with north India and therefore seen as non-Dravidian (Samuel 2015).

These shifts in naming marked the consolidation of a unified movement around transfeminine subjectivity, and it is evident that the conditions that enabled this mobilization also constitute the conditions under which thirunangais become illegible as political theological subjects—subjects formed through engagements with both divine and secular authorities. Even as state recognition increasingly characterized thirunangai religiosity as problematic practices on the wane rather than as constitutive of thirunangai identity and politics, it is evident that thirunangais have articulated their modern subjecthood precisely by using long-standing and coexistent ritualistic communal spaces, and they continue to do so.

Regimes of Body Modification: Castration and SRS

Castration as a term has gained preeminence to the extent that the *nirvan* (hijra term for the process) and nirvanam are defined as "ritual castration" or are conflated with castration even in academic studies seeking more capacious understandings of hijra and thirunangai lives. According to Lawrence Cohen (1995), the idea of castration is simultaneously reduced to a marker of bodily otherness and emptied of its material and embodied aspects in multiple ways: through the understanding of castration as always enforced upon unsuspecting recruits; and by reading castration as only ever serving larger sociocultural logics of gender/sexual difference with no space for exploring lived experience. In this framing, hijras are understood in functional terms as standing for a "thirdness" that scaffolds binary gender systems.

The meaning of *castration* has been produced within cis heteronormative biomedical, psychoanalytic, and legal discourse. In the context of South Asia, the widespread association of hijras with castration (and the colonial category of "eunuch") relates to colonial and postcolonial biopolitics. The colonial Criminal Tribes Act of 1871 (Hinchy 2019) found its postcolonial successors in laws such as the Habitual Offenders Act—which defines *emasculation* as a "grievous bodily harm"—and in laws against begging. These continue to criminalize not just the gender-variant body but the specific and communal forms of labor—such as sex work, ritual performance, and begging—in which transfeminine subcultures engage (Saria 2019). Similarly, the popular depiction of transfeminine communities as criminal groups that kidnap and castrate children continues to have purchase in the contemporary, marking anxieties about the "uncontrolled mobility, unintelligible kinship arrangements, and sexual corruption" of hijras and similar transfeminine groups (Nataraj 2017: 531). Court cases in various Indian states involving natal families attempting to "rescue" their "kidnapped" children are widely covered in the media, relying on lurid descriptions of castration and featuring brainwashed inductees and scheming transfeminine "traffickers."

As SRS became part of the vocabulary of transgender rights, the irrational violence and unintelligibility of castration were contained within the curative logics of gender dysphoria. Despite locating genital modification as part of a more holistic perspective on well-being, SRS came to take the place of castration as marking authentically transgender bodies. In spite of recommendations by activists and medical practitioners to the contrary, many Indian government agencies continue to demand proof of SRS in order to allow persons to choose their gender in documents. There are now good and bad forms of genital modification, with the dayamma nirvanam being associated with backwardness and risk and SRS signifying a secular technology of self that produces the modern, healthy, individuated, and rights-bearing transgender person. In sum, castration and SRS make the world of nirvanam illegible within the biopolitics of the nation-state in ways that supplement the erasure and/or criminalization of nonsecular thirunangai practices.

Recuperating Nirvanam: Thirunangais as Political Theological Subjects

As the vocabulary and politics of a Westernized LGBTQ identitarian framework proliferate in urban India, jamaath traditions are increasingly seen as outdated and unnecessary by thirunangais themselves. Our work here is to illustrate how nirvanam nevertheless remains a powerful imaginary around which thirunangais construct narratives of self and life, even when they define themselves against it. Our interlocutors were involved with public undertakings like HIV/AIDS prevention or community outreach initiatives for transfeminine persons in the city and were deeply invested in secular projects to secure citizenship. These ventures, however, were not separate from their equally substantial efforts to secure their positions within the jamaath, which are granted not just through an assumption of kin relationships but also through participation in advocacy work and activism. The values articulated in thirunangai narrations of the nirvanam speak to their lived realities in a more effective manner than existing expert-driven policy and welfare discourses that primarily use the developmentalist lens of sexual health, human rights, and empowerment in assessing community needs. By recuperating nirvanam as a means to understand thirunangai politics, we draw attention to the significance of faith—whether it is acknowledged, resisted, or enacted. Thirunangais actively negotiate their relationships with natal and jamaath kin, with the state, and with divine entities in establishing viable political and social futures for themselves. Thirunangai enactments of the nirvanam offer a rereading of modern narratives on desire, pain, risk, and care in thirunangai subculture, and they challenge the marginalization of faith-based practices that occurs in the space of the CBO, the hospital, or government-sponsored welfare.

Mobilizing Desire and Affect

Reddy (2006) argues that hijras selectively deploy certain aspects of their histories—like asexuality and celibacy—to establish their legitimacy. In contrast, thirunangais fashion themselves as always desiring subjects, using the event of the nirvanam as central to such a subjectivation. They draw on the origin stories of Santhoshi Matha when narrating themselves. We were told several versions of myths surrounding Santhoshi Matha. In most of them, Santhoshi Matha is a man born to an affluent family who cuts off her genitalia in a spontaneous act of enraged indignation or despair and is invested with divine femininity, as a boon for her sacrifice, by the goddess Shakti as she lies bleeding to death. In one version, she castrates herself when she is spotted applying turmeric on her body—a feminine routine of care—by a guard, who reports this to her family. In another, she desires the husband of her sister, who rejects her derisively. In both stories, we see that the goddess is an idealization of the thirunangai: one who is socially perceived as male and who undertakes the nirvanam out of the desire to be a woman. Unlike the origin stories of hijras (Nanda 1990; Reddy 2006), asceticism and celibacy as ideals are entirely absent, and what is celebrated is the willingness of the thirunangai to sacrifice her life for her desire to live and be loved as a woman. Respect, legible gender, and beauty are granted by the goddess through the nirvanam, which is a reenactment of the origin myth. Pain and sacrifice are understood as actualizing the desires of the thirunangai under the protection of the goddess and with the support of her adopted family. This framework of desire, blessing, and acceptance was also used by our interlocutors to articulate their desire for SRS and for equal opportunity.

The rearticulation of pain and suffering during the nirvanam as an affective and embodied indicator of sacrifice, effectiveness, authenticity, and self-actualization—rather than as a signifier of risk or of things gone wrong—is integral to thirunangai narratives. This reading contradicts secular understandings of pain as irrational or something to be eradicated (Asad 2003). Even when it involves medicalized forms of body modification, the nirvanam works with distinctly non-biomedical understandings of pain. The changes wrought by the nirvanam process are described in such terms: manly blood and hormones flow out, facial hair falls, and muscles get broken down, producing instead a desirable and feminine body. As a mode of engagement with the world, this invokes not just a disembodied, transcendent self but a "bioavailable" self (Cohen 2013), where the giving over of bodily components to something other than the self brokers relationships not just with human others but with extrahuman others like Santhoshi Matha. In the case of dayamma nirvanam, the increased levels of pain and the possibility of loss of life increase the value of this excision. It is important to note that such understandings of bodily commitment are othered not only within secular understandings of health and subjecthood but within secular prescriptions of the proper relationships between the human and the divine, where it is immaterial aspects of the self, such as the mind or the soul, that are given over to the divine (Ramberg 2014).

Contrary to developmentalist perspectives that identify nirvanam and thirunangai religious traditions as barriers to safe transition methods (Singh et al. 2014), thirunangais follow nirvanam prescriptions and rituals precisely to *mitigate* risk, which is articulated beyond purely medical terms. Even for jamaath outsiders like Nikki, the nirvanam offered a fuller affective experience of transition through its provision of religious and social protections without impairing her deliberate stance of independence. For Navya, jamaath relationships were carefully negotiated and maintained at a necessary minimum to avoid her parents' censure. But it remained an important avenue of support, information, and care. It was through Navya's guru that she was directed to a hospital for surgery, and it was her guru who cared for her immediately after the operation. Such instances offer a counter to prevailing dominant (popular and legal) perspectives on jamaaths as wholly coercive or violent or as obstacles to achieving modern citizenship. As we have seen, jamaath relationships permeate the spaces of CBOs and state undertakings for transfeminine communities in Chennai. The social space of the jamaath and the CBO are often blurred, as outreach work, crisis intervention, and support in accessing identity cards and other forms of state recognition are accessed often by means of the informal knowledge and social networks formed through jamaath connections. Veena noted that only "real" thirunangais could access CBO services like crisis intervention, where "realness" implied communal acceptance; Ramani told us that previous jamaath and NGO/CBO connections are crucial in verifying transfeminine applicants' claims for identity cards or other forms of government support, pointing to both the ongoing relevance of the jamaath and intracommunity anxieties about impostors and regulation of resources.

Imaginaries of Transition

Unlike liberal-secular narratives of transsexuality that celebrate the modern capacity for transformation and self-determination (Aizura 2018), thirunangai narratives of transition also emphasize affects like sacrifice, faith, and communal belonging.

They reflect not just normative and aspirational ideals of femininity and personhood but also transact in nonsecular values like auspiciousness, sacral embodiment, sacrifice, and submission. Even within the highly regulated and biopolitically mediated space of the contemporary development sector, where employees are routinely encouraged to participate in liberal political projects of citizenship, the nirvanam persists as a constant in thirunangai imaginaries of valuable lifestyles and futures. Jamaath insiders like Ramani emphasized the social aspect of the rituals—how it brought together community members and how it offered thirunangais an opportunity to celebrate a personal moment, often denied to them in their public lives outside the jamaath.

Contemporary performances of the nirvanam also demonstrate how faith is expressed and enacted in "living" religious practice (Cohen 1991). Adherence to nirvanam customs was never uniform or uncontested; some thirunangais noted that not all regulations were convenient, necessary, or relevant. Since thirunangai traditions were orally passed down to younger members and because local religious customs influence such practices as the paal function, our interviewees often had different and flexible notions of what constituted "tradition." This is most evident in their discussion of the dayamma nirvanam. None of the thirunangais we spoke to had done the dayamma nirvanam, nor did they plan to do so. Rather, some of them suggested that if practiced now at all, it was done only in "backward" rural areas, emphasizing their own separate performance of urban, modern transition practices. Almost all of them acknowledged that they preferred hospital-based procedures for themselves, even if not performed by licensed practitioners. Some thirunangais—like Satya—went to Thailand for SRS. Our interlocutors considered Thailand surgeries to be highly effective; the ability to access Thailand signaled socioeconomic capital, the foreign setting suggested greater medical expertise and better standards of care, and it was seen by thirunangais as the apotheosis of avenues for transformation and the performance of transness (Aizura 2018). SRS in Thailand and the dayamma nirvanam, performed in a rural elsewhere, constituted spatialized and quasi-mythical ideals of what it meant to achieve authentic femininity within a tradition-modernity dichotomy. Importantly, even in their discursive construction of Thailand as the secular antithesis to the dayamma nirvanam, the thirunangais used the terminology of blessing, respect, and submission (to both foreign doctors and the goddess), indicating the pervasive power of nirvanam values in their world-making.

Conclusion: Why Political Theology?

Whereas aspects of our argument have been studied in different contexts within the disciplines of anthropology, political science, development studies, and so on, we take up the incitement of this special issue to frame these questions within the discourses of queer political theology. While we find political theology, and queer political theology in particular, an apt discursive space to both historicize and foreground the mutual co-constitution of religion and secularism, we also use our study to consider how far the interventions of queer political theology can travel beyond its naturalized contexts, that is, Judeo-Christian religiosity in Euroamerica. Queer theologians invest in the value of queering as an analytic and of queer as identity in challenging boundaries and questioning essentialism, but only within the understanding that theology is equivalent to Judeo-Christian theology (Cavanaugh and Scott 2019). The one boundary that queer theologians seem unwilling or unable to consider surrounds the multiple forms of knowing the world that can be studied under theology. Queerness, therefore, is safely constrained within the permitted bounds of theology as a discipline that evolved within Judeo-Christian traditions of religion. Even postcolonial perspectives only go so far as to consider non-Western forms of Judeo-Christian theology as a product of European colonialism (Moore and Rivera 2011).

The purpose of this article, however, is not to ask what political theology can learn from queer spaces, or what Judeo-Christian political theology can learn from "third world" spaces. Such an orientation itself reifies the United States and the West in general (as a discursive world rather than a geographic one) as the center for both political theology and queer theory (Arondekar and Patel 2016; Shohat 2002). Rather, we aim to provincialize the canonical habits of thought of the area while also recognizing the usefulness of the unique epistemological orientation of political theology: that it makes analytic investments in the organization of society through the authority of god(s); or more broadly defined, that it works with a capacious view of ontology that includes the power exerted by divine entities on the lives of people and societies. Taking political theology's cue to step back from seeing faith as a "serious fiction" (Cavanaugh and Scott 2019), we begin to consider what it might mean to undo the presumption that critique and analysis—as well as more praxis-oriented discourses about the best normative frameworks for social organization—must always locate themselves as a secular practice (Brown et al. 2009). We also find productive the move from queer political theology as a focus on the religious practices of subjects framed as queer or protoqueer, to queer political theology as examining the ways in which the prescribed relationship between the religious and the secular are queered in different contexts. Therefore, what interests us is not how well thirunangais sustain anti-normativity (Jagose 2015) but the conditions and histories under which thirunangai mechanisms of norm production are shaped and rendered unintelligible—queered—in mainstream discourse.

Thirunangai performances of the nirvanam demonstrate that although it functions as a norm, it is dynamic and can accommodate many professions of faith and belief. By this, we refer to the strategic adoption of nirvanam by thirunangais who are not just invested in their relationship with the goddess but also deeply concerned with their place within the jamaath and its extended networks of support, information, and care. Kept alive through variegated practice and retellings, the nirvanam and the authority of Santhoshi Matha continue to contribute toward the thirunangais' dialogue with the state and its neoliberal affiliates, articulating community concerns in a more comprehensive manner than existing policy and government prescriptions for community well-being. We do not wish to romanticize the nirvanam as a more authentic reality for thirunangais by characterizing it as traditional. Unlike spectacular occasions like the Koovagam festival, which are often valued in academic analyses only to the extent that they subvert dominant Hindu religiosity, the nirvanam is a more quotidian referential reality. It is less amenable to readings of liberal emancipatory potential and prone to the violence of norm production. Its value as a concept, both for thirunangais and researchers—lies in the fact that it demands a more careful mapping of how thirunangais live with, through, and against various kinds of norms.

Notes

We thank Aaron Devor for extensive comments on early versions of this project. Thanks to T. D. Sivakumar and Delfina of Nirangal, an NGO in Chennai, for their generous research assistance in conducting the second set of interviews, and to the thirunangais who took the time to speak to us. We thank the three anonymous reviewers for their insightful suggestions, which have greatly helped us to refine the article. Any errors or oversights are ours.

1. Transfeminine communities like the hijras are believed to be invested with special powers to bless and curse; begging and blessing work are important sources of income. However, among the thirunangais we met, these practices were not as common.

2. The patron goddess of the hijras and thirunangais is variously known as Bahuchara Matha, Bhedraj Matha, or Santhoshi Matha. Minor deities of the Hindu subculture of goddess worship, they are understood to be the same or seen as different divine

entities by our interlocutors. Santhoshi Matha, for example, is otherwise known as a goddess who was newly popularized by cults of worship in Gujarat. This lack of agreement on who the goddess is signifies the ways in which divine actors live—as dynamic and context-based rather than as distortions of canonical religion by "the masses" (Cohen 1991).

3.   We use the term *transfeminine* as opposed to *transgender* to avoid the loaded implications of the latter and to foreground the implicit and widespread conflation of *transgender* with transfeminine identities and the consequent elision of transmasculine identities.

4.   Kothis are individuals who are assigned male at birth but present as feminine and prefer receptive sexual positions. *Kothi* may be seen as an identity distinct from *hijra* and *thirunangai*, or in some contexts, as an umbrella category for various feminine identities. The ways in which the term *kothi* has come to signify a reified identity within NGO terminology have been widely studied (Boyce 2007; Cohen 2005).

5.   All names used here are pseudonyms.

6.   Most excerpts from interviews are originally in Tamil, which we translated to English. We have, however, retained terms of self-identification without modification. Some of our interlocutors used "third gender," "transgender," or "woman" to describe themselves along with the term *thirunangai*.

7.   The anti-Brahmanical Dravidian cultural nationalist movement in Tamil Nadu, made most visible by E. V. Ramasamy's Self-Respect Movement, has been the subject of several historiographies and commentaries (Geetha and Rajadurai 1998).

8.   In November 2019, the Tamil Nadu government released a notification changing all uses of *thirunangai* to *moondram palinathavar* (those of the third gender), inciting widespread protests against the use of an outdated term (Nadja 2018).

References

Aizura, Aren Z. 2018. *Mobile Subjects: Transnational Imaginaries of Gender Reassignment*. Durham, NC: Duke University Press.

Arondekar, Anjali, and Geeta Patel. 2016. "Area Impossible: Notes toward an Introduction." *GLQ* 22, no. 2: 151–71.

Asad, Talal. 1993. *Genealogies of Religion: Discipline and Reasons of Power in Christianity and Islam*. Baltimore, MD: Johns Hopkins University Press.

Asad, Talal. 2003. *Formations of the Secular: Christianity, Islam, Modernity*. Stanford, CA: Stanford University Press.

Bernal, Victoria, and Inderpal Grewal. 2014. *Theorizing NGOs: States, Feminisms, and Neoliberalism*. Durham, NC: Duke University Press.

Boyce, Paul. 2007. "'Conceiving Kothis': Men Who Have Sex with Men in India and the Cultural Subject of HIV Prevention." *Medical Anthropology* 26, no. 2: 175–203.

Brown, Wendy, Talal Asad, Saba Mahmood, and Judith Butler. 2009. *Is Critique Secular?* Berkeley, CA: Townsend Center for the Humanities.

Cavanaugh, William T., and Peter Manley Scott, eds. 2019. *Wiley Blackwell Companion to Political Theology.* 2nd ed. Hoboken, NJ: Wiley.

Cohen, Lawrence. 1991. "The Wives of Ganesha." In *Ganesha: Studies of an Asian God*, edited by David Brown, 115–40. Albany: State University of New York Press.

Cohen, Lawrence. 1995. "The Pleasures of Castration: The Postoperative Status of Hijras, Jankhas, and Academics." In *Sexual Nature/Sexual Culture*, edited by Paul R. Abramson and Steven D. Pinkerton, 276–304. Chicago: University of Chicago Press.

Cohen, Lawrence. 2005. "The Kothi Wars: AIDS Cosmopolitanism and the Morality of Classification." In *Sex in Development: Science, Sexuality, and Morality in Global Perspective*, edited by Stacy L. Pigg and Vincanne Adams, 269–304. Durham, NC: Duke University Press.

Cohen, Lawrence. 2013. "Given Over to Demand: Excorporation as Commitment." *Contemporary South Asia* 21, no. 3: 318–32.

Dutta, Aniruddha. 2013. "Legible Identities and Legitimate Citizens: The Globalization of Transgender and Subjects of HIV-AIDS Prevention in Eastern India." *International Feminist Journal of Politics* 15, no. 4: 494–514.

Dutta, Aniruddha, and Raina Roy. 2014. "Decolonizing Transgender in India: Some Reflections." *TSQ* 1, no. 3: 320–37.

Geetha, V., and S. V. Rajadurai. 1998. *Towards a Non-Brahmin Millennium: From Iyothee Thass to Periyar.* Calcutta: Samya.

Govindan, Padma, and Aniruddhan Vasudevan. 2011. "The Razor's Edge of Oppositionality: Exploring the Politics of Rights-Based Activism by Transgender Women in Tamil Nadu." In *Law Like Love: Queer Perspectives on Law*, edited by Arvind Narrain and Alok Gupta, 84–112. New Delhi, India: Yoda.

Hiltebeitel, Alf. 1995. "Dying before the Mahābhhārata War: Martial and Transsexual Bodybuilding for Aravhāṇ." *Journal of Asian Studies* 54, no. 2: 447–73.

Hinchy, Jessica. 2019. *Governing Gender and Sexuality in Colonial India: The Hijra, c. 1850–1900.* Cambridge: Cambridge University Press.

Hossain, Adnan. 2018. "De-Indianizing Hijra: Intraregional Effacements and Inequalities in South Asian Queer Space." *TSQ* 5, no. 3: 321–31.

Jagose, Annamarie. 2015. "The Trouble with Antinormativity." *differences* 26, no. 1: 26–47.

Mahmood, Saba. 2011. *Politics of Piety: The Islamic Revival and the Feminist Subject.* Princeton, NJ: Princeton University Press.

Moore, Stephen D., and Mayra Rivera. 2011. *Planetary Loves: Spivak, Postcoloniality, and Theology.* New York: Fordham University Press.

Nadja, Nadika. 2018. "Self-Respect Weddings to Transgender Rights: Karunanidhi, a Leader of Minorities." *News Minute* (blog), August 7. thenewsminute.com/article/self-respect-weddings-transgender-rights-karunanidhi-leader-minorities-86159.

Nagar, Richa. 2014. *Muddying the Waters: Coauthoring Feminisms across Scholarship and Activism*. Chicago: University of Illinois Press.

Nanda, Serena. 1990. *Neither Man nor Woman: The Hijras of India*. Belmont, CA: Wadsworth.

Nataraj, Shakthi. 2017. "Criminal 'Folk' and 'Legal' Lore: The Kidnap and Castrate Narrative in Colonial India and Contemporary Chennai." *South Asian History and Culture* 8, no. 4: 523–41.

Ramberg, Lucinda. 2014. *Given to the Goddess: South Indian Devadasis and the Sexuality of Religion*. Durham, NC: Duke University Press.

Reddy, Gayatri. 2006. *With Respect to Sex: Negotiating Hijra Identity in South India*. Chicago: University of Chicago Press.

Samuel, Aaron Theodore. 2015. "Performing Thirunangai: Activism, Development, and Normative Citizenship in Tamil Transgender Performances." PhD diss., American University.

Saria, Vaibhav. 2019. "Begging for Change: Hijras, Law and Nationalism." *Contributions to Indian Sociology* 53, no. 1: 133–57.

Saveri, Shabeena Francis. 2013. "History, Identity, and Politics: Aravani Movement in the State of Tamilnadu, India." PhD diss., Tata Institute of Social Sciences.

Shah, Svati P. 2014. "Queering Critiques of Neoliberalism in India: Urbanism and Inequality in the Era of Transnational 'LGBTQ' Rights." *Antipode* 47, no. 3: 635–51.

Shohat, Ella. 2002. "Area Studies, Gender Studies, and the Cartographies of Knowledge." *Social Text* 20, no. 3: 67–78.

Singh, Yadavendra, Abhina Aher, Simran Shaikh, Sonal Mehta, James Robertson, and Venkatesan Chakrapani. 2014. "Gender Transition Services for Hijras and Other Male-to-Female Transgender People in India: Availability and Barriers to Access and Use." *International Journal of Transgenderism* 15, no. 1: 1–15.

Towle, Evan B., and Lynn Marie Morgan. 2002. "Romancing the Transgender Native: Rethinking the Use of the 'Third Gender' Concept." *GLQ* 8, no. 4: 469–97.

Weston, Kath. 1993. "Lesbian/Gay Studies in the House of Anthropology." *Annual Review of Anthropology*, no. 22: 339–67.

DIVINE MONARCHY, SPIRITED SOVEREIGNTIES, AND THE TIMELY MALAGASY MSM MEDIUM-ACTIVIST SUBJECT

Seth Palmer

$\mathcal{S}$prawled out on the cool cement floor, Balou Chabat Rasoanaivo worked with her coterie of fellow *sarimbavy*—same-sex-desiring and/or gender-expansive, male-bodied persons—to finalize plans for their upcoming soiree.[1] Some participants practiced their dance routines, while others made painstakingly difficult sarto-rial selections, and still others prepared the midday meal. Balou had purposefully planned for the Men Who Have Sex with Men (MSM) Ball to coincide with the *fanompoambe* ("Great Service")—the popular annual ritual return by pilgrims, supplicants, and spirit mediums alike to the royal shrine of Ndramisara in the city of Mahajanga, in northwestern Madagascar.[2] In fact, the MSM Ball was held on the evening before the final day of that periodic ritual gathering and thus was concurrent with festivities that continued at the shrine late into the night. Many of the male-bodied mediums and supplicants who arrived from across the island to attend the fanompoambe were same-sex desiring and/or gender nonconforming (and traveled to the site at considerable personal expense); mediumship was in fact central to the burgeoning regional collectivity of self-identified sarimbavy, MSM, and *dossier*, a term used interchangeably with the previous two in the in-group lexicon used by community members.[3] Balou, who permanently resided far away in the capital, Antananarivo, often scheduled activist efforts such as roundtables, town halls, and participatory workshops to correspond with pilgrimage dates at spirit shrines throughout the northwest (fig. 1). Still, despite Balou's best inten-tions, sarimbavy mediums cognizant of the Ball were torn between participating

GLQ 27:1
DOI 10.1215/10642684-8776862
© 2021 by Duke University Press

Figure 1. Balou Chabat Rasoanaivo (center), seated in front of a rainbow flag and
interviewed by journalists in Marovoay, 2015. Photograph by the author.

in the nocturnal merrymaking at the pilgrimage site and taking part in the MSM
event.

Possession by Sakalava royal sovereigns is common throughout northwestern Madagascar, given that the monarchic polity and ethnic identity are considered indigenous to the region.[4] Balou herself was among those sarimbavy who were
also mediums to *tromba*—spirits of deceased members of the Sakalava monarchy
and their diviners who return to life through the corporeal forms of their (often
female-bodied) human mediums. She was also the sole public figurehead of LGBT
activism in Madagascar and Présidente of the only active nationwide MSM rights
organization, Solidarité des MSM (hereafter Solidarité). Preparations for the Ball
unfolded in the two-story home of Julien, a fellow MSM, renowned spirit medium,
and leader of the newly formed regional MSM youth health association that collaborated with Solidarité to address rising HIV rates in the city. Clients regularly
visited Julien's abode to consult with one of the many tromba spirits of former
reigning monarchs that "sat upon" him, and his residence simultaneously acted as
a place for MSM to socialize.

MSM as an activist site and identity category emerged throughout Madagascar precisely because of the higher prevalence of HIV among the recently conceived MSM population on the island. Furthermore, given that Solidarité devel-

oped out of sexual health schemes, the organization often prioritized a biomedical concern with disease over intersectional understandings of sex/gender stigma and readily switched between employing "LGBT" and "MSM" rights discourses.[5] Still, MSM activist social networks forged through Balou's labor as a medium were largely integrated into her work with Solidarité; like other LGBT rights organizations in poor nations targeted for HIV prevention, Solidarité was born out of transnational public health funds and had developed in tandem with the global AIDS industry. Western nongovernmental organization (NGO) workers interested in sexual health and foreign diplomats invested in Malagasy LGBT rights projects were left largely unaware of the fact that possession circuits came to implicitly inform the burgeoning Malagasy MSM rights movement and HIV prevention programming, both of which are largely supported by foreign political actors. The Ball, which was the first of its kind organized on such a scale, was realized through funds provided by the United States Embassy and Population Services International (PSI), an NGO focused on public health initiatives. Several members of Julien's extended family attended the event, which included a dance party, a beauty pageant (designated a "Miss" Competition)—in which contestants were asked to respond to an array of trivia questions, including what the initialisms *LGBT* and *HIV* stood for—and free HIV testing (fig. 2). Most health care professionals present at the Ball had just arrived from the shrine, where they provided complimentary HIV testing throughout the day.[6]

While supported by MSM activists interested in fighting HIV, the desire to provide testing at the shrine also resulted from increasing demonization of Sakalava ritual practice on the part of conservative Christian publics. These Protestant Christian communities, which are particularly vibrant in the central highlands, have imparted connotations of sexual licentiousness and immoral bodily pursuits onto the pilgrimage circuits of *fanompoa*—a term perhaps best described as "royal work" that refers to the ritual labor that accompanies the annual series of pilgrimages to spirit shrines, including the most popular of them all, the fanompoambe.[7] This decidedly Christian moral puritanism, which renders "traditional" Malagasy religiosities as "behind the times" of medical, economic, and sexual development, was even reflected in the 2007–2012 *National Malagasy Action Plan to Effectively Combat HIV/AIDS*, which specifically noted that "traditional, periodic ritual gatherings encourage risky sexual behavior, including . . . the Fanompoambe" (Comité National 2007: 27).

Drawing upon the lived experience of Malagasy MSM medium-activists such as Balou and Julien, this article invites renewed critique of those tacit forms of liberal humanism that have supported the emergence of the queer secular sub-

Figure 2. The contestant who was later crowned "Miss" Mahajanga MSM performs
for the audience at the MSM Ball, 2015. Photograph by the author.

ject in human rights discourse and HIV prevention schemes. While the work of
Balou and her colleagues was inextricably tied to the global power structures of
AIDS cosmopolitanisms, its effervescence was the unique result of its willful and
imaginative incorporation into the spirit possession milieu.[8] As a spectacle wedded
to royal origins and a genre that has blossomed into vibrant queer of color worldings in North America, the Ball seems a salient juncture from which to articulate the complex cross-fertilizations between possession by the spirits of ancestral
monarchs and the political imagination of MSM.[9] Over the course of twenty-four
months of ethnographic research between 2012 and 2015, I learned that the Malagasy MSM activist movement flourished primarily through the social networks of
tromba "spirit possession," by which I refer to the process whereby tromba spirits
come to "sit upon" or "live within" (*mipetraka*) the bodies of human mediums,
including hosts who may also identify as Christian or Muslim. In contrast to much
scholarship and popular representation of African LGBT rights activism, which
automatically pits religiosity against same-sex desire and gender-expansiveness,
possession and this novel sex/gender rights project were mutually constitutive
rather than antagonistic (cf. Gaudio 2009; van Klinken 2015).

　　Through these religio-political entanglements, medium-activists in Mahajanga, the neighboring rural Betsiboka Valley, and the capital Antananarivo experienced shifting temporal allegiances through their roles as mediums to spirits of former reigning monarchs but also as MSM rights activists focused on achieving social and legal recognitions not yet realized. The former necessitated an onerous dedication to Malagasy history (*tantara*) and tradition (*fombandrazana*) while the latter required a deep commitment to move beyond the stigma-ridden past and present in which, as sarimbavy activists lamented, "there are not yet any rights" (*mbola tsisy zo*). Balou and Julien are examples of MSM medium-activists heavily invested in the ethical obligations presented by mediumship who also used these shared duties to animate a national activist project.

In light of queer theories staunchly wedded to death-drive presentism and asocial nonreproductivity, most famously furthered in the influential work of Lee Edelman (2004), it may be fruitful to consider those sarimbavy mediums I came to know who surrendered to—indeed, themselves reproduced—the transgenerational fetishization of heteroreproductive genealogy and divine queen-kingship.[10] Interlocutors' ritualized maneuvers into the past unfolded alongside the future-oriented medico-political projects of LGBT rights work and HIV prevention. These activist engagements—rooted in the call to honor international sexual rights and public health regimes—and those emergent MSM counterpublics and "secret" sociolects they produced were uncannily facilitated through mediumship social networks (rooted in ancestral religio-political devotion).[11]

In upsetting facile secular feminist notions of personal liberation, freedom, and agency, the scholarship of Saba Mahmood (2005) and Carolyn Rouse (2004) perhaps most clearly resonates with the ethnographic depiction of Malagasy MSM medium-activists that I tell here. Their accounts of Muslim women in strikingly different cultural contexts attest to the productive ways in which a collective political imagination may be spurred by ethical acts of pious submission, as seen in surrendering to one's fate as a medium and to the sacred authority of ancestral royalty, for those interlocutors whom I befriended. Furthermore, my intervention gestures to the generative potentialities forged at the intersection between, first, queer theory that remains simultaneously open to yet critical of religion-as-object and, second, anthropological work on mediumship that envisages possession-as-politics-otherwise yet bypasses easy, instrumentalist interpretation. In placing this scholarship alongside the lived experiences of MSM medium-activists, I illustrate how they challenged Western expectations that sex/gender rights movements must emanate through grammars of secular liberalism that presume, to draw from Wendy Brown (2002: 431), "an ontologically autonomous, self-sufficient, unencumbered subject." Their social activism transpired through the celebration of "traditional" Sakalava monarchical rule and its "possessed" subjects invested in those pilgrimage circuits described below.

Tromba, Pilgrimage, and Laboring for Monarchy

> *Nizara roa ary ny fitondrana, ao amin'ny firaisan'i Madirovalo.*
> *Nizara roa izy ireo, anefa samy mitondra vahoaka.*
> *Ny iray fitondram-panjakana, izay ho entin'ny lehiben'ny firaisana.*
> *Ny faharoa dia ny fitondran'ny razana ka i Adamalandy no mitondra*
>   *an'izany.*
> *Izany no tromban'i Madirovalo any Ambato-Boéni.*
> *Tromba mitondra vahoaka no sady tromba ho entim-bahoaka.*

> The local government is split in two, as is the community in Madirovalo.
> It is split in two, however both carry/guide the people.
> The first is the state, which is the head of this community.
> The second is the ancestors' government, which Adamalandy carries/guides.
> This is the *tromba* of Madirovalo over in Ambato-Boéni.
> *Tromba* carry/guide the people at the same time that *tromba* are carried/
>   guided by the people.
> —(Mahaleo, "Madirovalo")

The popular song "Madirovalo," which was written by Dama (Zafimahaleo Rasolofondrasolo) and performed by his band Mahaleo, describes the magical but "true tale" of a "place where taboos are kept." Widely recognized across Madagascar, the ballad identifies this site as the shrine of Anelobe, a spot from which "clean water" magically emerges from the earth. "Madirovalo" recounts the adventure of a group of university students who visit the town of the same name under the auspices of an internship and are "ruminating over what they observed." In this rural outpost, they find ethnic outsiders (*vahiny*, literally "guests") like themselves who have settled down in Madirovalo for good, and tromba—those spirits of deceased members of the royal Sakalava monarchy—that "carry/guide the people at the same time that tromba are carried/guided by the people."

The prominence of "Madirovalo" in the Malagasy national soundtrack is indicative of three popular conceptions of the Betsiboka Valley held by those with even the most passing familiarity with the region. For ethnic outsiders, but particularly the Merina and Betsileo from the central highlands, the fertile landscape is understood first as a place where the extraordinary, mythical, even slightly terrifying world of Sakalava spirit possession is alive and well; second, as a place where the precolonial, ethnopolitical institution of Sakalava monarchical power continues to captivate the hearts and minds of its subjects; and third, as a place where guests, motivated principally by the search for economic gain but also by the desire to visit spirit shrines and royal tombs, continue to temporarily sojourn to or permanently migrate into the region.[12] During fanompoa, all three pursuits are consummated when spirit mediums and supplicants participate in the yearly series of pilgrimages to shrines of deceased Sakalava sovereigns and their ancestors across the Betsiboka Valley. At these events, mediums and supplicants alike are understood to labor for the divine queen-kingship through the cyclical care and cleaning of sacred ancestral relics and by offering prestations at sites across the region (Lambek 2002).

Even if not articulated as a conscious decision—for tromba spirits choose their hosts, not vice versa—mediums implicitly express allegiance to the Sakalava monarchy, which continues to reign at the time of this writing. The Sakalava religio-political system is considered somewhat exceptional throughout Madagascar given the continued vibrancy of its monarchy. Oral histories detail the migration of people now united under the Sakalava ethnonym, from the southwest of the island northward, eventually reaching contemporary Mahajanga and the greater Betsiboka Valley by the late seventeenth to early eighteenth centuries under the tutelage of their royal sovereigns. However, the indigenous Sakalava monarchy lost its absolute sovereignty over the course of the nineteenth and twentieth centuries, first due to military takeovers by the Merina empire from the central highlands and later under French colonial rule. This historical legacy endures, as Sakalava royalty currently have no juridico-legal authority within the secular Malagasy nation-state.

However, just as the French colonial administration placated Sakalava monarchs to win over their subjects, so too do contemporary Malagasy politicians consociate with Sakalava royalty when campaigning for office, and, according to spirit medium interlocutors, some elected officials struggling with political stratagem also seek the advice of tromba through human hosts. In summoning tromba, state bureaucrats supplicate before the central figures in Sakalava religio-political life. Like these politicians, clients throughout the Malagasy northwest regularly seek mediums in order to communicate with tromba to locate solutions to personal problems, including physical ailments or interpersonal dilemmas. In turn, royal ancestral spirits that have come back from the past into the present—like those that emerge through Balou and Julien—provide supplicants with sage advice and practical suggestions.

In this sense, tromba comprise a therapeutic system; but as with the sarim-bavy category, which itself traffics between the logics of gender and sexuality, tromba "possession" is multivalent, crossing over multiple Western categories of academic inquiry and transcending distinct experiential planes. At once, tromba mediumship can be described as a religious ordeal, a healing art, a system of communication, a practice of indigenous historiography, and a display of come-dic entertainment. This article, however, attends principally to the significance of mediumship as a sign of political allegiance to Sakalava royalty, for both mediums and supplicants to tromba spirits celebrate the monarchical tradition through their spirit work.

The act of becoming host to tromba spirits is an intimate act of offering oneself to a higher authority, either a contemporary royal sovereign or a deceased monarch in spirit form. Notably, this higher authority is not the Malagasy nation-state but that of divine ancestral spirits, with the most senior ancestors taking precedence. Throughout, possession is considered a burdensome yet esteemed act of "travail" (*asa*) that commoners execute for royalty. Mediumship-as-labor is paradigmatic of fanompoa—a concept that, again, includes the labor that accom-panies the annual series of pilgrimages to spirit shrines. Ethnographer Gillian Feeley-Harnik's (1985: 293) assertion that "labor for monarchy is the most suc-cinct expression of citizenship" in Sakalava communities holds true well into the early twenty-first century.[13]

Elsewhere, Feeley-Harnik (1984) has charted the French colonial admin-istration's desire that Sakalava monarchy eventually die off. In response, the regional monarchy shifted the ritual emphasis of divine rule from easily stolen royal relics to the burial of deceased sovereigns in fixed tombs, as overseen by spirit mediums and other ritual actors. Subsequently, mediumship rapidly prolifer-ated, expanding to commoners and thus broadening the focus of monarchical polit-ical power outward to a wider public. The sovereign body of divine succession was thus "democratized"—it was extended out to the mortal subjects of both French empire and regional Sakalava monarchy who would soon form the newly indepen-dent Malagasy Republic. In this sense, contemporary mediums of tromba uphold a long-standing religio-political structure—a precolonial monarchical tradition that requires their subservience as subjects of royal power—but one that has shifted over time in response to competing sovereignties.

The call to replace divine succession with the "People's" will—perhaps the most distinctive feature of Enlightenment-era Western Europe—has since come to be indicative of the only appropriate "modern" political condition.[14] Eric Santner has nevertheless convincingly argued that political theologies of royal succession remain infused in postmonarchical, "modern" Western European societies more than is readily acknowledged or realized. Human obsession with the fleshly divine—so effectively embodied in systems of divine monarchy—and the religio-political desire to completely surrender oneself to a greater power—"do not disappear from the world once the place of the royal personage has been emptied and the principle of sovereignty relocated in the will, life, and fate of the 'People'" (2011: 50).

In the early twenty-first-century Malagasy postcolony, the ostensibly anti-democratic veneration of monarchy remains alive and well. And yet, while their position is seemingly antithetical to the "equality" concept embedded in LGBT rights activism, interlocutors in the 2010s did not envision their commitment to monarchic religio-political authority as in opposition to their political ideals. Dynastic reign was not regarded as in absolute contradistinction to grassroots governance, for any human could act as a host for tromba, and furthermore, the possession structure itself relied upon the participation of the people, as expressed in the lyrics of "Madirovalo": ". . . *tromba* are carried/guided by the people." One could thus argue that tromba mediumship embodies decidedly republican elements, given that the sovereign body of the "People" was precisely the medium that energized divine succession.[15]

Rather than acting in stark opposition to democratic principles, monarchic rule existed parallel to—if at times in friction with—popular forms of sovereignty in northwestern Madagascar. There, as throughout much of the island, the "People" were not united in their support for (or even informed of) the fight for sex/gender rights. As scholars have illustrated, in attempting to defy transphobic and homophobic structures, African LGBT activist movements have largely produced incipient subjectivities squarely invested in disseminating a distinctly neoliberal brand of sexual sovereignty—a limitation of rights-based projects more generally (Awondo, Geschiere, and Reid 2012; Hoad 2007; Lorway 2015; Otu 2016; Brown 2004). While Malagasy MSM activists participated in the push toward democratic ideals as espoused in the language of sexual "liberation" and "choice," most interlocutors I engaged remained skeptical of the promises of republicanism. They were critical of the failures of the postcolonial democratic project in Madagascar that, like foreign-funded LGBT rights projects, has been deeply entangled in neoliberal economic ideologies since the 1990s.[16] Even if MSM medium-activists were interested in local and national politics, interlocutors were likely to see the poisonous nepotism of morally bankrupt state representatives as more in opposition to their activist work than in support of it. Literally becoming "possessed" by political organizations irreducible to the modern nation-state and its colonial genealogies, though such was left unarticulated by interlocutors, MSM medium-activists engaged political imaginaries that existed alongside and well beyond the conceit of citizenship.[17]

Epistemologies of Religio-sexual Surrender

The public association between spirit mediumship and sex/gender nonconformity in the Malagasy northwest is perhaps best described as a soft or ambivalent one, for the connection between being sarimbavy and being a host to tromba is only rarely explicated in deterministic terms. Sarimbavy interlocutors (both medium and not), regularly explained to me that mediumship was not central or necessary to the articulation of same-sex desire or gender nonconformity, either for male or female-bodied persons. Thus despite the structural similarities between possession and sex/gender variance (i.e., both allow for a separation between physical embodiment and individual expression/identification/desire), the association between nonheteronormative experience and mediumship was never articulated as primordial, ahistorical, or permanently entrenched within the "Sakalava psyche."[18]

Since the consensus is that tromba seek their mediums and not vice versa, humans who found that a tromba had decided to "sit upon" or "live within" them did not describe any innate desire to become a medium. Rather, hosts narrated their journeys to mediumship as twists of "fate" (*anjara*) or "destiny" (*vintana*), in the same way that sarimbavy or heteronormative interlocutors might describe same-sex desire or gender variance as a question of one's "lot in life" (*anjara*). Male-bodied, gender-expansive interlocutors did not consider it a worldly or otherworldly mistake that they were born in a physical form incongruent with their gender expression; rather, it was an act of divine intervention based on their "weak destiny" (*malemy vintana*).

Tromba, in turn, are understood to select human mediums based on their own fickle desires. This affinity is described as *fitiavana*—attraction that may include but is not limited to sexual desire.[19] Physical attraction between humans is also understood in terms of fitiavana—both heteronormative affinities and those that defy their norms—just as a tromba spirit is attracted to a particular medium. Mediums possessed by an opposite-sex spirit refer to the spirit as their spouse (*vady*), the same term used for one's human partner, and possession rituals are ridden with idioms, dances, and jokes that riff off sexual tropes. Mediumship and nonconforming genders and sexualities are rhetorically and phenomenologically linked to somatic experience, rooted in the flesh of the human host, who—like the tromba spirit that "sits upon" him or her—is both a desiring and a gendered subject. Tromba mediumship, and the spirit worlds that it encompasses, thus exhibits a sexuality of its own, one that possesses affective attachments that complicate and overlay existing human ones.

Mahajanga is particularly well-known for its vibrant community of same-sex-desiring and/or gender-variant male-bodied mediums. Furthermore, many of the most prominent and successful tromba hosts in the city (including Julien) are sarimbavy or publicly recognized as same-sex desiring, and heteronormative mediums readily acknowledge that sarimbavy count among their ranks. Unlike Solidarité, which primarily attracts middle-aged and young MSM into its fold, socialities produced through mediumship facilitate dynamic, multiscalar, transgenerational sarimbavy networks that extend beyond Mahajanga and other regional centers to rural villages located near spirit shrines; these networks are forged in part in the collective experience of pilgrimage but also in relational ties produced through shared *tromba*.

The serendipitous nature of mediumship mirrors the suprahuman raison d'être for gender nonconformity and same-sex desire provided by both sarimbavy and heteronormative interlocutors. Across the board, human and tromba interlocutors usually responded to my questions regarding the etiology of both mediumship and queerness with the ubiquitous response: "I don't know." Far from flippant dismissal, this philosophical recognition of not-knowing reflects the unequal distribution of knowledge and agency between human and suprahuman forces and the opacity of identification and desire within both possession practice and human genders and sexualities. In this formulation, the hermeneutics of mediumship and nonconforming genders and sexualities were both tethered to the realm of divine intervention and celestial mystery, located well beyond the liberal, humanist ideals of individual agency and conscious choice so central to homonormative LGBT identity politics.[20] I refer to this as engaged religio-sexual surrender, a recognition of the limits of the human subject rather than a passive disavowal or apathetic orientation to the world.

In conceptualizing mediumship as a form of surrender, I draw from Rouse's (2004) articulation of "engaged surrender." Like the African American female converts to Sunni Islam described by Rouse, in enacting "engaged surrender" sarimbavy mediums become "part of a particular community of practice" that conjures "their political consciousness and produces not only a spiritual but a social epiphany" (9–10). For sarimbavy mediums, surrender to tromba "masters" is far from submissive acquiescence; it is an active, embodied embrace of one's destiny and of the power differentials between medium and spirit. Instead of attempting to rid themselves of "agency"—which interlocutors defined in subtle terms and which they recognized as consisting of both human and spirit actions—MSM medium-activists I came to know engaged a formative, ethical coproduction between human and tromba. In surrendering to the power of their tromba "masters" (*tompony*), mediums succumb to or recognize the repetitive role of power in the (re)produc-tion of the self, in keeping with the poststructuralist insistence that personhood is constituted through multiple axes of subjugating powers (see Butler 1997; Foucault [1976] 1990).

The self-identifying MSM subject, embodied and reproduced through the activism of Solidarité, was thus complicated by relationship to possession; MSM medium-activists enacted human-spirit relationalities irreducible to Western juridico-legal visions of the rights-bearing subject that affirms individuality, free-dom, autonomy, and other "democratic" values. Similarly, while homonormative LGBT rights frameworks are tethered to a bounded, self-possessed person, MSM medium-activists who took up the call to protect this emergent figure carried the profound ethical burden of maintaining spirit relationalities—at once historical, political, and religious—alongside their sense of sexual personhood.[21]

Reassessing Religiosity and Ritual in Queer Theory-Ethnography

Spirit-human relationalities are central to anthropological scholarship on phenom-ena labeled "spirit possession," scholarship that was itself haunted by the ques-tion of gender difference at the onset of second-wave feminism. Ioan Lewis (1966: 310) then famously explained the cross-cultural prevalence of mediumship among women as "compensation for [women's] exclusion and lack of authority in other spheres." Lewis asserted that possession acted as a "weapon of the weak" from which subaltern female mediums—marginalized in relation to Abrahamic reli-gions and patriarchal sociopolitical formations—could seek social redress for their "relative deprivation" through their possessing spirits. Subsequent generations of feminist anthropologists challenged such explanatory scholarship that reduced mediumship to functionalist intentionality and instead detailed how possession becomes holistically and noninstrumentally integrated into female spirit medi-ums' subjective lifeworlds, labor practices, and kinship networks.[22] Given that the language of marginalization and deprivation (often of human rights) overwhelm-ingly marks popular Western accounts of African same-sex-desiring and gender-expansive communities—similar to rhetoric that pervaded early androcentric readings of female spirit mediums' social standing—the scholar may be invited, once again, to ask, through whose eyes are such sexed/gendered subjects "marginal" or "deprived"?

Concerns regarding the representation of the queer-possessed-racialized figure are especially fraught given the position it has occupied within the Western academy. Recent scholarship in queer anthropology has confronted the long-romanticized relationship between religion, ritual, and non-Western same-sex-desiring and/or gender nonconforming persons and now has, in the words of Tom Boellstorff (2007: 22), "little patience for nostalgic approaches that . . . seek instead ritualized forms of transgender or homosexual practices." Boellstorff joins a more widespread critique of the troubling ways in which subjects occupying "indigenous" nonconforming sex/gender categories have been rendered more "authentic" than those non-Western activist-subjects who claim LGBT identities.[23] These necessary and trenchant assessments appropriately flag the dangers of an anthropological obsession with ritual and/or an unwarranted repudiation of activism in the lives of racialized gender-variant and/or same-sex-desiring persons (see also Morgensen 2011; Towle and Morgan 2002).

Similarly, given the prevalence of mediumship in African and African diasporic religiosities, these "traditions" are particularly vulnerable to reductionist readings of possession-as-premodern spectacle. As queer of color theorists such as Roderick Ferguson (2004: 91–92) have noted, racist logics that hypersexualize black bodies also reduce spirit possession and other "African traditional religions" to irrational emotionalism.[24] Scholars cognizant of these academic legacies recognize that attending to Black queer subjects' relationship to religiosity and ritual—categories largely constructed through Christian frameworks of nineteenth- and twentieth-century anthropological thought—is a significantly difficult undertaking.[25]

Taken to an extreme, however, literature on queer life that bypasses religiosity altogether tacitly performs a secularizing erasure in otherwise discerning scholarly work. In avoiding the romanticizing move, ethnographers foreclose the potentially important role that religion plays in queer subject formation by imparting what Jasbir Puar (2017) has termed "queer secularism," which, following Ann Pellegrini (2009: 208), "implicitly smuggles a white, liberal, avowedly secular LGBT subject at the center of its analysis." As others working at the intersections of queer theory and religious studies have argued, religiosity is often hastily written off as a "bad object" for queers, rendering it in opposition to both sexual freedom and liberal, secular thought; this move, Pellegrini rightly insists, leaves "to the side women of color and transnational feminisms whose relationships to religion have historically been far more complex and variegated" (208).[26]

Queer theory that shirks the sacred, including its suprahuman relationalities and divine obligations, risks suggesting that ritual practice is somehow static and of secondary importance to gender/sexual difference in the production of subjectivity. Scholarship that conceptualizes ritual life as obsolete or accessory in global accounts of same-sex-desiring and gender-expansive communities proffers myopic analyses of LGBT activism that do not attend to its intersectional obligations, which may include religious commitments as well as the myriad ways in which religious roles and experiences may "queer" otherwise normative subject positions.[27]

Edelman's (2004: 27) provocative, nuanced, and universalist portrayal of queerness's "rejection of spiritualization through marriage to reproductive futurism" offers one avenue through which to explore the secular impulses embedded in some strands of queer theory. *Shrine*, *ritual*, and *sacred* repeatedly reappear in Edelman's text in pejorative terms; nevertheless, his understanding of queerness's opposition to "spiritualization" somewhat ironically presumes that there is no "spiritualization" embedded in his prophetic call to rebuff reproductive futurism. One wonders if, despite his best intent, Edelman's imperative to abandon naive hope for future political liberation is not a shrine of another sort: are, in fact, his romantic urgings as devoid of "spirit" as he himself hopes?

As other critics have noted, shrouded in the facade of subjectless queer critiques resides a living, breathing privileged queer subject who freely opts out of the political (Eng, Halberstam, and Muñoz 2005). If politics is not "the only game in town," as Edelman (2004: 26, 44) asserts, sarimbavy mediums of ancestor spirits may retort that neither is his "refusal to embrace the genealogical fantasy that braces the social order." The call for a presentist vision of queer life—firmly embedded in a rejection of reproductive futurism—implicitly consigns both future-oriented political aspirations of rights work and backward-facing ancestor worship among Malagasy MSM to the dustbins of false consciousness.

And yet, in his powerful urge to reject "politics as we know it" and those liberal humanist fantasies that propel such projects, Edelman nevertheless brilliantly challenges the reader to consider "the space outside the framework within which politics as we know it appears" (3). Following in the tradition of Leo Bersani's (2010: 30) work, scholarship in queer theory that locates the power of male same-sex sexualities in its "risk of self-dismissal, of *losing sight* of the self" here collides with the lived experience of Malagasy mediums in trance states. The body politic(s) of possession is perhaps one such space outside the normative framework of queer identity politics in which the endgames of sexual sovereignty unfold and where "dreams of self-dissolution" are made real through acts of surrender to powers greater than oneself (Benedicto 2019: 276; see also Brintnall 2017).

Edelman's articulation of queer surrender to deathly desires resonates with the thanatological overtones central to possession in northwestern Madagascar, where tromba reemerge through the bodies of their mediums just as the once living royal sovereigns passed away from their earthly existence—coughing if the death was by choking, for example, or gasping if by drowning. Mediums follow a strict series of taboos that are often linked to the death stories of the individual tromba spirit(s) that "live within" them; if a human host fails to closely respect these prohibitions he or she may fall ill, even unto death. The labor of fanompoa presages the "death" of fertile fields along the Betsiboka River as they are left fallow before flooding over during the rainy season; furthermore, possession pilgrimage centrally involves the ritual cleaning of, among other items, the physical, bodily remains of deceased members of the Sakalava royalty. Thus as subjects marked for HIV in a devastatingly debilitated national economy, MSM medium-activists engaged deathly rituals while they themselves were squarely situated within the necro- and biopolitical structures of contemporary Malagasy life.

In embracing mediumship and its deathly customs, however, MSM medium-activists ironically have preserved the vitality of divine monarchy, reenergizing the agricultural and religio-political cycle of life and death reproduced though its ancestral rituals. As Feeley-Harnik (1984: 5) has noted, Sakalava queen-kingship "has persisted in the face of serious political, economic, and military losses, not by denying the death of kings . . . but by celebrating it." If through possession deceased figures are returned to the living, so too do mediumship pilgrimages provide opportunity for both reproductive and nonreproductive forms of celebratory sociosexual regeneration and ancestor veneration.

Conclusion

Balou and her entourage of fellow sarimbavy activist friends all stayed at Julien's home when visiting Mahajanga for the annual fanompoambe and, in 2015, as they prepared for the MSM Ball. During these visits, Balou usually sought advice from tromba that "sat upon" their host, Julien. One evening at Julien's residence, Balou called upon the tromba Mbotimahasaky, a princess and sex worker who tends to possess female-bodied women and sarimbavy. When she appeared in Julien, Mbotimahasaky brandished a large wooden dildo. In her hands, the phallic prop used by MSM sexual health educators to model appropriate condom use was transformed into a regal scepter. Wanting to know more about her relationship with sarimbavy mediums, I asked her to explain why so many sarimbavy are host to tromba.

Surrounded by several images of the nineteenth-century Merina queen Ranavalona I and a small statue of Shiva as the Nataraja, Mbotimahasaky noted that while any person could become a spirit medium, tromba had to seek approval from the medium's ancestors before they could "live within" them. Balou agreed, adding that for a person to become a host, tromba had to "beg from the mediums' ancestors," thus asserting that human ancestors played a role in the production of mediumship just as ancestral royal tromba spirits did.

Like other tromba and many human interlocutors, Mbotimahasaky recognized that worldly attempts to explain what is inexplicable—the capricious desires and demands of the spirit world—is a foolhardy pursuit and beyond the realm of appropriate human epistemological inquiry. These anthropocentric concerns have little meaning within Sakalava meditations on both nonconforming genders/sexualities and the art of mediumship, given that knowledge and power are primarily located in suprahuman and ancestral domains. Potential anxieties over human difference—in this case the unexpected divergence from heterosexual desire and/or from normative gender presentation—is not cause for undue concern but, rather, an expected occurrence located beyond sites of human comprehension. As queer-possessed subjects, MSM medium-activists and their royal "masters" reproduce political imaginaries enabled through such an epistemology of divine surrender.

These political imaginaries continue to be produced while MSM are increasingly rendered opportune subjects ripe for intervention across Madagascar by HIV prevention industries, homonationalist LGBT rights projects backed by foreign governments, and many Christian publics. Such dynamics infused the MSM Ball, where a simple five-color rainbow flag was hung at the center of the room, under which Balou opened the event by thanking the United States Embassy and PSI for their support. Julien gave a short speech, which he began by acknowledging Andriamanitra—the all-powerful being often glossed as "God" by Christian-identified Malagasy such as himself—and enthusiastically ended his speech with the French phrase: *Vive la verité, vive la liberté!* (Long live truth, long live liberty!). A medical doctor who worked for PSI followed, pledging to continue to work with the MSM community by providing condoms and lubricant, as the organization had done for the past ten years.

The MSM medium-activists who traveled by motorized rickshaw from shrine to Ball that evening embodied the surprising means by which the forward-facing projects of HIV prevention and MSM rights activism manifested through a queer temporal turn toward the past and, furthermore, how the democratic vision of gender and sexual minority rights work developed through the idiom of queen-kingship. Because MSM networks in the Malagasy northwest were largely fostered through the socialities of possession practice, LGBT activism unwittingly emerged through the logics of pedigree and monarchical hierarchy. The interplay between the fanompoambe, the MSM Ball, the coronation of the "Miss" pageant winner, and Balou's call upon Mbotimahasaky all reveal the ways in which queer activist networks in Madagascar were brought to life precisely through rituals of divine succession rooted in, as sarimbavy medium-activists themselves described: "Malagasy tradition" (*fomba gasy*). MSM medium-activists did so by surrendering to the weight of royal sovereignty as mediums and supplicants. In so doing, sarimbavy mediums such as Balou and Julien did not exhibit passivity or a lack of willfulness but, rather, intellectually assented to the mystical and astrological rhetoric of destiny both as medium and as sarimbavy.

Queer African studies—a field within which Madagascar is itself queerly situated—is nicely positioned to rethink queer aversions to both religiosity and (hetero)reproductive dynasty, given the pervasiveness of ancestor worship and divine succession throughout (and beyond) the continent. Rather than outright thwart reproductive futurism's embrace of spiritualization and political aspiration, we may consider how queer African subjects—including Malagasy MSM medium-activists—enact queer "politics in unusual places," which, as Mahmood (2005: 192) asserts, requires the ethnographer to turn "not to the usual spaces of political struggle (such as the state, the economy, and the law) but to arguments about what constitutes a proper way of living ethically in a world where such questions were thought to have become obsolete." Just as Mahmood has questioned the notion that Egyptian women's political agency must develop through the subversion of social norms, the lived experiences of MSM medium-activists challenge the idea that queer social movements must emerge through a repudiation of traditional, dynastic, hierarchical, religio-political formations. Instead of yearning for that which lies beyond the political or the religious, MSM interlocutors who graciously allowed me to participate in their activist-mediumship work have constructed rich, self-reflexive lifeworlds centrally around their ethical obligations to the "reproductive futurism" of royal ancestral lineage.

Notes

This article is based on ethnographic research conducted with the generous financial support of a Wenner-Gren Dissertation Fieldwork Grant, the Ruth Landes Memorial Research Fund, and the Less Commonly Taught Languages Grant at the University of Toronto. During the period of its writing, I greatly benefited from a predoctoral fellowship at The Carter G. Woodson Institute for African-American and African Studies at the University of Virginia. I wish to thank Ashon Crawley, Celeste Pang, Letha Victor, William Hébert, David K. Seitz, and the anonymous reviewers for their insightful comments on previous versions of this work. Most important, I extend my deepest gratitude to those *tromba* and human interlocutors who generously welcomed a complete stranger into their homes, relationships, personal histories, and collective futures: *misaotra betsaka daholo!*

1. Biological essentialism is embedded in the category of sarimbavy, which literally translates to "in the image of a woman." During my research, most interlocutors who identified under the term—including gender-nonconforming, male-bodied persons—understood themselves as occupying a distinct identity category from that of female-bodied women (*vehivavy*). This position, curiously, sometimes places them in conflict with contemporary global transgender politics.

2. See Lambek 2002 for an authoritative ethnography on the fanompoambe. Boellstorff 2011 cogently noted the irony of deploying "MSM" as a self-identifier, given that the category was created precisely to circumvent identitarian constructs such as "gay" or "bisexual." Nevertheless, public health officials and LGBT rights activists in Madagascar have come to accept this category as a transparent marker of individual personhood as indicated in the primary activist organization's very name: Solidarité des MSM.

3. The *kinou* sociolect likely developed among sarimbavy sex workers in Antananarivo in the 1970s and 1980s. Its presence in Mahajanga signaled that the sarimbavy/MSM/dossier community had blossomed into a thriving counterpublic, marked by a mutual sense of belonging based on their nonconforming genders/sexualities.

4. On tromba spirit mediumship, see Feeley-Harnik 1991; Lambek 2002; Ramamonjisoa 1987; and Sharp 1993.

5. The privilege afforded to HIV within the global culture of public health, including the exceptional funding it has received in comparison to other public health challenges—so thoughtfully articulated by Adia Benton 2015—reinforced the exceptionalism of "MSM" persons in relation to their female-bodied counterparts in the struggle for Malagasy LGBT rights, for the latter were not seen as a "vulnerable" or "key" population in the fight against HIV. On the biomedicalization of the MSM category, see Reddy 2005.

6. Since the early 2000s, free HIV testing has been provided at the "Great Service" on

an almost annual basis—a controversial decision given that the purification of royal relics is the primary goal of the ritual and that HIV is widely considered polluting (see Lambek 2016: 326).

7. These Christian publics have driven Malagasy national politics for the past several decades, aligning themselves with politicians from the central highlands who continue to maintain political and economic power across the island. See Gingembre 2011; Randrianja 2003.

8. See Cohen 2005 on AIDS cosmopolitanism.

9. Thinking monarchy alongside queer politics brings new meaning to drag "kings" and "queens." One is tempted to draw parallels to the salience of "queen" in queer North American cultures and "queenly" figures in queer theory more generally, as in Lauren Berlant's (1997) trenchant scholarship. On North American ball culture, see Bailey 2013. See Besnier 2002 and Ochoa 2014 on globalization and queer beauty pageants.

10. Sakalava history is replete with reigning queens, hence my use of "monarchy" or "queen-kingship" over the androcentric concept of "kingship." See Ruti 2017 on the acrimonious debates between the so-called antisocial and relational schools of queer theory.

11. On counterpublics, see Warner 2002.

12. As the ancestral land of the Sakalava people, only those with Sakalava lineage identify as "the owners of the land" (*tompontany*). Although Merina and Betsileo ethnic outsiders who originate from the central highlands have long since seized or purchased fertile fields in the region, they can never ascend to the category of "owner of the land" despite the declarations of any legal deed (Dubourdieu 1989; Sharp 1993).

13. As a concept, fanompoa has existed in other monarchies across the island. The French colonial administration appropriated the indigenous institution in their attempts to force Malagasy to labor for the imperial regime (see Feeley-Harnik 1984; Palmer 2014).

14. This even though the sovereign, "democratic" nation-state is often activated by a troublingly charismatic cult of ethnic nationalism (see Arendt 1973).

15. Lambek 2013 explores the relationships among mediumship, Sakalava royal succession, and the categories of "religion" and "law" as embedded within the contemporary, secular Malagasy state.

16. See Jackson 2013 and Cole 2010 (42–44) on neoliberalism and democratic reform in Madagascar.

17. It is important to note, however, that some members of the royal Sakalava family actively collaborated in projects undertaken by the French colonial administration. Thus not all tromba express anticolonial sentiment.

18. This diverges from some of the rich global scholarship on spirit mediumship in which possession is offered as the etiology of a medium's sex/gender nonconformity by prac-

titioners and/or analysts. For example, see Lescot and Magloire 2002; Wekker 2006: 116.

19. For more on fitiavana, see Cole 2009. Sharp (1993: 122–23) has described how fitiavana is connected to the art of mediumship. Lambek (2002: 239) rightly notes that this attraction cannot be reduced to sexuality but reflects, rather, the "complexity and serendipity of personal attraction."

20. I draw from Lisa Duggan's (2003: 50) articulation of homonormativity.

21. Literature on the Afro-Atlantic world, for example, is replete with scholarship that attends to the imaginative possibilities that possession affords to Black queer experience. See Allen 2012; Strongman 2019; Tinsley 2018; Wekker 2006.

22. See, e.g., Boddy 1989. This diverse and nuanced literature on mediumship rarely interrogates the heteronormative assumptions at play in the cultural contexts in which the ethnographers work.

23. See also Dave (2012: 16–17), who notes that in much queer anthropology "a more authentic cultural subject is privileged over the less authentic queer activist."

24. "African traditional religions" is a problematic umbrella term regularly employed within religious studies. On the denigration of Black embodied religiosity, see also Crawley 2017.

25. On the construction of the anthropological category of "religion," see Asad 1993.

26. See Crawley 2017; Jakobsen and Pellegrini 2003; Seitz 2017.

27. For a moving ethnographic example on this point, see Ramberg 2014.

References

Allen, Andrea Stevenson. 2012. "'Brides' without Husbands: Lesbians in the Afro-Brazilian Religion Candomblé." *Transforming Anthropology* 20, no. 1: 17–31.

Arendt, Hannah. 1973. *The Origins of Totalitarianism*. New York: Harcourt Brace.

Asad, Talal. 1993. *Genealogies of Religion: Discipline and Reasons of Power in Christianity and Islam*. Baltimore, MD: Johns Hopkins University Press.

Awondo, Patrick, Peter Geschiere, and Graeme Reid. 2012. "Homophobic Africa? Towards a More Nuanced View." *African Studies Review* 55, no. 3: 145–68.

Bailey, Marlon M. 2013. *Butch Queens Up in Pumps: Gender, Performance, and Ballroom Culture in Detroit*. Ann Arbor: University of Michigan Press.

Benedicto, Bobby. 2019. "Agents and Objects of Death: Gay Murder, Boyfriend Twins, and Queer of Color Negativity." *GLQ* 25, no. 2: 273–96.

Benton, Adia. 2015. *HIV Exceptionalism: Development through Disease in Sierra Leone*. Minneapolis: University of Minnesota Press.

Berlant, Lauren. 1997. *The Queen of America Goes to Washington City: Essays on Sex and Citizenship*. Durham, NC: Duke University Press.

Bersani, Leo. 2010. *Is the Rectum a Grave? And Other Essays*. Chicago: University of Chicago Press.

Besnier, Niko. 2002. "Transgenderism, Locality, and the Miss Galaxy Beauty Pageant in Tonga." *American Ethnologist* 29, no. 3: 534–66.

Boddy, Janice. 1989. *Wombs and Alien Spirits: Women, Men, and the Zār Cult in Northern Sudan*. Madison: University of Wisconsin Press.

Boellstorff, Tom. 2007. "Queer Studies in House of Anthropology." *Annual Review of Anthropology* 36: 17–35.

Boellstorff, Tom. 2011. "But Do Not Identify as Gay: A Proleptic Genealogy of the MSM Category." *Cultural Anthropology* 26, no. 2: 287–312.

Brintnall, Kent. 2017. "Desire's Revelatory Conflagration." *Theology and Sexuality* 23, nos. 1–2: 48–66.

Brown, Wendy. 2002. "Suffering the Paradoxes of Rights." In *Left Legalism/Left Critique*, edited by Wendy Brown and Janet Halley, 420–34. Durham, NC: Duke University Press.

Brown, Wendy. 2004. "'The Most We Can Hope For . . .': Human Rights and the Politics of Fatalism." *South Atlantic Quarterly* 103, nos. 2–3: 451–63.

Butler, Judith. 1997. *The Psychic Life of Power: Theories in Subjection*. Stanford, CA: Stanford University Press.

Cohen, Lawrence. 2005. "The Kothi Wars: AIDS Cosmopolitanism and the Morality of Classification." In *Sex in Development: Science, Sexuality, and Modernity in Global Perspective*, edited by Stacy Leigh Pigg and Vincanne Adams, 269–303. Durham, NC: Duke University Press.

Cole, Jennifer. 2009. "Love, Money, and Economies of Intimacy in Tamatave, Madagascar." In *Love in Africa*, edited by Jennifer Cole and Lynn M. Thomas, 109–34. Chicago: University of Chicago Press.

Cole, Jennifer. 2010. *Sex and Salvation: Imagining the Future in Madagascar*. Chicago: University of Chicago Press.

Comité National de Lutte Contre le HIV/Sida. 2007. "Plan d'Action de Madagascar pour une lutte efficace contre le VIH/Sida 2007–2012." hivhealthclearinghouse.unesco.org/sites/default/files/resources/iiep_psn_2007_2012_final.pdf.

Crawley, Ashon. 2017. *Blackpentecostal Breath: The Aesthetics of Possibility*. New York: Fordham University Press.

Dave, Naisargi. 2012. *Queer Activism in India: A Story in the Anthropology of Ethics*. Durham, NC: Duke University Press.

Dubourdieu, Lucile. 1989. "Territoire et identité dans les cultes de possession de la basse Betsiboka." *Cahiers des sciences humaines* 25, no. 4: 461–67.

Duggan, Lisa. 2003. *The Twilight of Equality? Neoliberalism, Cultural Politics, and the Attack on Democracy*. Boston: Beacon.

Edelman, Lee. 2004. *No Future: Queer Theory and the Death Drive.* Durham, NC: Duke
University Press.

Eng, David, Jack Halberstam, and José Esteban Muñoz. 2005. "What's Queer about Queer
Studies Now?" *Social Text* 84–85, nos. 3–4: 1–17.

Feeley-Harnik, Gillian. 1984. "The Political Economy of Death: Communication and
Change in Malagasy Colonial History." *American Ethnologist* 11, no. 1: 1–19.

Feeley-Harnik, Gillian. 1985. "Issues in Divine Kingship." *Annual Review of Anthropology*
14: 273–313.

Feeley-Harnik, Gillian. 1991. *A Green Estate: Restoring Independence in Madagascar.*
Washington, DC: Smithsonian Institution Press.

Ferguson, Roderick. 2004. *Aberrations in Black: Toward a Queer of Color Critique.* Minneapolis: University of Minnesota Press.

Foucault, Michel. (1976) 1990. *An Introduction.* Vol. 1 of *The History of Sexuality*, translated by Robert Hurley. 3 vols. New York: Vintage.

Gaudio, Rudolf. 2009. *Allah Made Us: Sexual Outlaws in an Islamic African City.* Malden,
MA: Wiley-Blackwell.

Gingembre, Mathilde. 2011. "Match religieux en terrain politique: Compétition entre
Églises chrétiennes et chute du régime Ravalomanana à Madagascar." *Politique Afric-
aine*, no. 123: 51–72.

Hoad, Neville. 2007. *African Intimacies: Race, Homosexuality, and Globalization.* Minneapolis: University of Minnesota Press.

Jackson, Jennifer. 2013. *Political Oratory and Cartooning: An Ethnography of Democratic
Processes in Madagascar.* Chichester, Sussex: Wiley.

Jakobsen, Janet, and Ann Pellegrini. 2003. *Love the Sin: Sexual Regulation and the Limits
of Sexual Tolerance.* New York: New York University Press.

Lambek, Michael. 2002. *The Weight of the Past: Living with History in Mahajanga, Madagascar.* New York: Palgrave Macmillan.

Lambek, Michael. 2013. "Interminable Disputes in Northwestern Madagascar." In *Religion in Disputes: Pervasiveness of Religious Normativity in Disputing Processes*, edited
by Franz von Benda-Beckmann, Keebet von Benda-Beckmann, Martin Ramstedt, and
Bertram Turner, 1–18. New York: Palgrave MacMillan.

Lambek, Michael. 2016. "On Being Present to History: Historicity and Brigand Spirits in
Madagascar." *HAU* 6, no. 1: 317–41.

Lescot, Anne, and Laurence Magloire. 2002. *Des hommes et des dieux.* Watertown, MA:
Documentary Educational Resources.

Lewis, Ioan. 1966. "Spirit Possession and Deprivation Cults." *Man* 1, no. 3: 307–29.

Lorway, Robert. 2015. *Namibia's Rainbow Project: Gay Rights in an African Nation.*
Bloomington: Indiana University Press.

Mahaleo. 1990. "Madirovalo," on *Madagasikara Two: Current Popular Music of Madagascar*, track 3, compact disc. London: GlobeStyle, Ace Records.

Mahmood, Saba. 2005. *Politics of Piety: The Islamic Revival and the Feminist Subject.* Princeton, NJ: Princeton University Press.

Morgensen, Scott Lauria. 2011. *Spaces between Us: Queer Settler Colonialism and Indigenous Decolonization.* Minneapolis: University of Minnesota Press.

Ochoa, Marcia. 2014. *Queen for a Day: Transformistas, Beauty Queens, and the Performance of Femininity in Venezuela.* Durham, NC: Duke University Press.

Otu, Kwame Edwin. 2016. "Amphibious Subjects: Sassoi and the Contested Politics of Queer Subject-Making in Neoliberal Ghana." PhD diss., Syracuse University.

Palmer, Seth. 2014. "Asexual Inverts and Sexual Perverts: Locating the *Sarimbavy* of Madagascar within Fin-de-Siècle Sexological Theories." *TSQ* 1, no. 3: 368–86.

Pellegrini, Ann. 2009. "Feeling Secular." *Women and Performance* 19, no. 2: 205–18.

Puar, Jasbir. 2017. "Homonationalism in Trump Times." In *Terrorist Assemblages: Homonationalism in Queer Times*, 223–42. Durham, NC: Duke University Press.

Ramamonjisoa, Suzy-Andrée. 1987. "Symbolique des rapports entre les femmes et les hommes dans les cultes de possession de type tromba à Madagascar." In *Transformations of African Marriage*, edited by David Parkin and David Nyamwaya, 155–69. Manchester, UK: Manchester University Press.

Ramberg, Lucinda. 2014. *Given to the Goddess: South Indian Devadasis and the Sexuality of Religion.* Durham, NC: Duke University Press.

Randrianja, Solofo. 2003. "'Be Not Afraid, Only Believe': Madagascar 2002." *African Affairs* 102, no. 407: 309–29.

Reddy, Gayatri. 2005. "Geographies of Contagion: *Hijras, Kothis*, and the Politics of Sexual Marginality in Hyderabad." *Anthropology and Medicine* 12, no. 3: 255–70.

Rouse, Carolyn Moxley. 2004. *Engaged Surrender: African American Women and Islam.* Berkeley: University of California Press.

Ruti, Mari. 2017. *The Ethics of Opting Out: Queer Theory's Defiant Subjects.* New York: Columbia University Press.

Santner, Eric. 2011. *The Royal Remains: The People's Two Bodies and the Endgames of Sovereignty.* Chicago: University of Chicago Press.

Seitz, David. 2017. *A House of Prayer for All: Contesting Citizenship in a Queer Church.* Minneapolis: University of Minnesota Press.

Sharp, Lesley. 1993. *The Possessed and the Dispossessed: Spirits, Identity, and Power in a Madagascar Migrant Town.* Berkeley: University of California Press.

Strongman, Roberto. 2019. *Queering Black Atlantic Religions: Transcorporeality in Candomblé, Santería, and Vodou.* Durham, NC: Duke University Press.

Tinsley, Omise'eke Natasha. 2018. *Ezili's Mirrors: Imagining Black Queer Genders.* Durham, NC: Duke University Press.

Towle, Evan B., and Lynn Marie Morgan. 2002. "Romancing the Transgender Native: Rethinking the Use of the 'Third Gender' Concept." *GLQ* 8, no. 4: 469–97.

van Klinken, Adriaan. 2015. "Queer Love in a 'Christian Nation': Zambian Gay Men Negotiating Sexual and Religious Identities." *Journal of the American Academy of Religion* 83, no. 4: 947–64.

Warner, Michael. 2002. *Publics and Counterpublics*. Cambridge: Zone.

Wekker, Gloria. 2006. *The Politics of Passion: Women's Sexual Culture in the Afro-Surinamese Diaspora*. New York: Columbia University Press.

THE QUEER NARRATOR

Violence, Ethics, and Sexuality

Vaibhav Saria

The Film

The 2012 Bollywood film *Agneepath* (*The Path of Fire*), directed by Karan Mal-hotra, has a scene in which a villain is auctioning the hero's sister as a sex slave. His dialogue—addressed to nobody in particular—informs us that he is doing so to avenge the death of his son who was murdered by the hero. Suddenly, the scene breaks off to show hijras armed with swords and butcher knives running toward the villain and the crowd of bidders and henchmen around him (fig. 1). They start hacking and killing, quickly carving a path through this mob to allow the hero to reach the villain with relative ease. But there are so many immoral people either facilitating the auction or clamoring to bid, all ignoring the pitiful cries and pleas of the young girl, that neither the hijras nor the hero get the job done quickly. The next scene shows hijras forming a protective circle around the hero, and they move in tandem rhythmically, killing and hacking everyone surrounding them, and eventually killing the villain and saving the innocent virgin (fig. 2).

In India, *hijras* is now translated as "transgenders" in popular English-language dailies; but at various points during the colonial regime of policing, the term has also been translated as "eunuchs," "hermaphrodites," and "sodomites." Hijras have been and continue to be identified as the "third gender" in scholarship that has studied ideas of sex and gender in Hindu, Buddhist, and Jain religious texts. The exigencies of the HIV epidemic brought hijra bodies and practices into secular understandings of disease and risk. Moreover, epidemiologists and public health officials identified hijras as a "high risk" population and absorbed them into the category of men who have sex with men (MSM). Concomitant with these understandings of hijras has been their absorption as historically and religiously legitimizing figures into LGBT politics in India. The various myths associated with

GLQ 27:1
DOI 10.1215/10642684-8776876
© 2021 by Duke University Press

Figure 1. Hijras entering the scene and hacking the immoral crowd. Screenshot from *Agneepath* (dir. Karan Malhotra, 2012).

Figure 2. Hijras forming a protective circle around the hero and they move toward the villain. Screenshot from *Agneepath* (dir. Karan Malhotra, 2012).

hijras in the various recensions of the two great epics of India, the *Mahabharata* and the *Ramayana*, have laid the groundwork for them to make religious claims of citizenship on the Indian state.

The current moment of Hindu nationalism, often shorthanded as "saffronization," has also resulted in the state's attempting to absorb the figure of the hijra. The aim of this ostensibly sympathetic stance is to reframe hijras as evidence of Hinduism's long history of tolerance and celebration of gender variance, in contrast to Muslim intolerance and violence. The recent spate of legislative actions concerning hijras is often presented as a remarkable coming of age of Hindu liberalism, but a close reading shows this to be nothing but alibis for increased policing of a population that has historically proved resistant to being cleaved for surveillance and discipline (Saria 2019).

The scene described from *Agneepath* stands out from previous depictions of hijras in Bollywood films because it shows their participation in an economy of violence and because it reflects a larger shift in the relationship between violence, ethics, and the state. There have been two distinct ways that hijras have been deployed that reflect the moral universe of the Bollywood cinema. The first has been didactic—to preach an idealized moral order of syncretic democratic liberalism through Gandhian notions of tolerance, peace, and coexistence. Mani Ratnam's *Bombay* (1995) has a hijra sheltering a child from religious riots, followed by a form of platonic dialogue in which the hijra observes that religious riots are politically orchestrated and violence is therefore pointless. Moreover, the hijra explains that Hinduism and Islam are both different ways to reach god and, hence, are essentially the same. Films that have used hijras as comic relief tend to prevent the jokes from becoming cruel by invoking their sacred powers to bless good fortune. *Maine Pyar Kiya* (*I Fell in Love*) (1989) is a good example of this trope.

The second way in which hijras have been deployed is as villains who deal in violence and psychic threats and thus as figures who must be defeated. Two films from the 1990s, *Sadak* (*Road*) (1991) and *Sangharsh* (*Struggle*) (1999), present the death-dealing and threatening hijra. The evildoer in *Sadak* is Maharani, a brothel owner, who does not think twice about trapping, trafficking, and torturing young women and who will go to any length, even murder, to prevent any girl from escaping her clutches. The villainous hijra in *Sangharsh* is a cannibalistic, child-sacrificing Kali worshiper.

To put it another way: hijras have been depicted either as life-affirming (because of a certain ethic of nonviolence), or as death-dealing (because they are morally corrupt and pathologically aggressive). This difference is erased in *Agneepath*, where participation in violence ends up being a life-affirming choice. Participation in violence is presented as the only moral action to take to establish sovereignty, and to be life-affirming is presented as the only way to be queer in India. Tracking the change in the ethical and moral work the hijra does by dispensing violence reveals the theological underpinnings of contemporary popular Indian political life.

The Song-and-Dance Number

A song from the Bollywood film *Amar Akbar Anthony* (1977) provides one of the most iconic representations of hijras. Akbar, the hero, dances with hijras singing "Tayyab Ali Pyar Ka Dushman" ("Tayyab Ali is the Enemy of Love"), while hijras join him in the refrain "*hai hai*," which is a curse. Akbar and hijras are swearing at Tayyab Ali because he will not let his daughter marry Akbar, who is her sweet-

heart. William Elison, Christian Lee Novetzke, and Andy Rotman's 2016 mono-
graph on this landmark film examines the complex moral position put forward by
the song and dance: that only poor hijras and poor lovers can see, understand, and
expose the "shameful truths" of our hypocritical society.[1] They write:

> Having assembled his scandalous chorus of hijras, the poet hero calls out
> the [father of his girlfriend]. Tayyab Ali's [self-presentation] is revealed to
> be false on two counts. The outwardly respectable businessman is himself
> a lover. And beyond that, he can't recognize the right of those humbler than
> he to experience love, because the very pride and comfort that come with
> his social standing have blinded him to their plight. (112–13)

The song was recreated for the film *Once Upon a Time in Mumbai Dobaara* (2013).
While the film's narrative and the song's lyrics were changed, the hijras' refrain
was kept intact. More than four decades later, hijras are still seen as truth-telling
figures, ever ready to side with lovers and to curse the enemies of love. What has
changed, though, is that hijras no longer function as comic relief. They are given
a certain dignity, to the extent that they facilitate heterosexual coupling by holding out for an ideal of love that can conquer, defeat, and overwhelm anything that
stands in the way.

We can see this in *Tera Kya Hoga Johnny* (*What's Gonna Happen to You
Johnny*) (2010), which has a hijra character, Begum, who is not a brothel madam
but, rather, runs an agency for domestic workers. The narrator, a young boy forced
to sell drugs as well as coffee on the streets, explains that when he came to the
city from his village all he had was the contact of Begum, and through her he got a
place to stay and a job to support himself. The work was not very nice, he reveals,
but Begum "gave [him] the love of a mother." The film depicts the morally dubious
acts the various characters have to perform to fulfill their desires in the cutthroat
competition that defines modernity and Mumbai. Begum is one of the few characters who is not seen as morally compromised, and that is because she functions as
a person in love. Although her boyfriend is violent toward her, she is kind toward
everybody, including the drug-selling street urchin. Her lover eventually kills her
when she tries to break up with him, after catching him cheating on her.

Tera Kya Hoga Johnny is an anomaly in that it gives a lot of screen time
to Begum and makes the hijra a prominent character in the story, thereby illus-
trating her life-affirming position. The elaborate song-and-dance routine and the
morality of maternal/feminine tenderness are often condensed in other films into
a few scenes, rendering the clarity and durability of the life-affirming position of

the hijra in narratological codes. For example, in the film *Tamasha* (*Spectacle*) (2015), the protagonist's offer of marriage and gift of a diamond engagement ring are refused by the heroine because the suitor is an unexciting product manager. Sad and melancholic, he usually ignores the hijra who knocks on his car window every day when he is on the way to work. Begging for alms, she teases him, pleads with him, taunts him, "Oh, hero, today also won't you give anything," and "I'll pray from my heart for you to get your favorite heroine," and "don't you have a heart," and "when will you give me something." These blink-and-miss scenes serve to communicate the boring quality of the hero's corporate life; the only break in the repetition comes from the hijra's various one-liners and tones. One day, we see the hero ignoring her while he is on the phone trying to persuade the jeweler to let him return the rejected diamond ring for the same price he paid for it. The hero's argument with the jeweler drowns out the hijra's begging. We hear him making the case that the manufacturing charges should not be deducted, since the jeweler will sell the ring to the next buyer at the same price and hence will recuperate those charges. The next day, when the hijra comes knocking, the heartbroken man impulsively gives her the ring without even looking at her. In their next interaction, she is not knocking on the car window and begging; instead, she is standing in front of his car, praying and then blowing the blessing (*barkat*) his way, removing the evil eye. A while later, after the hero seems to have conquered his personal demons and regained his equanimity, he once again encounters the hijra. She then retrieves the diamond ring from a knot in the corner of her saree and returns it to him. She tells him, "Nobody has ever given such a big gift. I was so happy, but what will I do with it? The ring will fulfill whatever desire is in your heart." The hero takes back the ring, and soon wins the heart of the heroine.

The hijra's role in *Tamasha* is so minor that the hijra does not even get a credit or a name, and the character visually communicates nothing beyond an anthropological reality of India that hijras beg on the streets. Yet the fact that a poor hijra who earns her livelihood by begging at a traffic stop claims to have no use for a diamond ring besides a sentimental one throws the entire moral universe of the film into relief. Indeed, her actions illuminate the hidden gaps between value, price, profit, and loss and their relationship to moral personhood, all of which the hero learns eventually in order to win the heroine and live happily ever after. The hijra in *Tamasha* carves a space for the truth of living one's dreams, even if they do not entail bringing home a corporate salary. She represents a life-affirming principle in the context of the everyday capitalist realities of India.

The Action Sequence

The villain in *Murder 2* (2011) is a man whose modus operandi is to hire, trap, and murder "call girls"[2] while dressed in full feminine attire, including jewelry and makeup. His weapon of choice is the *chimta*, a popular musical instrument associated with groups of folk, ascetic-mystic, wandering singers and performers, of which hijras are members (Hinchy 2014; Roy 2016). The villain's hijra-ness seems to be further consolidated when he reveals that the goddess came to him in a vision and told him to castrate himself, citing the myth of origin for hijras. He then goes to a hijra called Nirmala Pandit, who is also an elected politician, and asks to be castrated. Nirmala Pandit depicts one of the many elected hijra politicians who have won offices on the basis of the ascetic incorruptibility that hijras claim, especially during election campaigns (L. Cohen 1995, 2004). It is the juxtaposition of these two individuals that differentiates the real hijra from the fake.

After the villain is arrested as a serial killer and is in prison, Nirmala Pandit sends lawyers to rescue her presumed sister/friend/community member. In fact, Nirmala goes to the police station herself and threatens the police officer, saying, "You are making a mistake by trapping the goddess's disciple. I will curse you so that you won't be able to piss properly. I am going to take her with me. And close that case of murdered girls. Remember, I too have a red beacon on top of my car."

After using her political connections and power to get the villain released, Nirmala and the villain go to a temple together to pay their respects and gratitude to the hijra goddess, Bahuchara Mata. At the temple, the priest informs them about the serial murderer, and the politician starts putting two and two together. It is noticeable that she immediately starts referring to the villain using masculine pronouns and his male names, asking him, "Boy, have I unwittingly/unknowingly committed a sin in rescuing you?" The villain then murders Nirmala. The short exchange in the temple saves Nirmala from accusations of moral corruption. Regardless of what she did to save a fellow disciple of the goddess, Nirmala knew that killing women was evil and that saving a serial murderer of women was a sin. While she was not beyond ignoring due process—very much like the typical hero—she was looking after her people and her community, a familiar way of doing politics in India (Witsoe 2011). The fact that she dies at the hands of the villain, in the temple of the hijra goddess, further cements her authenticity as an ascetic hijra. Like the murdered "call girls," she too is an innocent victim, taken in by the tricks of an inauthentic hijra who both hates and desires women. The villain's addiction to/obsession with women eventually causes him to feel powerless, and he cannot find a cure besides castration. But after he commits the bloody act, his desire remains; he can find no way to slake it besides murder.

Murder 2 illustrates a crucial fact about how contemporary liberal hijra personhood has become delinked from their castrated status. Both the villain and the hijra politician are without male genitalia, but it is the nature of their desire that defines them. The villain's emasculation results from his murderous desire for women, whereas the hijra politician's status and sense of self are defined by asceticism. Along with their asceticism and incorruptibility, it is also a desire *to be* women that defines hijras, as opposed to a murderous desire *for* women. This distinction is carried over when popular Indian dailies refer to hijras as "transgenders," which reflects a liberal aspiration to make hijras respectable and to solder the local to globalizing categories rather than to a universal understanding of transgender women (Valentine 2007). Such homonationalist aspirations explain the seamless shift from the historic definition of hijras as men who have been castrated to one of persons desirous of gender affirmation surgeries.

In other words, the translation of *hijras* as "transgenders" is dependent not only on redefining castration from a status that makes hijras but also on a desire for gender-affirming body modification. This resignification of castration is most clearly seen in the film *Mom* (2016), about a stepmother who avenges her stepdaughter's rape and battery. Devki, the titular mom, who is a high school biology teacher, also teaches hijras on the side as part of her "social service." These hijras tell Devki that it was because of her gift of education and respect that they are now independent and running their own tie-and-dye business. Devki first seeks justice by following the rule of law, but her stepdaughter's rapists are so rich and powerful, and the world is so corrupt, that they are able to tamper with the evidence, buy themselves the "not guilty" verdict from the courts, and get off scot-free. In her pursuit to deliver divine justice, Devki starts killing the rapists one by one. A bit of dialogue in the movie goes:

Devki: God cannot be everywhere, Mr. DK.

Mr. DK: I know, that's why he created mothers.

For the first murder—that of the watchman, Baburam—Devki is aided by her hijra students. While Baburam is drunk, they seduce and kidnap him. The next morning, he wakes up with a hangover, assaults his wife, and then goes to the bathroom to pee, but can't find his penis. He sees he has been castrated and starts screaming. He punches his image in the mirror, slips on the bathroom floor, hits his head on the water tap, and dies.

Hijras in this film are worthy and deserving social citizens who can run respectable businesses with the help of allies. They desire a more globalized version of corporeal modification, and their identity extends to their desire for transformation, even when the film repeats an old trope of rape and revenge that centers on castrating men against their will. The scene in which hijras seduce the drunk Baburam emphasizes their breasts and femininity. It seems to be inserted in the film for the purpose of clarifying that castration does not make a man into a hijra, nor is a hijra merely a castrated male. The colonial imagination argued that, since no man would willingly undergo such a corporeal transformation, hijras were kidnapping and forcibly castrating young children and hence needed to be criminalized. Hijras in *Mom* are not men who have been castrated against their will, and in their castrating a man who later dies, *Mom* argues that castration does not make a man into a hijra; rather, hijras are those who desire a more globalized version of this corporeal modification. But men like Baburam die of it. This change is clearer when we compare *Mom* to the 1988 film *Zakhmi Aurat* (*Wounded Woman*) (1988), which also portrays a group of women castrating men. The castrated men in *Zakhmi Aurat* cannot bear the shame of being emasculated, and they come close to becoming unwilling hijras, whereas *Mom* makes sure to point out that castrating men does not make them into hijras. Rather, hijras exceed castration—both physically, as the presence of their breasts on screen show, but also psychically, as they are not made or unmade by it. It is no coincidence that this liberal recognition of hijra interiority comes freighted with their willing participation in delivering divine justice in India. In other words, hijras become trans citizens, but they remain life-affirming ascetics, and their participation in violence must be to restore the moral order of the universe.

The Role

The small roles that hijras play in these films are analogous to the ones enacted by the figure of the *sutradhar* in Sanskrit drama, which has been carried forward in modern theatre. The meaning of the word *sutradhar* as holder (*dhar*) of the strings (*sutra*) of the dramatic elements refers to the puppeteer as well as the architect, or master builder, who measures and thus formulates the plot. He is the "one who knows," who "'carries,' (has memorized) the rules" (Steiner 2012: 6, cited in Binder 2015: 21). This moral duty of the sutradhar makes it possible for the figure not just to narrate the play for the audience but also to participate in the drama, bringing the text or the drama to the correct moral ending if the narrative threatens to deviate otherwise. Robert P. Goldman (1986) gives us some nuanced understanding of what a sutradhar does; more specifically, of their position in the eighth-century play *Uttararamacarita* (*Rama's Last Act*) by the Sanskrit dramatist Bhavabhuti. The sutradhar interacts not just with the audience but also with the play's characters to influence their decisions. Using the trope of a play within a play, Rama hears about Sita's despair from the sutradhar in Valmiki's play, which is being performed in Bhavabhuti's play, and reunites with his wife. Sheldon Pollock (2001: 197) writes that the dramatic narrative must unfold in such a way that all unpleasant realities and conflicts are resolved, and a single moral vision of the world stands out. He quotes Bhoja, an eleventh-century philosopher: "In literature if not in life . . . 'it must be the good guy, not the bad guy, who wins.'" One of the quandaries of the dramatic narrative is that in order to make the hero heroic, the villain must equal him in all respects but moral high-mindedness. Both author and reader must remember that they must not be like the villain in desiring the morally improper object but rather like the hero. This lesson is important because it allows for the sacred to absorb the profane, even if only for a short duration.

Pollock masterfully traces how the languages of the hero and the villain must have the same *rasa* (aesthetic sensibility) but must also differ in their ethical positions and have opposing goals—that is, moral and immoral. Once again, however, the difference cannot be sustained due to the chance that the object might not be inappropriate, as in the case of unrequited love that a villain might harbor. One of the possible solutions is that the responsibility for recognizing the intensity of the passion (and also its inappropriateness) must be shared with the *rasika*, the knowing reader. The text must then have a larger point (*mahavakyarth*) that works through suggestion and that requires from the reader an "innate receptivity" (*upahitasamskara*) about right and wrong. This, in turn, requires yet another, larger realm of meaning that the reader and the text share, *paro mahavakhyaikarthah*.

Interpreting the hijras' presence in the films discussed above as similar to that of the sutradhar explains not only the films' moral and ethical burden but also how queer figures have been understood in the context of contemporary Indian liberalism. Their role is somewhat similar to that of the Greek chorus: unrelated to the narrative arc yet a crucial element for driving home the moral message of the film, making hijras figures of interruption. They appear as a form of parabasis at moments when the protagonist, who must deliver justice, is painted into a corner, defeated, and possibly dead. Yet to understand why hijras are particularly suited to play their singular role in the economy of violence, we must turn to myths from the Indian epics.

Two myths from the epic *Mahabharata* have striking similarities to the scenes of life-affirming violence in the films discussed earlier. Wendy Doniger (2009: 23) gives us a helpful, if ironic, summary of the epic:

> The bare bones of the central story (and there are hundreds of peripheral stories too) could be summarized like this, for our purposes: The five sons

of King Pandu, called the Pandavas, were fathered by gods. . . . All five of them married Draupadi. When Yudhishthira [the eldest of the five] lost the kingdom to his cousins in a game of dice, the Pandavas and Draupadi went into exile for twelve years, at the end of which, with the help of their cousin the incarnate god Krishna, who befriended the Pandavas and whose counsel to Arjuna on the battlefield of Kurukshetra is the Bhagavad Gita, they regained their kingdom through a cataclysmic battle in which almost everyone on both sides was killed.

One of the many myths concerning hijras involves Arjuna killing his grandfather/great-uncle, Bhishma. Bhishma had abducted three princess sisters to get them married to his half-brother. The eldest of the princesses, Amba, is in love with another prince. She convinces Bhishma's advisors that she should not be forced to marry the half-brother. Her request is granted, but her lover refuses to take her back. Shunned by everybody, Amba vows revenge on Bhishma and is born a man, Shikhandi, in her next life so that she can fight, defeat, and kill him. During the battle that eventually ensues, Bhishma refuses to fight Shikhandi since they both remember Shikhandi's female past, and Bhishma cannot pick up a weapon against a woman. To finally defeat the great warrior Bhishma, Arjuna hides behind Shikhandi and slays him.

Shikhandi, described as the "man child who is a woman," is seen as one of the prototypes of hijras—men who are women—and is often cited as a figure of religious and historical importance to hijras (Custodi 2007). What is intriguing in this myth, and what has gone hitherto unremarked, is the participation of Shikhandi in this economy of violence. In an episode very much like the scene in *Agneepath*, Shikhandi helps the morally righteous hero, Arjun, fight against an equally strong but morally questionable villain. Yet another popular myth that has over the last thirty years become increasingly associated with and celebrated by hijras also takes place during the great war of the Mahabharata. As Alf Hiltebeitel (1995: 453) explains, Aravan, son of Arjuna, has agreed to sacrifice himself and die a heroic death, but:

> Aravan does not want to die a bachelor, since dying unmarried would prevent him from receiving the ancestral rites of a "Father," or Pitr. Krsna, asking, "Who would marry someone just about to die," solves this difficulty by taking the form of Mohini, the Enchantress, and marrying Aravan in a last-minute wedding. This is the version of Aravan's marriage reported in scholarly literature on South Indian popular Hinduism.

During the festival of Koovagam, hijras perform a ritual enactment of Mohini's marriage to Aravan and then of her subsequent widowhood. By doing so, they make not only a place for a form of god that was male and then female but also an argument for their position in the Hindu cosmology. It is intriguing that the context of war once again crops up in this myth, together with the relationship it signals between violence and masculinity as brokered by and through hijra personhood. As before, the hijras facilitate the morally correct conclusion for a hero, and the sacrifice and the violence are for the victory of the greater moral good.

Statecraft

The myths associated with gods who transform from one gender to another allow hijras to be recognized in religious and historical registers. The frequent citation of this recognition is seen in the roles that hijras play in films and is made possible only through a particular understanding of contemporary life in Indian politics. It is no coincidence that the various versions of the Transgenders Rights Bill that has been rattling around the various houses of parliament also cite these myths to make a case for ensuring that trans persons are equal citizens and should thus enjoy the same rights as everybody else. Yet the allegory presented in the films and myths goes deeper: hijras gain a certain salience largely because of the flexing of the Hindu right-wing muscles in the political arena. The rereading of Carl Schmitt's *Political Theology* (2005) and its modification for the non-Christian context allow us to understand the allegory of violence that Bollywood reflects, if not represents. In his writings on Schmitt, Hent de Vries makes the case that, rather than repressing its theological foundations, worldly politics was always about the theological. Talal Asad's (2011) recuperation of political theology by way of cautioning against reducing secularism to Christianity is particularly helpful in unpacking the secular understanding of queer citizenship that the enactment of morally justified violence elides in the case of hijras. He writes: "If I am skeptical of the claims made for secularism's essential roots in Christianity, this is not because I argue that its *real* historical roots lie elsewhere, that secularism has no connection with Christianity whatever, but because I don't think we are entirely clear about what we are seeking to explain with such confidence" (673). Several scholars have attempted to understand the theological underpinnings of sovereignty in postcolonial contexts as laboring under other burdens, such as moral striving (Khan 2012), polytheism (Singh 2012), and everyday life (Das 2004, 2011). Building on these interventions, we can begin to understand the presence of hijras vis-à-vis sovereignty in India as reflected by the recursive tapping into the mythic register in various domains, including films, lives, and legislation.

In January 2019, news broke that Laxmi Tripathi, a familiar face of queer rights in the media, had reached the banks of the Ganges in the city of Allahabad (now known as Prayagraj). She was staking a right to participate in the Kumbha Mela, one of the most important pilgrimages for Hindus, which takes place every three years in one of the four holy sites by the river Ganges. One of the rituals of the Kumbha Mela is the *Shahi Snan*, the first dip into the holy river, and the various religious orders (*Akharas*) of the various sects (*sampradaya*) proceed in sequence to bathe in the holy river. Laxmi demanded recognition for her order, the *Kinnar Akhara*,[3] which she established to reclaim the importance of the religious position of hijras and to which the Hindu nationalist discourse had hitherto only been paying lip service. The body that governs the thirteen orders, the *Akhil Bharatiya Akhara Parishad*, refused to recognize Laxmi's order and forbade her from taking part in the ritual dip. Laxmi, deploying an impressive political tactic, convinced the largest of the orders, the *Juna Akhara*, that joining forces would be in the best interest of everybody. Thus she managed to take a dip along with the others in the procession, achieving a historic victory and consolidating the recognition of hijras as religious figures. Laxmi's act and the recognition of her order were celebrated by the liberal media as well as by the religious groups in an uneasy alliance (fig. 3). Laxmi was well received by the conservative Hindu religious groups because she no longer tied either her political aspirations or the political emancipation of her community to the political Left or to leftist discourse.

Seizing the political opportunity that the religious groups had made available to her through their recuperation and citation of the myths associated with the hijras, Laxmi made many people in the nascent queer rights movement uncomfortable with her alliance with the Hindu right-wing parties. She supported their demands to build a temple on the site of a mosque that been destroyed by hardline Hindus in 1992. The demolition of the mosque and the ensuing riots that took thousands of lives have seared themselves in the social, cultural, and political consciousness as an emblem of postindependence India. Laxmi is quoted in the *Hindustan Times* (2019) as saying, "Where my Lord Ram was born, there the temple has to come, [The Mughals] brought [the temple] down, and then they enslaved us all." The sovereign power exhibited by the state under the burden of creating a Hindu nation created opportunities for Laxmi and her followers not only to demand their place in the political order that was citing them but also to link their personal

Figure 3. Laxmi at the Kumbha Mela. *Hindustan Times*, "Kumbh 2019: Inside the Unique Kinnar Akhada," YouTube video, 3:35, February 12, 2019. www.youtube .com/watch?v=SdW4VJLoWCM&list=LL1tngTOXbI1zpOu2DKeO04A&index =27&t=0s.

ambitions to this project. The presence of hijras and their participation in violence to balance the world's moral ledger gains a "resonant meaning" (Das 2016) only when considered together with these other discourses about political life in India.[4]

The other great epic of India, *Ramayana*, has consistently provided ample material to fashion political sovereignty in India. The epic has made particularly felicitous the modern narrative of a mythic Hindu kingdom that was and is the Indian state and that must be saved from the constant defacement by Muslims that began in premodern India and continues today (Mehta 2015). Pollock (1993: 264) writes that the *Ramayana* offers "unique imaginative instruments—in fact, two linked instruments—whereby, on the one hand, a divine political order can be conceptualized, narrated, and historically grounded and, on the other, a fully demonized Other can be categorized, counterposed, and condemned." The condemned Other in the current political climate in India is the Muslim, usually the Muslim male, as a result of which hijras have been appropriated into the "divine political order." Yet this appropriation has not been without its tension, since the canniness of this political maneuver is difficult to hide, given the widespread violence, discrimination, and poverty that hijras suffer on a daily basis. Hijras have seized the opportunity that current statecraft offers to make demands for various types of recognition—political, religious, and economic.

The Field

The relationship presented in the films and the myths gives us a glimpse of how hijras brokered violence to create victorious heroes. The mythic role of hijras is baked into contemporary understandings of "transgenders," as revealed in the films, and this seamless transition is made possible by the resounding encouragement that hijras receive from Hindu religious groups. Actual lived realities were also sutured to this understanding of hijra desires; in other words, this role of consolidating masculinity was also how hijras formulated ordinary ethics and crafted everyday lives. Based on fieldwork I conducted in India between 2008 and 2018, in the rural districts of Bhadrak and Bhawanipatna in the eastern state of Orissa, a very specific reasoning emerged among hijras regarding their participation in the economy of violence that kinship, masculinity, and patriarchy entails. One day in 2012 there was great excitement in the hijra community in Bhawanipatna because of the visit of Julie, a petite and pert-looking hijra and a cause of good-hearted teasing because she insisted on wearing very high heels, which made her totter and trip all the time. Julie also had a speech impairment, and since she had grown up with some of the other hijras, learning the tricks of sex work together, they had developed a language of their own—partly sign language and partly grunted-out words—that was comprehensible because of their shared world of abject poverty.

Julie's way of speaking was not the only reason she attracted a large amount of good-hearted teasing. Someone would say, "She is so short, the men treat her like a doll. They just carry her off to fuck in the middle of the night." Someone else would say, "She is mad. She has no fear at all. She goes wherever she wants to, with whomever she wants, without any worries as to what might happen to her. At night, after our work, we would look for her, but we could never find her. In the morning we would ask her where she was last night, and she would say, 'Oh a group of truck drivers picked me up and took me away.'"

Julie's face, hands, and body were covered with scars. She showed and counted them for me, there were twenty-seven in total. I asked her for the story behind them, and she told me that groups of drunken men would just carry her off in the middle of the night and, while fucking her, they would stub out their cigarettes on her body. I learned that this was a common act of violence many men meted out to hijras. I asked her why she kept on going with these men if they harmed her, and she replied, "It's okay. They do it because they are drunk. When they sober up, they are very sorry—they give me food, money, and sweets—they are so loving." At that point in the narration, Jasmine, who was acting as translator between Julie and me, started laughing hysterically with the other hijras. She said, "then later that night they get drunk again and carry her off again and stub cigarettes out on her body again" (pers. comms., December 4, 2011).

Hijras did not see the men's violence as a legal or moral wrong but rather as an inextricable variable of masculinity and not necessarily one that could be controlled. The men in these villages did not consider the women they were married to or courting correct or proper recipients of this form of violence. But that is not to say that other forms of domestic abuse were lacking in this poor village. For example, one of the ways hijras would amuse themselves was by watching a woman scream at and beat her husband in the morning when he was sober, and then watch the husband scream at her and beat her in the evening when he was drunk. There was a way in which the hijras recognized and controlled the inescapability of the violence of kinship, either by colluding with sisters and sisters-in-law or by taking care of the widowed women of the family, the aged, and the orphans. They would put up with a lot of violence by the men in their lives as the inherited moral responsibility of the feminine, excusing and explaining it as one of the painful conditions of life and love rather than deeming it illegal and remediable.

Hijras would often amplify the masculinity of a man they were trying to seduce by complimenting him on his penis, his prowess, and his virility (Saria 2015). Their desires as seen in the films, myths, and personal narratives were not antinormative, and this largely explains their absorption in the universe of the Hindu Right. Cathy J. Cohen (1997: 442), in what would become a foundational text of queer theory, asked, "How would queer activists understand politically the lives of women—in particular, women of color—on welfare, who may fit into the category of heterosexual, but whose sexual choices are not perceived as normal, moral or worthy of state support?" In other words, Cohen shifts the division between normative and queer sexualities from the hetero-and-homo binary to the racialized relationships that the state has with its citizenry. Borrowing this analytic move, we may then see that the relationship that the Indian state has with hijras has not pivoted on their queerness or pathology at all but on their religious significance and import that can be mined for nationalism (Saria 2019). The new role of hijras in the political sphere builds on an older history of the hijra politician who because of their asceticism was also incorruptible. Given the emphasis on the purity of the state as a Hindu nation, it is not surprising that various claims of incorruptibility and ascetic ethics have been pressed into service.

The current moment of globalized sexual categories and identities might allow us to celebrate the forms of visibility that I have discussed above. However, the different histories of trans people across cultural contexts give very different valences to these visibilities. Andrea Long Chu (2018: 10) writes, in the context of "sissy porn," that "most disruptions do not have the patina of the political." I would like to argue that the reverse can also hold true; in the films, the myths, and hijras' own desires, the patina of the political makes us believe that there is disruption at work. And perhaps there is—it is just not the kind of disruption we wanted or expected. The paradoxical role of hijras—as those who are beckoned to fix the breaches in the social fabric and as those who themselves never acknowledge the violence the social order inflicts on them—is better understood not through an ontological notion of generosity but through the moral position of the sutradhar. Their participation in the economy of violence must not be seen as a political problem to be overcome or explained away but as an instantiation of how queer and political theologies can come together in deeply unsettling ways.

Notes

1.   The issue of class is crucial for hijras to be recruited in shameful truth-telling. The film *Kunwara Baap* (1974) has a particularly poignant song-and-dance routine in which the hijras come to the protagonist's house to collect alms for a newborn baby. When they find out that the baby is an orphan who has been adopted by the protagonist, the lyrics of the song are changed to make "the street" the orphan's mother.

2.   "Call girls" perform sex work, but they also signal a very particular intersection of class and sexuality and hence reveal emerging anxieties of middle-class respectability endangered by young women expressing the sexual freedom offered through internal migration to urban centers.

3.   *Kinnar* is a term that has come into use in the last fifteen years and is replacing *hijra* in order to accrete respect to hijras, given that the term *hijra* is also used as a pejorative, sometimes by hijras themselves. Though *Kinnar*, too, is contested by some as evidence of the saffronization of hijra identity and politics.

4.   Veena Das (2016) studies a famous passage from tenth-century scholar Abhinavagupta that has been widely studied, including by Jacques Lacan, to argue that the grammar of poetics makes sense or gains life because of "resonant meaning." Also see Jean-Luc Nancy 2007 for another interpretation of resonant meaning.

References

Agneepath. 2012. DVD. Directed by Karan Malhotra. Mumbai: Dharma Productions.

Amar Akbar Anthony. 1977. DVD. Directed by Manmohan Desai. Mumbai: Hirawat Jain and Company, M. K. D. Films, and Manmohan Films.

Asad, Talal. 2011. "Thinking about the Secular Body, Pain, and Liberal Politics." *Cultural Anthropology* 26, no. 4: 657–75.

Binder, Katrin. 2015. "No Strings Attached? The Use of a Sutradhhāra in Modern Kannada Drama." In *In ihrer rechten Hand hielt sie ein silbernes Messer mit Glöckchen (In Her Right Hand She Held a Silver Knife with Small Bells)*, edited by Anna Aurelia Esposito, Heike Oberlin, B. A. Viveka Rai, and Karin Juliana Steiner, 21–28. Wiesbaden: Harrassowitz.

Bombay. 1995. DVD. Directed by Mani Ratnam. Mumbai: Aalayam Production, Amitabh Bachchan Corporation, Jhamu Sughand Productions, and Madras Talkies.

Chu, Andrea Long. 2018. "Did Sissy Porn Make Me Trans?" Paper presented at the conference "Queer Disruptions 2," Columbia University, New York, January 12.

Cohen, Cathy J. 1997. "Punks, Bulldaggers, and Welfare Queens: The Radical Potential of Queer Politics?" *GLQ* 3, no. 4: 437–65.

Cohen, Lawrence. 1995. "The Pleasures of Castration: The Postoperative Status of Hijras, Jankhas, and Academics." In *Sexual Nature, Sexual Culture*, edited by Paul R. Abramson and Steven D. Pinkerton, 276–304. Chicago: University of Chicago Press.

Cohen, Lawrence. 2004. "Operability: Surgery at the Margin of the State." In *Anthropology in the Margins of the State*, edited by Veena Das and Deborah Poole, 165–90. Santa Fe, NM: School of American Research Press.

Custodi, Andrea. 2007. "Transsexuality and Gender Bending in the Characters of Arjuna/ Brhnnada and Amba/Sikhandin(i)." In *Gender and Narrative in the Mahabharata*, edited by Simon Brodbeck and Brian Black, 208–30. New York: Routledge.

Das, Veena. 2004. "The Signature of the State: The Paradox of Illegibility." In *Anthropology in the Margins of the State*, edited by Veena Das and Deborah Poole, 225–52. Santa Fe, NM: School of American Research Press.

Das, Veena. 2011. "State, Citizenship, and the Urban Poor." *Citizenship Studies* 15, nos. 3–4: 319–33.

Das, Veena. 2016. "Aesthetic Emotion: Fleeting Moments that Might Last Forever." Lecture presented as part of the Durham Castle Lecture Series 2016/17, Durham University, Durham, UK, December 7.

De Vries, Hent, and Lawrence Eugene Sullivan, eds. 2006. *Political Theologies: Public Religions in a Post-secular World*. New York: Fordham University Press.

Doniger, Wendy. 2009. *The Hindus: An Alternative History*. New York: Viking Penguin.

Elison, William, Christian Lee Novetzke, and Andy Rotman. 2016. *Amar Akbar Anthony*. Cambridge, MA: Harvard University Press.

Goldman, Robert P. 1986. "The Serpent and the Rope on Stage: Popular, Literary, and Philosophical Representations of Reality in Traditional India." *Journal of Indian Philosophy* 14, no. 4: 349–69.

Hiltebeitel, Alf. 1995. "Dying before the Mahhābhhārata War: Martial and Transsexual Bodybuilding for Aravhāṇ." *Journal of Asian Studies* 54, no. 2: 447–73.

Hinchy, Jessica. 2014. "Obscenity, Moral Contagion, and Masculinity: Hijras in Public Space in Colonial North India." *Asian Studies Review* 38, no. 2: 274–94.

Hindustan Times. 2019. "From Pariah to Demigod: Transgender Leader a Star at Kumbh Mela." May 11. hindustantimes.com/india-news/from-pariah-to-demi-god -transgender-leader-a-star-at-kumbh-mela/story-hc6gv01YMiuyglbAB1YMHI.html.

Khan, Naveeda. 2012. *Muslim Becoming: Aspiration and Skepticism in Pakistan*. Durham, NC: Duke University Press.

Kunwara Baap. 1974. DVD. Directed by Mehmood. Mumbai: Balaji Arts.

Maine Pyar Kiya. 1989. DVD. Directed by Sooraj Barjatya. Mumbai: Rajshri Productions.

Mehta, Deepak. 2015. "Naming the Deity, Naming the City: Rama and Ayodhya." *South Asia Multidisciplinary Academic Journal*, no. 12. journals.openedition.org/samaj/4053.

Mom. 2016. DVD. Directed by Ravi Udyawar. Mumbai: MAD Films and Third Eye Pictures.

Murder 2. 2011. DVD. Directed by Mohit Suri. Mumbai: Prime Focus and Vishesh Films.

Nancy, Jean Luc. 2007. *Listening*, translated by C. Mandell. New York: Fordham University Press.

Once Upon a Time in Mumbai Dobaara. 2013. DVD. Directed by Milan Luthria. Mumbai: Balaji Motion Pictures.

Pollock, Sheldon. 1993. "Rāmāyaṇa and Political Imagination in India." *Journal of Asian Studies* 52, no. 2: 261–97.

Pollock, Sheldon. 2001. "The Social Aesthetic and Sanskrit Literary Theory." *Journal of Indian Philosophy* 29, no. 1: 197–229.

Roy, Jeff. 2016. "Translating Hijra into Transgender: Performance and Pehchhān in India's Trans-Hijra Communities." *Transgender Studies Quarterly* 3, nos. 3–4: 412–32.

Sadak. 1991. DVD. Directed by Mahesh Bhatt. Mumbai: NH Studioz.

Sangharsh. 1999. DVD. Directed by Tanuja Chandra. Mumbai: NH Studioz.

Saria, Vaibhav. 2015. "The Pregnant Hijra: Laughter, Dead Babies, and Invaluable Love." In *Living and Dying in the Contemporary World: A Compendium*, edited by Clara Han and Veena Das, 83–99. Berkeley: University of California Press.

Saria, Vaibhav. 2019. "Begging for Change: Hijras, Law, and Nationalism." *Contributions to Indian Sociology* 53, no. 1: 133–57.

Schmitt, Carl. 2005. *Political Theology: Four Chapters on the Concept of Sovereignty*. Chicago: University of Chicago Press.

Singh, Bhrigupati. 2012. "The Headless Horseman of Central India: Sovereignty at Varying Thresholds of Life." *Cultural Anthropology* 27, no. 2: 383–407.

Tamasha. 2015. DVD. Directed by Imtiaz Ali. Mumbai: Nadiadwala Grandson Entertainment.

Tera Kya Hoga Johnny. 2010. DVD. Directed by Sudhir Mishra. Mumbai: Medient Studios and Pixion.

Valentine, David. 2007. *Imagining Transgender*. Durham, NC: Duke University Press.

Witsoe, Jeffrey. 2011. "Corruption as Power: Caste and the Political Imagination of the Postcolonial State." *American Ethnologist* 38, no. 1: 73–85.

Zakhmi Aurat. 1988. DVD. Directed by Avtar Bhogat. Mumbai: Manta Movies.

QUEER POLITICAL ASTROLOGY

Problems and Potentials

Alexa Winstanley-Smith

*M*ainstream contemporary discourses of political theology are frequently staged within philosophy as an exigency: Make a decision! Behold, a messiah! Behead the king—in theory, at least! A modern political astrology, for which we presently have more empirical evidence than theories, does not and cannot really emerge likewise from such a powerful, if often somewhat mystical, intellectual demand. As Theodor W. Adorno (2002) once observed, modern astrology actually tends to drag the stars too much "down to earth"—pro forma, down to the margins of tabloid newspapers; and, *ad populum*, down to the ranks of complacently powerless publics—if only, in turn, to project a manageable and banal quotidian agenda onto the cosmos and so to produce the ideal schematic underpinnings of a popular dialectics for idiots. This is both an arrestingly acute criticism and a somewhat unfairly acute analysis, since modern astrology seems to be an amorphously occasional pursuit—even when it is characteristically political, even when its own political turn is taken as a queer one.

For this reason, we probably should think that the cause for a return of astrology, for its becoming the subject and object of both political interests and cultural critique, cannot be accessed in abstractions. Rather, following Adorno, at least to a certain extent, we must instead find evidence in the concrete but ignoble outskirts of mass public discourse and journalistic circulation from which the contingency paradigms of today's astrologers have taken their contemporary shapes. Indeed, to judge from the quantity of articles about it in both specialized and mainstream North American magazines and popular online publications, astrology recently has become a significant public phenomenon. In its mainstream form, it is described in terms that range from "belief" to "therapy" to a "refuge" in times of political and economic instability—none of which is terribly novel or specific, much less very interesting (Beck 2018; Ewens 2018). More to the point: to judge

GLQ 27:1
DOI 10.1215/10642684-8776890
© 2021 by Duke University Press

from the social media accounts of its practitioners and followers, a new and more community-determined astrology is taking a self-reflexive form that has begun to transform it into a sometimes critical and sometimes poetical practice.

This form of modern astrology, especially centered on the zodiac and creative overspill from daily readings, has become a resource of language and thought-shapes, even a kind of auxiliary practice for political activism, especially among queer-identifying persons and their allies: for example, the website and Instagram account of Chani Nicholas and the Twitter account @poetastrologers will be familiar to some readers. With reference to this latter type, astrology has been variously described as a "shorthand" social jargon for millennials and queer folks (both separately and in coincidence); as a worldview and vocabulary that are the enemy of "straight men"; as a relational system whose internal logic is ideally reducible to the space of a "meme"; and not least, as a language of "power and magic" for claiming the "predestination" of selfhoods and ways of being that cannot yet (and perhaps will never want to) rely on established normative heft for the purposes of political persuasion or a determinate conventional status among the general public (Dockray 2018; Ish 2017; Jones 2018; Santoro 2019).

If indeed political astrology is having a moment right now—if astrology itself is taking new shapes or being put to new uses by distinct communities who accordingly are seeking or interrogating new arguments for its validity as a relevant cultural form—it might be asked how this phenomenon does or should comport with the chiefly academic vocabulary and concept cache of political theology. Are the increasingly visible theological-academic and astrological–mass-public frameworks for sorting out a figurative shadow-language of contemporary politics even strictly separable? Leaving aside the premodern or merely occult-ish trappings of (post-)modern "theology" or astrology, can we find anything to clarify the current state of affairs in the proximal histories of either approach in its distinctly modern relationship to contemporary political imaginations? These are oversized questions, of course, but they deserve a timely airing. Moreover, crucial to ask, how might a sketch of some important interrelations and historical nodes inform the current use and renovation of astrology, especially among queer-identifying persons? Contradictory to Adorno's view of modern astrology as a kind of papier-mâché portrait of conservative and consumerist cravings for mystical authoritarian supervision over private life, does present-day queer astrology represent what Michael Warner (2005: 124) has called a "counterpublic"—that is, a kind of interventionist subgroup of the general reading public that transgresses and disrupts its norms in order to perform the possibilities of "[inhabiting] a culture with a different language ideology, a different social imaginary"? Or—a risky question to begin an article with—is it silly and ultimately pointless to go under the nose of political theology only in order to indulge a vaguer and less demanding variation on its patterns? Is it simply too late and not enough to attempt publicly oriented interventions that challenge the rules and ever more definitive nonrules of political theology in its self-entitled role as a metapublic philosophical domain? Perhaps the apparently burgeoning reformation of astrology is fated to fantasize only within the limits of its own birthplace—that is, within a rather useless public that has been almost irretrievably processed and packaged by our newest eschatological categories: late capitalism and neoliberalism. After all, in a time when those combined forces are suppressing reactions to environmental catastrophe in favor of campaigns for outer-space adventurism—whether Jeff Bezos or the president of the United States will broker the first trip to Mars seems moot—we might as well howl along with Hamlet: "This majestical roof fretted with golden fire—why, it appeareth no other thing to me than a foul and pestilent congregation of vapours" (Shakespeare 2006: 257).

Whatever its future trajectory, the proximal history of modern astrology can be viewed vis-à-vis the academically dominant discourse of political theology from at least two perspectives, neither of which entails anything very enchanted or esoteric. Both of these views go only as far back and as wide as the twentieth-century Protestant-majority West (though not without internal difference and dissent). The first perspective is marked by a general distinction that appears to separate the academic concept and study of the singular, theologically derived figure of the sovereign from the historical development of a mass public, especially under the banner of a politically malleable but sometimes unpredictable reading public: the long history internal to modern political theology bends more toward Roman and medieval sources, whereas the late-emerging "public" domain of modern astrology makes necessary at least some reference to Early Modern and Enlightenment intellectual and print cultures. Not unrelated to this, even though political theology is clearly a cluster of ideas that are familiar from published books and journals, those forms remain quietly in tension with conceptual content that fixes on temporal exclamation marks—"crisis," "emergency," "kairos," "now"—even if these must be understood as somehow "permanent" registers (Agamben 2005). On the other hand, the content of modern astrology tends to cohere with its forms in passing, ceding the distance or deferral required for delivering any oracular shocks, and instead actually functioning in a fast-paced, self-renewing present-tense of periodical time, in step with daily newspapers or even Twitter feeds. In other words, the conventional outlets for political theology and modern astrology respectively favor decisive statement and subsequent contemplation or a rapid procession of unstable reflections and revisions. Further, whereas political theology, clearly, has a dangerous element in its own right, some have hoped that its darker temptations might remain sequestered within the purview of theory and among relatively concept-inebriated but effectively power-neutered academicians (Taubes 1983: 5). In fact, astrology's distinctive appeal to mass publics is highly visible in mid-century sociological examinations like Adorno's famous "Stars Down to Earth" essay (2002). Such mass appeal can also be seen several decades earlier in the context of a public address by the equally influential and idiosyncratic art historian Aby Warburg. This second perspective is connected with the same group of discussants from which we get the first view—and this is really less a distinctively separate perspective than a wrinkle, in the sense of a lingering little problem and a minor overlap. The Benjaminian—and, per political-theological trendsetter Giorgio Agamben (2009: 73–75), equally Warburgian—method of "constellation" has certainly retained something from its astrological milieu. In short, we cannot entirely dismiss the astrological interference that is built into political theology, even if it remains visible only in a vague, latent analogy between negative magnitudes and critical distance or, more cynically, as a bit of rhetorical relief from the theopolitical sovereignty of method and tone that is arguably sometimes taken in political-theological discourse (Derrida 2009: 92–96).

Mostly skipping over its better-known usage, a stranger side of constellation will be seen in sections from Karl-Günther Heimsoth's 1928 book, *Character-Constellation: With Particular Reference to Homosexuality*. Given the popularity of "constellating" and the comparatively negligible appeal of Heimsoth's work to most readers, perhaps it is unfortunate that this overfamiliar academicized usage has left little attention to spare for the politicization, secularization, or even theologization of present-day astrology itself: a dispassionate, full-scale inquiry into the modernity of astrology seems to remain for us a desideratum (but see Campion 2012). At any rate, it seems necessary to at least get a glimpse at the short history of modern astrology as a public phenomenon, along with its relationship to the same background that gives us modern political theology, before we can work together to address generally "left" and specifically "queer" angles on astrology given its current reprise within the North American mass public.

The birth of modern astrology, in the form of the horoscope, is placed by popular consensus under the ever-churning signs of the public time of circulation—that is, in the newspaper. On August 24, 1930, the English astrologer R. H. Naylor provided the *Sunday Times* with a reading of Princess Margaret's birth chart. Despite (more likely, because of) the vagueness of Naylor's royal reading, there was an immediate demand for the democratization of horoscopy among the *Times*'s readers (Campion 2012: 77). Naylor had judiciously observed that "the Princess will share basic characteristics common to all people born in the present month," and probably this alone is enough to explain the instant mass appeal. Still, Naylor had also mixed the gossip-column mood of his royal reading with some political forecasting that equally reflected the "front page" content of the newspaper: "A sudden outbreak of revolutionary activities may be expected in Germany." In the meantime, although the American general public had been earlier to embrace astrology, with mainstream newspaper features appearing already in the late nineteenth century, it really hit its stride in England only during and after the First World War. The effect of the war on the anticipated audience for and content of astrology columns can be seen from a sample of their titles. The 1894 piece in a Utah newspaper that cozily indicated "Modest Women Deeply Engaged in Studying Stars" is typical of its time. A few decades later, equally typical is the overly optimistic revelation "Mars Will Sway World Until 1944, Astrologer Reveals" (in the *Washington Times* at the end of 1921). An explicitly political-theological use of astrology—more rare than one might think—can be seen in 1914, when the astrologer for the *Times Dispatch* of Richmond, Virginia, announced that the Star of Bethlehem itself was returning overhead—"the same celestial visitor that has heralded the most momentous events in history."

As to the lasting presence of daily astrology columns, it probably was less the predictions of global crises and more the personal touch in an otherwise public forum that did the trick, although it might have helped that Naylor himself famously failed to predict the Second World War. Nonetheless, by 1937 Naylor's technique of combining broadly personal forecasts for those born on this day with a few more or less near-sighted predictions for the fate of Europe had expanded its rather basic astro-personal hermeneutics over the now-familiar field of the twelve "sun signs." The very familiar format of the twelve signs is a construction of modern newspaper astrologers, an arrangement that allowed them to address as many readers as possible within a manageable space and using a minimum of specificity (Campion 2012). Still, whatever charlatanry characterized the populist format or the oracular vagaries of these columns, they must have suggested to their readers a gentle belief that no person is born beneath a black hole. This almost invisible assertion—atavistic to call queer, but one that certainly appealed to the margins of mass readership—is a subtle but still-remarkable trick of astrological representation when it reaches mass public consciousness. Even now, whether or not it is defensible by reference to astrological hokum, neither its appeal nor its manipulability should be underestimated.

With the expansion and popularity of astrology columns came a subtle shift in the way a general public could participate with the newspaper: now, any-one could flip to a certain page and find themselves represented under a sign, according to which the events of their lives were directly (if always quite vaguely) addressed, interpreted, and speculated upon. Even if the prognostications were dubious or silly—indeed, even if more serious astrological adepts would stick to complex natal charts and spurn the generalized format of the sun-sign column— the quick transition of astrology from a source of information on the royal family and the fate of Europe to a paradigmatic reflection on the lives of a mass public is a notable aspect of the modern history of astrology. It would be too much to sug-gest that newspaper astrology straightforwardly developed the idea that marginal members of the public were members of an astrological "in-group"; much less that these public-personal forecasts were ever meaningfully coordinated with the fore-bodings of "revolution" in a way that had any recognizably positive social or politi-cal effects. Nonetheless, the encoded representation of a general-yet-niche reading public along with the interpretive and prognosticative attention that this public received in early to mid-twentieth-century newspaper astrology columns probably brought with it a range of new possibilities and limitations, at least as far as public fantasies of the quotidian were concerned.

So far in our account there is no great source for much paranoia about or contest between this kind of newspaper astrology and the religious or cultural claims of public or political theology: the Church of England had long incorpo-rated or tolerated strands of so many Christian traditions that it was badly poised and probably disinclined to take umbrage at a hokey newspaper feature. On the other hand, the United States had had no established state church since 1833, and astrology could be taken seriously as only one contentious force among many spiri-tualisms and occultisms that had openly operated vis-à-vis theology, politics, or both since the nineteenth century (Gutierrez 2009). The indeterminate exoticism of astrology was, in fact, likely easier to absorb into predominantly Protestant cul-tures than into actual other religions: one could cast it in the role of propounding a weak providence, a vague pluralism, a vulgarized and uncontroversial version of American transcendentalism, or almost anything else, depending on the function it served to a given group of readers. Nonetheless, a similar increase of astrologi-cal interests received a different contemporary reading in Germany, where a pro-liferation of "magical" or "superstitious" content in the newspapers appeared to suggest—more furtively and threateningly than Naylor had done—that "an out-break of revolutionary activities" of one kind or another could be expected (Cam-pion 2012: 78).

In the 1910s, ahead of the 1917 anniversary of Martin Luther's Protestant Reformation, German-Jewish art historian Warburg had begun a collection of documents in order to gain a kind of double-headed view of broadly "magical" and specifically astrological thinking, both in his own time and in the early sixteenth century. Jane O. Newman (2008: 86) has observed that Warburg's preparation of an essay on Luther's reactions to contemporary catastrophe-boding astrological pamphlets and single-page flyers coincided with the period in which Warburg collected "seventy-two file boxes" that "[tracked] the resurgence of . . . various kinds of 'magical thinking' in the World War I years." Warburg's work on "Luther's Birthday" traced a use and abuse of "celebrity birth-charting" that was far less politically naive than Naylor's later contribution but that equally found its greatest potentials in the mundane sphere of popular appeal. Whereas, according to Warburg and for the purpose of his own argument, Luther had maintained a kind of 'religiously reasonable' objection to the prognostication value of astrology, his erudite humanist sidekick Philip Melancthon had both a fascination with and a cynical use for it. Turning popular enthusiasm for predicting catastrophe to favor their cause, astrologically minded reformers tried to finagle Luther's less-than-auspicious true birthdate to fit with a portentous arrangement that would cosmically authorize and ex post facto "predict" his growing religious and political power. These scholars and strategists were not above taking their political cues from a public mood easily discovered in pamphlets and flyleaves, even if such scholars also had other more bulky and esoteric sources from which to draw.

In the fractious sixteenth-century scenario examined by Warburg, the authorizing power of astrology may appear to be serving as a mere handmaiden to higher and more powerful theopolitical purposes. But, at least in Warburg's reading, there was more at stake. Certainly, Luther's name alone indicates a theopolitical heavyweight, and we do read that Melancthon was condescendingly allowed to indulge his astrological interests specifically because Luther considered these things to be more or less "a load of shit" ("es ist ein dreck mit irer kunst") (Warburg [1932] 1999: 607). Then again, when Warburg describes Melancthon as working in three different capacities at once—"as a humanist, as a theologian, and as an astropolitical journalist"—we should take note to which term the "political" is appended (601). Clearer still in Newman's work on Warburg's readings is the gist of his piece that the political-theological and the "astropolitical journalistic" were (and perhaps once more would become) two different and equally forceful discourses that were not necessarily fated to be harmoniously cooperative. Without being able to go into a closer reading here, we might loosely follow Newman in suggesting that astrology offered the apparently appealing difference of a material and observable relation to natural causality, a more close-ranging and proximate scope of "prediction" than the lofty oversight of God's providential plan or a universally divisive concept of predestination. The astrology under discussion here is, no doubt, a specifically Protestant astrology, but its visible power dynamics are significantly ulterior to those drawn from the familiar "theological" regime. An argument could even be made for the legitimating value of the almost proto-journalistically "neutral" or "impartial" numb oversight of the planets and stars, especially as compared with that strangely overpersonal and wholly unworldly Christian God who was himself undergoing various renovations at the time. At the same time, even if our theological mascot, Luther, in fact disliked the usurpation of divine predestining power by the chartable predictive patterns of the planets—that is, he begrudged them an ungodly insight into politics—he was no enemy of astrology on the whole. Newman quotes from Luther's *Table Talk*, a collection of sayings gathered from his more informal conversations, where Luther glamorized his conventionally Protestant wretched human state by referring to himself as an unhappy child of Saturn (Newman 2008).

As the much later development in newspaper astrology has shown in its prevailing transition from the forecast format to a delineative sun-sign model, not everyone who rejects astrological prediction of world events also resists astrological reflections of personality and character traits in the same motion: it simply remains up to the reader to decide if the latter has any political function when it is held aloof from a higher or more specifically theologically derived paradigm. It can at least be said, given the examples above, that strictly theological, political, humanist, and astrological (not to mention monarchical or democratic, religious, or journalistic) interests and vocabularies do not appear to necessarily fall into a strictly fundamental order of priority in times of crisis or even of mere opportunity. For now, it can be observed that any of these discourses might prove itself rhetorically limber enough to take on or slough off bits of another at any one time, borrowing or attacking one's capacity to legitimate another in a given scenario. This is true not least because any strict separations among them are from the outset entirely unstable and difficult to sustain without the artificial means of philosophy. Nonetheless, while moving from the touch-and-go workings of "astropolitical journalism" to the critical and constructive arena of theory does change the complexion of this mess, it does not really unspool the entanglements. And despite our late-modern purview, we are not yet dealing thoroughly or vigorously enough with these very long-lasting entanglements.

Looking at birth charts and fervid letters about pending cosmic disasters, Warburg seems to have stressed the dangers of the forecasting model of astrology, especially in its sixteenth-century pamphlet format and, as we know from Newman, its twentieth-century reprise in the daily newspaper. Fears of the irrational and cynical "authorizing" power of astrological prediction, which roused understandable feelings of instability and dependence in a less technologically advanced age, seem to suggest that there is at least one demonstrably "wrong use" of astrology, which is, if not strictly reducible to a mere product of ultimately theopolitical manipulation, then at least perhaps broadly and eventually reconcilable with it. It might be asked: perhaps can we help ourselves to the interesting potential of astrology if we simply clean up our ideological commitments and clarify the role of astrology as a methodological resource? This question has already been asked and answered with lasting success—albeit not so much in the old mass-public outlets of pamphlets and newspapers but mainly, so to speak, "in theory." In his *Signature of All Things*, Agamben has cited Warburg as one resource for a "constellating" approach to conceptual history. This entails an Agambenian conceptual history, whose many concepts and senses of history tend to depend on a bid to ontologize secularization itself, thus rendering the sword of theo-politics—once shown to have always contained the ploughshare of its latently economic form—a potentially indeterminable tool, even a toy (Agamben 2009). The late Paul Colilli (2015: 84) made a concerted effort to delineate "the astrological file of the allegorical mode of analogy" in Agamben's work in order to get a clearer view of the political-theological uses of astrology for theory-invested people today. Unfortunately, while Agamben's method draws on a potentially playful and marginal strain of astrological imagery found chiefly in undervalued texts of the Renaissance, he is only one among many thinkers—not the least of whom is the extremely astrology-allergic Theodor—who have drawn on Walter Benjamin's somewhat more deracinated, modern use of "constellation" (Adorno 1973: 52–53). As will be seen below, this theoretically authorized idea of astrology as constellation actually forms a rather shaky foundation for modern practices, especially for queer-identifying people and their allies.

The term *constellation* and its uses appear throughout Benjamin's work right up to his finally unfinished *Arcades Project* (1999). Given our present aims, one interesting aspect of Benjamin's "constellation" is little more than a disastrous fluke: the first major public appearance of Benjaminian constellation coincided with the far less auspicious birthday of its own evil terminological twin in Heimsoth's *Character-Constellation* of 1928. Completed but rejected in 1925, Benjamin's dissertation, *The Origin of German Tragic Drama*, was finally published in 1928. Here we get our early formulation of "constellation" as technique in the famously difficult "Epistemo-Critical Prologue," a text that Benjamin promised would be comprehensible only to kabbalists (it goes without saying: this, long before the Kabbalah itself had been broken down and made answerable to astrology in the North American postreligious marketplace of spiritualisms). As a way around the sediment of prevailing aesthetic and historicist approaches, Benjamin ([1928] 1998: 34–35) offered a somewhat gnomic formula: "Ideas are related to objects as constellations are to stars. This means, in the first place, that ideas are neither the concepts of objects nor their laws. They do not contribute to the knowledge of phenomena, and in no way can the latter be criteria with which to judge the existence of ideas." Although Colilli (2015: 78) has offered dozens of well-researched pages arguing a strong case for Benjamin's "rational astrology," I am going to risk pressing the point that these are hardly the words of an astrological adept. At least here, Benjamin does not invoke any possibly spurious validity of astrology itself, nor does he point to any particular ennobling episode in its history as a shadow-partner of theology. Rather, he presents a seductively imagistic sustained metaphor for what will become, for him, chiefly a textual and citational set of thinking, reading, writing, and collocating practices. As a technique, this kind of constellation can effectively disarm the typically theological tendency to illicitly invest contingent phenomena with ransacked, utterly foreign eternal meanings. Yet it remains difficult to measure the risk or success of translating the underlying astrological image of constellation into the fixed stars of a philosophical program not only for texts and artifacts but also for human life. Insofar as Benjamin's work goes, especially as early as 1928, astrological figures have provided an academic technique for disarming theopolitical certainties, but they have not been proved for their own sake by this singular use. This is important, because even if the light of a Benjaminian constellation arrives from a great distance to meet the highly personalized discourse of today's young astrologers, it is likely that the critical sheen once applied to astrological vocabulary has enabled its modern appreciators to claim a nonsuperstitious and even a somewhat philosophical attitude toward the meaning-laden stars. As will be shown below, it is unclear whether even the main line of our burgeoning political astrology does not derive as much from the vocabulary of twentieth-century theory as from the kitsch-habitus of twentieth-century newspaper columns. And one may wonder whether it is becoming no less difficult to gain decent critical distance from astrology than it once was—or still is—to find a philosophically remote purchase from the political and cultural spectral presence of Christian theological structures.

Suffice it to say that a hand-me-down astrological technique, if not astrology itself, has played a well-known and important role for contemporary political theology. The "constellations" and imagistic pastiche-networks borrowed from Benjamin and Warburg, respectively, are not least employed to disarm or to display the possibility for "inoperative" versions of absolutes that remain fundamental, at least on the order of description, to the task of political theology. But just as Warburg's comparison of sixteenth-century pamphlets with his modern-day newspaper clippings showed that astrology and its image-systems were hardly a surefire neutralizing form—nor even a noncontentious servant to better or worse political-theological agendas—likewise, the more astrology returns to public consciousness, so much the less the term *constellation* itself can be taken for a guaranteed anodyne or methodological crutch. In a book published in 1928, the same year that we first get Benjamin's "constellation" technique, we also find a less well-known and somewhat different view of things. The book, as noted above, was *Character-Constellation: With Particular Reference to Homosexuality*, the work of Heimsoth, a German medical doctor who was variously (and rather unexpectedly) a kind of gay-rights activist, an active member of the Nazi party, a semi-secret member of the Communist party, and, of course, an astrologer.

The varied field of study that *Character-Constellation* takes up makes the book an almost impossibly annoying and difficult read today: psychological and, elsewhere, specifically psychoanalytic vocabulary is correlated with a physiological-temperamental typology derived from the mostly forgotten work of the (also Nazi-affiliated) psychiatrist Ernst Kretschmer. The resulting combination is then tested and nuanced with reference to astrological star-charts and gonzo-learned discourses on planetary influence, the latter of which lean heavily on the astrological writings of Oscar A. H. Schmitz. Given the "particular reference to homosexuality" advertised in the book's title, Schmitz's vast repertoire of adjectives is ranged to special effect in Heimsoth's ([1928] 2015: chap. 1, 561) description of Uranus, which is typically "intuitive, explosive, volcanic, energetic, maturing, self-willed, unpredictable, obstinate, intellectual, bisexual, asexual, enigmatic, heroic, creative, hypercritical, sarcastic, disorderly, perverse, flashing, paradoxical, sometimes deceptively vacuous, sometimes extremely deep." Heimsoth quotes Schmitz copiously through the early sections of his book, which has the interesting effect of presenting the sun signs through a kind of one-note Nietzsche-enthused fondness for staunch pronouncement. No wasted rhetoric here: Nietzsche's birth chart appears in a later section, along with the gossipy claim that he was, to put it crudely, homosocially hot for Wagner (chap. 5, 1575). Once again cited on the topic of "Uranians," Schmitz asserts that these types control "the course of destiny" either as "destroyer" or "savior" of others; even their apparent modesty in fact "proceeds from an inner freedom which stands beyond law, morality, convention, mode and party" (chap. 1, 549). All of this at least has the virtue of readability, which itself makes a palpable belly-flop wherever Heimsoth mixes in Kretschmer's work on physiology and temperament. The absurdly crass euphemistic link between Uranus and gay men is almost preferable to the following statement, which goes some way to showing a less glamorous side of what happens when Renaissance emblematic thinking is conjoined with modern pseudoscientific theory: "The athletic-leptosomic constitution [read: muscular-slim], the basic temperament of fire-air—that is, choleric and sanguine—and the schizothymic character are masculine criteria, while the pyknic-lymphatic constitution [read: doughier torso and finer limbed], the basic temperament of earth-water—that is phlegmatic and melancholic—and the cyclothymic character are feminine criteria" (chap. 1, 403).

The thing to observe here is not that Heimsoth wholeheartedly embraced an extremely recondite mishmash of astrological-characterological-physiological-elemental descriptions to arrive at a bunk synthetic method for profiling gay men. This is actually almost exactly what he does, but he does it, as they say, with a difference. As Jack Halberstam has observed (2011: 148), "The role of homosexuality in fascism is very ambiguous and complicated"—in this case, certainly not least since Heimsoth's own political affiliation with National Socialism was likewise ambiguous and complicated. In other words, Heimsoth remains a largely unnoticed poster child for the enduringly "problematic" queer person: ambiguous and fluid in his affiliations, to be sure, but equally without real solidarity or elasticity for the sake of reciprocal vulnerability in accordance with any broader or higher aim at diverse sociality and coexistence.

Heimsoth's use of astrology largely aligns with Halberstam's observation regarding "homosexual masculinists" like Heimsoth's acquaintance Ernst Roehm; in other words, that they "resisted biologistic theories . . . in favour of culturalist notions of male homosexuality" (Halberstam 2011: 156). In fact, Heimsoth's short and inconclusive chapter on female homosexuality confirms this; although, still more complicated, he likewise distances himself from the "manly man" homosociality theories of his contemporary Hans Blüher, who falls in with the group mentioned by Halberstam. Comparing astrology with psychoanalysis in the final chapter of his book, Heimsoth claims that the former is "the most objective" science—a claim that looks quite bad following on the disturbing physiological-psychological theory above and even worse in light of the eighth chapter, where Heimsoth (chap. 9, 1930) uses the horoscopes of the English royal family to discern a creditable case for the "inheritability" of "characterological" traits (by Heimsoth's logic, including "homosexuality"). Even more unpleasant is one particular case study in the fifth and longest chapter, "Homosexuality as Constellation," which features a seemingly endless catalogue of birth-chart–based "case studies"—thirty-three of them in total, including a mixture of Heimsoth's analysands and prominent figures like Blüher, Edward VIII (then Prince of Wales), and, last of all, Nietzsche. The least conscientious and most interesting of these case studies describes an apparently bisexual young man who committed suicide after a romantic rejection. Heimsoth's analysis includes details from the autopsy report on the shape of the young man's skull—which perhaps served to confirm his "genius" and "cultivated aesthetic sense"—before mostly dismissing these findings in favor of his own extremely detailed description of the planetary arrangement at the time of the young man's death. To this extent, Heimsoth's "constellation" appears to be doing minor-key psychological work in what now might even be dismissed as a typical Nazi-aligned mishmash of symbolical occultism and human biology-obsessed pseudoscience, albeit with a marked emphasis on cultural and characterological data over and above the perhaps more familiarly sinister physical-biological profiles. We might be justified in calling this work the incipiently "half-woke" nadir of an ideologically broken "identity politics."

All of which is to say, this view from the Weimar is both familiar and alienating. From the outset of *Character-Constellation*, Heimsoth is careful to limit how much of either Kretschmer's or Schmitz's presuppositions he will take on. For instance, on the physiological front, Heimsoth (chap. 1, 273) asserts that "no connection exists between the constitution types described by Kretschmer and the different racial types." Indeed, he follows Kretschmer's belief that "pure types" are vanishingly rare, and in both his psychological-physiological and his astrological findings Heimsoth adopts something like a spectrum approach, which he likewise applies to his understanding of gendered traits and sexual preferences (chap. 1, 275). This is where the more seemingly inert, and thus more problematic, version of Heimsoth's titular "constellation" technique comes in. *Constellation* is, for Heimsoth (chap. 1, 187–88), a designation of "the organization of character and personality," which is "similar to the concept of the physical constitution *and* condition," hence the physiological-temperamental examples from Kretschmer. Despite the fact that Heimsoth appears to have subscribed to the physical legibility of psychological types, he invokes this stuff mainly for the sake of forcing a weak analogy. To wit, as in Kretschmer's physical "constitution *and* condition" matrix (if we agree to be mindful of its hypothetical "no pure types" proviso), so in Heimsoth's incredibly complicated "character *and* personality" constellations: any number of factors and conditions might make any combination a *pathological* type or, on the other hand, not. For Heimsoth, human character and personality are cosmically complex, and sexuality—"homosexual," "heterosexual," or otherwise—is formed, confirmed, and/or warped (the last of these, for Heimsoth, chiefly through repression or antagonism) in connection with innumerable factors. For him (chap. 1, 188), a "constellation" of differently corresponding aspects of origin and development, combined to form an observable whole picture, "is similar to a concept descriptive of an actual state and including past and present conditioning factors." This is reasonably modern and fair-minded, in its weird and off-putting way. It is really the fixity of astrological insights into the objective and fatalistic arrangements of the stars at birth and death that proves most unpleasant, as when Heimsoth (chap. 1, 191; chap. 3, 815) adds to the idea of a character "fixed at birth" and the personality traits that are "presently conditioned" that the "reality" of this "constellation" has "mechanisms and to some extent [a] destiny [that] can be ascertained." In other words, it is hard to get astrological insights to work beyond the fixities of birth dates and death dates that are taken as meaningful, symbol-laden markers that chart and essentialize the limiting characteristics of living persons from the domains of two equally overpowering horizons.

In its own way, Heimsoth's "constellation" is almost as vague and suggestive as Benjamin's. But clearly Heimsoth's definitive technique has aged much worse, and there is no small danger in simply ignoring its comparative illegibility. Combining what to us appears as a mixture of resuscitated "New Age" faux-sociology and now-outdated psychological and physiological vocabulary, Heimsoth (chap. 1, 191) employs the figure of constellation to yoke presuppositions about a meaning-laden origin point of human lives to the "mechanisms" of their development, even adding the shadowy suggestion that these together might offer a glimpse at "some destiny." To be clear: Heimsoth does this precisely in order to wrest that title-page "particular reference to homosexuality" away from binary approaches or the equivalents of vulgar "nature or nurture" arguments for the "cause" of gender identity and sexual preference that were available in his time. One need only glance at his oddly strident claims for the rational limits of astrology against those of psychoanalysis, as in the claim that "one can tell from the horoscope whether a man is avaricious or not but not whether he is anally erotic or not" (chap. 10, 2122). Heimsoth is arguing for a highly complex account of gender and sex identities that is, in places, almost as "queer-friendly" as it is blatantly offensive in others. Unfortunately, complexity becomes the victim of Heimsoth's constellation, in that he undertakes the interpretation of an unwieldy cosmic arrangement of spectrums, aspects, conjunctions, and multiple variable directions of orientation only to find the "fixed stars" that comprise a "constellation" that lays bare certain truths of "origin" and "destiny" that are just as singular and incontrovertible as they are intriguingly convoluted. In other words, Heimsoth's "constellation" gives evidence that the most dangerous aspects of political theology can be roughly performed according to a recognizable structure equally under the banner of something like cultural astrology. If anything, the latter displays a compelling and even more frightening realism in the difference of its inherently complex expectations for representations and their relations. When astrology is not made the handmaiden of theological concerns, it cannot organize political binaries like *friend* and *enemy* not as pure types. Rather, perhaps more frighteningly, it must produce only incomplete and almost metonymic existences, identified piecemeal in accordance with a contingent spectrum of different aspects, conjunctions, and arrangements of different characteristics—all of which can be given a strict "origin" and "destiny" only latterly by means of an interpretive methodology. In other words, astrology does not necessarily dumbly repeat theological-political concepts, but it can certainly accomplish strong interpretations of its own in fixing *whatever* dysmorphic "secular" typologies are present in its given milieu. Heimsoth was not the right person for this task, but glimpsing his work alongside more familiar academic astrological vocabulary may yet give us cause to wonder how the unique figure-system of astrology is equipped to provide additional metaphors for complicated, self-entailing, irreducibly inconclusive concepts that cannot be made easily or fully visible in political-theological language. Two examples that might be worth new and continued effort are the highly relevant sociopolitical concepts of solidarity and complicity, both of which are unthinkable without access to a language of spectrums, aspects, conjunctions, and the influence of changing times and tides.

Even after distancing ourselves from Heimsoth's clearly problematic model, exploring the representational and metaphorical potentials of modern astrology can still be quickly shipwrecked in at least two ways—and, again, one is a more academic tendency and the other an option that takes its case to broader publics. One can either Adornize about astrology—that is, reject it outright—or else, as it turns out, one can astrologize about Adorno. In a December 2015 piece for *Salvage*, a UK journal of the haute-pessimist Left, the journalist Sam Kriss (2015) presented "Twelve Theses on the Theory of Astrology." Here, the "theses"—a form made useful anywhere from Luther to Marx and beyond on the theopolitical spectrum—are creatively subsumed or transposed into the twelve sun signs. As with the quotations from Schmitz in Heimsoth's book, the high style makes for an enjoyable read even if one quickly tires of trying to pick apart the adopted hoopla of vaticination from the author's sincerely bad taste, an endeavor that will get you from the "blankness of subatomic chaos" to the "cloistered depths of humanity's screaming infancy." It is an interesting creative piece, not least in that it forces the reader to think the horoscope column as a politically charged performative text-space on the order usually associated with theological- or political-philosophical theses. Equally interesting, though perhaps less promising, is the laundry list of philosophers' and theorists' names that appear throughout the astrological theses: Saussure, François Wahl, Kristeva, Debord, Benjamin, Bataille, and Derrida, among others. The political-theoretical combination is not peculiar to the "Theses" example, and it is by no means always so artfully accomplished. In a post to his website, the American "author, speaker, and teacher of astrology and esotericism" Austin Coppock (2010) offered an analysis of twelve styles of "world domination" according to sun signs. Here the reader may be surprised to learn that the approved domination strategy for Pisces is "mythology," and that this "may be studied extensively in the works of Roland's Barthes' 'Mythologies'"! Those born under Cancer will probably have better luck with the "panopticon" strategy, which is explicitly drawn from Foucault's work and yet—somehow—also recommended as a personal strategy for "combat" and "control." The critical and creative potential on display here is admirable, even if there is a jarring astrological earnestness in the explicitly political "Theses" piece and, on the opposite side of things, a disconcertingly loopy embrace of "world domination strategies" in the astrological advice column.

To focus on the "Theses" piece, which is at least cogent in its aims, here astrology is used as a meta-academic structure in order to both embrace and critique philosophers and theorists who are now associated with mainstream academia. Still, so much is invested in the critico-vatic afflatus alone that modern astrology ceases to merely reflect and perhaps provide interpretive space for change in mass communities or their public dispositions; instead, astrology itself suddenly becomes the ideal object of its own liberating discourse. There is a language of activism that even acknowledges the limitations of astrology for political thinking, as in the astro-eschatological claim that "various mystical groups have put their faith in a rising Age of Aquarius, but the stars don't care, and they're not here to help us. The point is not to pass through Piscean oppression, and hope it never rises again, but to abolish it altogether" (Kriss 2015). Still, more annoyingly self-reflexive is the end of this same "Pisces" thesis, which acknowledges but also idealizes the historically contingent and public character of modern astrology in order to luxuriate in itself as the privileged backdrop for radical human meaning-making: "The night sky has always been the terrain on which we make and unmake our own social reality. One day, when we crawl out from the wreckage, we might look up, and see very different stars in the sky." The tone is similarly emphatic in Kriss's "Virgo" thesis, which "inverts" Adorno—perhaps even as Marx once famously upended Hegel—only explicitly for the sake of a truly revolutionary astrology: "If astrology has been pressed into the service of mundane power, to represent a world that can never change, our task is not to do away with it, but to fight for its liberation. We must—to employ an ironic inversion of the type Adorno was so fond of—put the stars *back in the sky*." Is this a beautiful sentiment? Perhaps, at least to those who are already invested in astrological imagery—but is it anything more than that? Really—do we have to save the secret potential of astrology, maybe even to save ourselves? What does taking such a position actually mean or entail? Those questions are barbed ones, but since there is presently no specific body of theory that examines or argues for these claims, the frustrations that arise from this kind of rhetoric might as well be infinite. It should be noted, in passing, that these same questions are and must be addressed unceasingly to works that fall under the heading of political theology. Still, it is interesting that they can be generated just as pointedly in response to a piece of "astropolitical journalism" (to borrow Warburg's term) and that the position undertaken in a piece like this—a kind of "Who constellates the constellators?" face-off with theory itself—is an exceptionally difficult one to answer on its own terms. I do not want to suggest that astrology is a waste of time for queer-identifying persons and their allies: I only ask that we continue to seek solidarity among the truly queer formal contingencies of our living, becoming friends and comrades, and that we continue to question and criticize false metaphoric systems that may only appear friendly to us as novelties. After all, wisdom once taught us that nothing is new under the sun—indeed, not even our stars.

References

Adorno, Theodor W. 1973. *Negative Dialectics*. New York: Seabury.

Adorno, Theodor W. 2002. *The Stars Down to Earth and Other Essays on the Irrational in Culture*. London: Routledge.

Agamben, Giorgio. 2005. *The Time That Remains: A Commentary on the Book of Romans*. Stanford, CA: Stanford University Press.

Agamben, Giorgio. 2009. *The Signature of All Things*. New York: Zone.

Beck, Julie. 2018. "The New Age of Astrology." *Atlantic*, January 16. theatlantic.com/health/archive/2018/01/the-new-age-of-astrology/550034/.

Benjamin, Walter. (1928) 1998. *The Origin of German Tragic Drama*. London: Verso.

Benjamin, Walter. 1999. *The Arcades Project*. Cambridge, MA: Belknap Press.

Campion, Nicholas. 2012. *Astrology and Popular Religion in the Modern West: Prophecy, Cosmology, and the New Age Movement*. London: Routledge.

Colilli, Paul. 2015. *Agamben and the Signature of Astrology: Spheres of Potentiality*. Lanham, MD: Rowman and Littlefield.

Coppock, Austin. 2010. "The Strategic Zodiac: A Mandala of Power." Austin Coppock professional website, May 31. austincoppock.com/strategy-zodiac/.

Derrida, Jacques. 2009. *The Beast and the Sovereign*. Vol. 1. Chicago: University of Chicago Press.

Dockray, Heather. 2018. "Astrology Is Booming and It's Queerer Than Ever." *Mashable*, May 4. mashable.com/2018/05/04/astrology-lgbtq-stars-resurgence-diverse-voices/.

Ewens, Hannah. 2018. "Why Straight Men Hate Astrology So Much." *Vice* (blog), November 15. vice.com/en_ca/article/qvq87p/why-straight-men-hate-astrology-so-much.

Gutierrez, Cathy. 2009. *Plato's Ghost: Spiritualism in the American Renaissance*. Oxford: Oxford University Press.

Halberstam, Jack. 2011. *The Queer Art of Failure*. Durham, NC: Duke University Press.

Heimsoth, Karl-Günther. (1928) 2015. *Charakter-Konstellation: Mit besonderer Berücksichtigung der Gleichgeschlechtlichkeit (Character-Constellation: With Particular Reference to Homosexuality)*. Translated by Richard S. Baldwin as *Homosexuality in the Horoscope*. Tempe, AZ: American Federation of Astrologers. Kindle.

Ish, Dru. 2017. "Astrology and the Importance of Queer Spirituality." *Archer Magazine*, May 11. archermagazine.com.au/2017/05/astrology-queer-spirituality/.

Jones, Baylea. 2018. "The Importance of Astrology in Queer Online Communities." *Hello Giggles* (blog), July 2. hellogiggles.com/lifestyle/importance-astrology-online-queer-communities/.

Kriss, Sam. 2015. "Twelve Theses on the Theory of Astrology." *Salvage*, December 7. salvage.zone/uncategorized/12-theses-on-the-theory-of-astrology/.

Newman, Jane O. 2008. "Luther's Birthday: Aby Warburg, Albrecht Dürer, and Early Modern Media in the Age of Modern War." *Daphnis* 37, nos. 1–2: 79–110.

Santoro, Nadine. 2019. "Queer Astrology: Why LGTBQ People Seek Answers in the Stars." LOGO, January 3. newnownext.com/queer-lgbtq-astrology-horoscope-stars/01/2019/.

Shakespeare, William. 2006. *Hamlet*, edited by Ann Thompson and Neil Taylor. London: Arden Shakespeare.

Taubes, Jacob, ed. 1983. *Religionstheorie und Politische Theologie, Band 1*. Munich: Wilhelm Fink Verlag.

Warburg, Aby. (1932) 1999. *The Renewal of Pagan Antiquity*. Los Angeles: Getty Research Institute.

Warner, Michael. 2005. *Publics and Counterpublics*. New York: Zone.

THE QUEER ARCHIVE IN FRAGMENTS

Sunil Gupta's *London Gay Switchboard*

Glyn Davis

The exhibition *Slide/Tape* was staged at Vivid Projects, Birmingham, England, from October 5 to November 16, 2013. Curated by Yasmeen Baig-Clifford and Mo White (2013: 2), the show attempted "a fresh appraisal of an abandoned medium," tape-slide, as it was used by artists across the 1970s and 1980s. As White (2007: 60) writes in her unpublished doctoral thesis, tape-slide was "technically crude, cheap and eccentric": its technical assemblage usually consisted of one or two carousels of 35 mm slides with an accompanying audio cassette soundtrack. The progression of the slide images could be activated by hand or set to advance at a pace controlled by the cassette. Tape-slide's precarious form made it susceptible to disassembly, its material components easily scattered and lost. It was also materially delicate: individual images could be scratched or burned, and audio tapes might snap or unspool. The instability and ephemerality of the medium contributed, in significant part, to a notable paucity of critical attention from historians and theorists. As White writes (60–61), "Tape-slide has not offered itself up to be collected, archived or even adequately documented making the task of providing an accurate retrieval of its history difficult. [As the artist Judith Higginbottom notes,] the unpredictable nature of tape-slide led to much of the original material not surviving and that which did is difficult to access in archives." The Vivid Projects exhibition included work by Black Audio Film Collective, Nina Danino, William Furlong, Sunil Gupta, Tina Keane, and Cordelia Swann. Gupta's contribution consisted of "fragments"—the curators' term—from his 1980 tape-slide project *London Gay Switchboard*. As the program for the exhibition noted of Gupta's piece, "The audio track remains missing, a reminder of the fragile nature of early slide-tape work" (Baig-Clifford and White 2013: 7).

GLQ 27:1
DOI 10.1215/10642684-8776904
© 2021 by Duke University Press

The image—or "fragment"—by Gupta used to illustrate his entry in the program and to adorn its cover was shot in the London nightclub Heaven. The gay "superclub" was launched in 1979 and swiftly became an enormous hit. Gupta's photograph (fig. 1) provides a bystander's perspective, inviting the viewer to join patrons arrayed in clusters or standing alone around the edge of the dance floor as they watch and cruise. The visual focus of the image is located halfway down and just in from the left of the frame where, in the receding perspective of the shot, a man is dancing, the exposure catching him in a pose with his legs akimbo. A strong white-yellow light emanates from behind the dancer, rays strafing the space and drawing the viewer's eye toward him. On the right of the frame, three men bathed in red and purple light stand nonchalantly. The shortest of the three, dressed in slacks and a white shirt, faces away from the camera; one of the others seems to have spotted Gupta and his camera. On the left of the frame, a fey figure in black leans against a ledge, watching the dancer. In the center of the photograph, five men are moving toward the dance floor; the attention of some of these men also seems to have been caught by the dancer. The composition of the shot is formally rigorous, the use of light and color vibrant and bold. The photograph has force and unity as a self-contained cultural text or object, a documentary record of a particular (sub)cultural space and its complex spatial and sexual dynamics. As a fragment of something larger, however—that is, as just one element of *London Gay Switchboard*—it tantalizes. What was this larger work, one that now seems to exist only as a phantasm? How much of the shattered work remains? What would be achieved through its reconstitution, however partial or incomplete? And what might the work, splintered, reveal about the place of the fragment in the queer archive and about the queer relation to the archival fragment?

To theorize or engage with the archive, any archive, is necessarily to confront fragmentation and the fragment. For Carolyn Steedman (1998: 67), the archive is "that prosaic place where the written and fragmentary traces of the past are put in boxes and folders, bound up, stored, catalogued"; it is also, more generically, "a name for the many places in which the past . . . has deposited some traces and fragments." Encounters with archives, that is, inevitably involve confrontations with gaps and ellipses, with fragments and ruins, whether of primary materials, documented record, or surviving memory. Queer archives are no different, but their fragmentation is often exacerbated by a lack of institutional recognition. Queer historical materials, that is, are often scattered, unordered, filleted; they frequently reside semihidden in personal collections, buried in lofts or basements, stuffed into closets or under beds. This is not to disavow the extraordinary work being done in many countries across the world by formal and semiformal orga-

Figure 1. Sunil Gupta, photograph of Heaven nightclub, from *London Gay Switchboard*, 1980. Image courtesy the artist and Hales Gallery. © Sunil Gupta. All Rights Reserved, DACS 2020.

nizations to archive queer history and materials, nor is it to ignore the complex relationships between queerness and the institutionalizing force of archives per se. (Derrida: "There is no political power without control of the archive, if not of memory" [1996: 4]). It is, however, to acknowledge the allegiance between the queer archive and the counterarchive. As Tim Dean writes (2014: 11; italics in original), "The term *counterarchive* refers less to a determinate place or archival content than to a strategic practice or a particular style of constituting the archive's legibility. Less an entity than a relation, the counterarchive works to unsettle those orders of knowledge established in and through official archives." My intention here is to explore the ways in which the queer archival fragment can activate those counterarchival relations or practices, using surviving elements of Gupta's *London Gay Switchboard* as emblematic of such dynamics.

The photograph of Heaven described above is one fragment of a much larger work. Photographs themselves, of course, can be understood as fragments. As Susan Sontag noted in an interview (Cott 2014: 57), "Photography comes in the form of fragments. The nature of the still photograph is that it has the mental status of a fragment. Of course, it's a thing complete in itself. But in relation to the passage of time, it becomes that telling fragment of what is left to us of the past." Whole, yet also partial: the form of the fragment oscillates, refuses to settle.

"Always," writes Brian Dillon (2018: 68) in his comments on written fragments, "there is this ambiguous shuttle between identity and dispersal, between formal, almost physical integrity and a fracturing or even pulverizing action." Beyond this ontological plasticity, valuable for its resistance to reification, it is necessary to interrogate what the fragment can do. That is, to pursue a line of questioning proposed by Camelia Elias (2004: 4): "What is a fragment when it is not a matter of form or content but a question of function, a philosophical concept, a manifestation of a theory, or a self-labeled 'thought'?"

Maurice Blanchot (1986: 7), in *The Writing of the Disaster*—a text written in fragmentary form—explores the political potential of the fragment. "The fragmentary," he writes, "promises not instability (the opposite of fixity) so much as disarray, confusion": disarray that is to be welcomed. The fragment "tends to dissolve the totality which it presupposes and which it carries off toward the dissolution from which it does not (properly speaking) form"; it carries within itself "the energy of disappearing" (60). Blanchot urges other writers to author fragments as a process or strategy for undoing writing. Breaking the structures of language, he argues, can enable access to a silence that has the potential to affect and shape future forms of community. (An alternative version of the essay you are reading would have been written in fragmentary form; unfortunately, I am no Roland Barthes or Wayne Koestenbaum, to identify just two exceptional queer fragmentists.) Jasmine Wallace (2016: 299–300) has nuanced Blanchot's argument, highlighted its omissions or lacunae. "We forget," she writes, "that fragmentation is not something we can all choose. We forget that fragmentary writing is, in some cases, symptomatic of fragmented histories." For oppressed and silenced communities, J. Wallace advocates a process of reassembly of fragments followed by a refragmentation. Before we can identify the value of the queer archival fragment, then, it is necessary first to try to reassemble the lost whole, then to pull that aggregate apart once more. Such a process strikes me as not only evidently counterarchival but also inherently queer: politically motivated yet also riotously playful.

Sunil Gupta's *London Gay Switchboard* is a work that can now be accessed only in fragmentary form. The original piece—an installation consisting of a thirty-nine-minute audio collage and dozens of slide images projected from two carousels—was staged once, in 1980, and has never been shown again. Over the years, its constituent components became separated, disappearing into the depths of Gupta's archive; as already noted, the audio track was seemingly lost. Gupta has included some visual components of the work in exhibitions and publications: five of the photographs, scanned in high resolution, were included in the handsome catalogue of his work, *Queer* (2011); a six-minute silent reconstruction, with new intertitles that attempted to give a sense of the project's form and intentions, was created for *Keywords* (Iniva, London, and Tate Liverpool, March 27–May 18, 2013), an exhibition inspired by Raymond Williams's landmark text of the same title; slivers were shown at the *Slide/Tape* exhibition in Birmingham (also 2013). The public exposure of these morsels has the ability to cause a shivering in the spectator, the agitation of fantasy or reverie in which the potential of a lost and unobtainable entity is engaged.

Gupta made *London Gay Switchboard* as a student at West Surrey College of Art and Design in Farnham, England. Born in Delhi in 1953, Gupta moved as a teenager to Montréal in 1969. At college in the city in the early 1970s, he became involved in a local gay scene and its politics; his interest in photography started to become more serious. In the mid-1970s he moved to New York, began and abandoned an MBA at Pace University, and studied photography at the New School for Social Research, where he was taught by Lisette Model, George Tice, and Philippe Halsman. Gupta moved to London in the late 1970s, taking up a place at Farnham soon after. In his second year at the College, he began looking for "a subject that would lead me into a gay world in London."[1] He was still relatively new to the city but had a history of local gay activism from his years in Montréal, including working on a gay helpline. "We got in touch with the local Samaritans who gave us training," Gupta remembers (2011: 24). "[This was] 1972–73. The trainings happened in our flat. I just did the weekends and people would ring up and threaten to kill you or something." London's Switchboard was launched in 1974; by the end of the decade, when Gupta approached them with the idea of making a work about the organization, it had around eighty volunteer staff contributing to its operations and offered its services twenty-four hours a day.

In his first year at Farnham, Gupta had some nuts-and-bolts film training; he learned how to edit to a metronome and the value of having an editing beat in a film. He was introduced to the medium of tape-slide by staff at the college: they "liked you to try and use the technology that they [thought was] all new and exciting; they want[ed] the students to do something with it." He was interested in the combination of distinct elements that tape-slide would allow: in Montréal, he had made *24 November 1977*, a series of photographs of an almost-naked man on a bed, accompanied by poetic, diaristic annotations, and has subsequently gone on to produce other series that combine text and image, such as *Exiles* (1986, published in 1999). Gupta also has a long-standing love of cinema: he grew up with Bollywood, a formative influence; Chris Marker's work is a touchstone for his own practice. "I am just a kind of frustrated filmmaker at heart," he told me. Gupta has in fact worked with film and video a number of times over the decades, including making a short piece on the artist Allan deSouza for the British lesbian and gay TV series *Out on Tuesday* in the late 1980s, and the thirty-minute film *(A World Without) Pity* (2003) about HIV/AIDS in India. At Farnham, Gupta chose to use tape-slide as "a poor man's film."

Tape-slide was used not only by artists but also in educational settings. One early evangelist for the format's use in schools and colleges compared it to cinema (Laun 1964: 173). "With a stereo tape recorder, an automatic slide projector, and a tape-slide synchronizer, it is possible to create an instructional program that will rival a sound motion picture. Even though still pictures are used, a well-planned program can move along with movie-like realism." In fact, he advocated for tape-slide's use over cinema, due to its simpler technological setup, faster speed of production, and easy duplication. As a format, tape-slide has been situated in relation to cinema by more than one theorist. Mo White frames the use of tape-slide by artists in the 1970s and 1980s in relation to Laura Mulvey's theoretical analyses of the workings of cinema. Exploring both tape-slide and photo-text approaches, White (2007: 58) proposes that the "meshing of photographs and text as much as the commandeering of an otherwise educational and presentational tool, the slide-projector, led to a moment when avant-garde art practices explored the separation of photographs and text, and images and sound." Drawing on commentary from the period by authors including Victor Burgin and Griselda Pollock, White argues that the artists who used photo-text and tape-slide "were responding to a legacy of ideas formulated in [film studies journal] *Screen* in the 1970s, including Mulvey's" (58). For artists, tape-slide served as an alternative to film, an adjacent technique for bringing images and sound into juxtaposition.

It is vital to recognize that tape-slide had distinct affordances and benefits that heightened its appeal for artists. It was a more affordable form than video: as Katy Deepwell notes (2018: 13), "The means to make the image and the tape were within most artists' reach." In contrast, "when artists hired, borrowed or loaned video cameras in the 1970s, video editing was largely only accessible for most artists in art school or as they joined or created new film and video co-operatives and associations" (13). Through the 1970s and into the 1980s, tape-slide was also a preferable alternative to evolving video technologies due to the superior quality of its separate channels. Video cameras at that time, Michael Archer writes (2018: 6), "were substantial, and the resultant image remained distinctly lo-fi"; 35 mm slides, in contrast, "gave a dense, tonally rich, sharply detailed image able to retain quality when projected at size." Analogue audio tapes, similarly, were "of higher quality and greater dynamic range than anything that could be recorded on videotape" (6). "With tape/slide," Archer summarizes, "you could make something visually sumptuous and audially striking relatively cheaply" (6).

For some educators and artists, one of the strengths of tape-slide was the possibility it allowed for images and sound to work abrasively against each other. "Cinema" was splintered into its two constituent channels, enabling a dismantling of—and commentary on—the ways in which movies create their meanings and effects. Maggie Humm used tape-slide in an educational setting to enable students to develop hands-on experience of assembling "cinema" in a crude form. She has argued for the political value of the technique: tape-slide, she claims (1994: 152–23), "offers a great flexibility and potential for dislocating existing regimes of political representations and for constructing new multiplicities of knowledges." She initially situates the form against cinema, with the latter understood as ideologically suspicious:

> Unlike film, tape-slide inherently carries a hostility to commercial representations, by, for example, often disrupting cause-and-effect narratives and privileging everyday experience. Tape-slide *makes* the viewer think about the sequencing of events and the viewer's place in similar events. The disparity between sound and image highlights the message that the personal is not being smoothly *re*-presented to *us*, but is part of a process we create. Thus sound can dominate more than vision. Revealing disjunctions in address, tape-slide's anti-seamless process can be a visual politics. (147; emphasis in original)

Ultimately, however, she suggests that it could be "fruitful" to "establish tape-slide as a film form operating within socially and historically produced visual processes, since the principle of juxtaposition at the heart of tape-slide is similar to the principle of montage in the cinema" (154).

Tape-slide is, I would suggest, quasi-cinematic. During the years that it was being used by a variety of artists and educators, film and video were also available as technologies, but tape-slide offered alternative opportunities and so sat alongside them. Tape-slide is not quasi in terms of being ersatz, inferior, or minor—though there is perhaps an interesting argument to make, following Patricia White's (2008: 413) exploration of the resonances between "minor" and "queer," for tape-slide as a Deleuze-and-Guattarian minor cinema, "making use of limited resources in a politicized way." Rather, I would posit tape-slide's quasiness in terms of its adjacency, its besideness. Less cinema's next-door buddy, more its brittle and caustic neighbor, the queer potentiality of tape-slide is wrapped up in its quasi-ness—indeed, the format invites us to interrogate the queerness of the quasi. Contiguous to cinema, rather than cinema per se, tape-slide's fractured and disruptive form enables a critique of seamlessness, homogeneity, tidiness.

Gupta was given free rein to take photographs at Switchboard: "I tried to make as much as I could out of the place. They gave me a lot of access. They didn't care what I took pictures of." At the time, the organization was housed in a small space above Housman's bookshop at 5 Caledonian Road in Islington. During his visits, Gupta took images of the cramped and cluttered location. On one wall, a map of London was dotted with colored and annotated pins marking the where-abouts of key queer venues; one small central area of the map, dense with social-izing opportunities, was afforded its own magnified section, layered on top of the bottom right of the main map. Pinned to the wall around this map were others, including a transport map of London. Shelves in alcoves on either side of these documents were used for mail, lever arch files, and other paperwork. The back of one door, painted white and taupe, had a few hangers for jackets and coats. Wall space was used for posting up hand-written lists and charts, clippings from news-papers, minutes of meetings, membership information, notes to staff. Gupta pho-tographed a clipping of two short condemnations of William Friedkin's *Cruising* (1980): "'Cruising' Sucks" and "Gays Curse 'Cruising.'" A whiteboard was used for topical developments. In Gupta's image of the board, this included a short list of venues that were "recently deceased" (including Beagles, Country Cousins, and the George and Dragon); a note warning "Beware the Gay Sun Club—a [Roger] Gleaves outfit being investigated by the police"; and guidelines for one venue ("No leather jackets should be worn—denim, western, uniform only").

Gupta also took photographs of some of the eighty-odd volunteers who worked at Switchboard as they answered calls, handled paperwork, or otherwise occupied the space. Almost all of these volunteers were white men in their twenties and thirties: as we looked through some of the photographs together, Gupta raised an eyebrow as an image of a Black man, around thirty years old, appeared on his computer screen ("Oh look, a non-white face"). He would take full reels of shots of a particular individual, shooting quickly, with an awareness that projecting these images in quick succession would enable an approximation of the cinematic, allow him to "fake a movie with stills." Sequences of these images give a sense of the tenor of the calls to which the staff were responding when photographed: Lisa Power, her black bobbed hair in a blue alice band, shot in close-up through a hatch that separated rooms in the venue, laughs while talking on a yellow telephone; Gus Cairns, in medium-shot framing, looks considerably more serious and concerned

Figure 2. Sunil Gupta, photograph of Gus Cairns, from *London Gay Switchboard*, 1980. Image courtesy the artist and Hales Gallery. © Sunil Gupta. All Rights Reserved, DACS 2020.

as he deals with another caller (fig. 2). The limited scope and variety of the photographs Gupta was taking concerned him, however: "They're on the phone, that was the activity. The other activity was that they had meetings above a pub in very bad lighting, where they had arguments about policy. So I did some of that." For instance, Gupta documented a Switchboard Annual General Meeting that took place on Sunday, April 13, 1980. "And then I thought I've got to expand this." He supplemented the portraits of Switchboard volunteers at work with images of them in their homes, where he would also interview them, recording their conversations.

He also started to photograph London's gay scene beyond Switchboard, the community context within which the organization was operating. "A huge percentage of the calls [they received] were about 'where shall I go, I'm in London.'" Gupta selected venues from Switchboard's map and photographed their exteriors: The Boltons, its shabby frontage graffitied with a doodle of a large-nosed figure; the more salubrious Salisbury; a sunlit Princess of Prussia; The Coleherne; The Sols Arms. These images, plainly framed, reveal the nondescript and unremarkable aesthetic of the exteriors of these queer venues, the extent to which they were hidden in plain view. Gupta took a series of images of performers on the South London drag scene, in glitzy and trashy incarnations, from one rake-like individual dressed smartly in a Weimer-era *Cabaret*-emcee outfit to a larger-bodied

Figure 3. Sunil Gupta, photograph of drag queen, from *London Gay Switchboard*, 1980. Image courtesy the artist and Hales Gallery. © Sunil Gupta. All Rights Reserved, DACS 2020.

queen in ill-fitting tan tights, roller skates, and a bright red wig (fig. 3). In addition, there were the images of Heaven, a sizeable series that serves as a cohesive body of work in its own right, a detachable fragment of the whole. In the club, Gupta photographed solitary men loitering, propped against walls, and cruising the space. He shot staff working behind the bar, punters parked on low seating around tables lit by candles, men playing pool. The main focus, however, was the dance floor, shot from a variety of angles and distances. In some images, the space seems quiet, but this was due to the exposure length Gupta had to use and the lighting available: "I had to shoot one second [exposure], so if you were moving quickly you disappeared. It was lit by the strobes." Looking back at these images in the wake of the AIDS crisis—HIV being discovered in 1981, the year after *London Gay Switchboard*—the ghostly presence/absence of many of the dancers takes on added resonance.

In order to assemble his tape-slide work, Gupta needed hundreds of images. To all of the material he had shot of Switchboard, its staff, and venues across London, he also added an array of black-and-white documentary images of London that he had been taking as a relative newcomer to the city. He then started to complicate the form that he was using: as he now acknowledges, "I was trying to be very structuralist and disruptive about the documentary part of it." This began with the addition of images by other, renowned photographers. "I had been developing a gay photographic history that hadn't been taught to me, but I had been making my own personal collection of it. So I included [images by] Arthur Tress and Robert Mapplethorpe—I had the cock on the slab, for example [Mapplethorpe's *Mark Stevens (Mr. 10 ½)*, 1976]." He also inserted slides featuring text: "Reversed-out type-writer, Courier, white-on-black, just a few lines, a bit like intertitles. I had quotes that I was getting from, I don't know, Duane Michals or Susan Sontag, whoever I was finding that was sort of relevant around the idea of "picture making and gay" and [related to the topic of] deconstructing documentary." For example, on separate slides were quotes by Dennis Altman ([1971] 1993: 238): "The price of solidarity, whether for blacks, women or gays, is separation"; and Allan Sekula (1978: 883): "I'm arguing then, for an art that documents monopoly capitalism's inability to deliver the conditions of a fully human life." The authors were identified, though not fully referenced or clearly attributed, in end–credits slides.

In order to make sense of Gupta's "structuralist and disruptive" inclusion of a number of provocative quotes and of images from his personal gay archive, it is useful to acknowledge the influence of Anne Williams, one of Gupta's tutors at Farnham (on Gupta's tutors, see K. Wallace 2011: 132). Williams, along with fellow Farnham tutor Karen Knorr, was taught by Victor Burgin at the Polytechnic of Central London, and both seem to have absorbed and adopted what John Roberts (1998: 152) has called Burgin's "framework for photography from which to attack the political credentials of the documentary tradition." Gupta's deconstructionist approach to *London Gay Switchboard* evidences the impact of the critical and theoretical perspective taught by Williams. It also makes clear that Gupta had identified a particular capacity of tape-slide: what Humm (to repeat a fragment of a quote used above) called the medium's "potential for dislocating existing regimes of political representations and for constructing new multiplicities of knowledges." Indeed, Gupta's "structuralist and disruptive" tactics served to fracture the work, to fragment any false unity toward which the bulk of the content might be seen to gesture.

Deconstructionist tactics can be identified throughout Gupta's oeuvre, in variously subtle or substantive forms, from the previously mentioned text/image relations of his series *Exiles* to the riffs on art historical references in the *Sun City* project (2010). As Natasha Bissonauth identifies (2019: 101), Gupta's "practice has been committed to decoding and recoding documentary photography as a way of calling out the medium for objectifying minoritarian lives, especially the lives of those at the intersections of race and sexuality." Race and ethnicity remain largely absent as topics of interrogation in *London Gay Switchboard*, the work offering instead a substantive and sustained engagement with the lesbian and gay culture and politics of its time. The project's purview extends far beyond the official voice of the volunteer-run organization named in its title, seeming to acknowledge that a telephonic switchboard enables mediated access to a plethora of people, to a variety of geographically dispersed locales, to numerous dissenting and contradictory perspectives. That dissent is registered in *Switchboard*'s rupturing and fragmentation of the documentary format itself, its questioning of the limitations of still images and sound as media for capturing and contributing to an archival record of minoritarian subjectivities, spaces, and cultural creativity.

As noted at the start of this essay, the program for the 2013 exhibition *Slide/Tape* claimed that the audio track for *London Gay Switchboard* "remains missing." In my first substantial interview with Gupta about *Switchboard*, he maintained this position, commenting on the dispersal of the work's components within his own archive, a dispersal compounded by the age of the work. On the train home to Edinburgh from London, however, my phone buzzed: an email from Gupta. "Found some original audio tapes . . . ," read the message, accompanied by a photograph of a plastic tray of audio cassettes, one of which—a TDK SA-C90—was clearly labeled "LONDON GAY SWITCHBOARD BY Sunil GUPTA" on the spine. The box of around thirty miscellaneous tapes contained several featuring lengthy interviews with Switchboard staff: Gus Cairns, Val Bott, Bob Harris, Peter Scott, David Seligman, Keith Mason.

The ninety-minute interview tapes had a particular format: on one side, Gupta would ask the sitter questions about London Gay Switchboard, their role at the organization, lesbian and gay politics, and so on; on the other, he probed them about their personal life and experiences. "I would ask everyone the same questions: really about coming to London, and how it was for them, and why they were at the organization—a little potted history of lesbians and gay men at that time. [Most of them were] between twenty-five and thirty; there were some who were a bit older, but it was a particular generation." The next time he and I met, we set aside two days to work through the tapes. Gupta's two cassette players were rather old; the first tape that he attempted to play—the interview with Gus Cairns—snapped immediately in the worn cogs. I think I was more concerned about this than Gupta, the sensitivity of the archival researcher to the fragility of objects of study triggering an overly cautious attitude, whereas the practicing artist approaches the same materials as operational or exploitable malleable components, which, if necessary, can be repaired. After borrowing a couple of Walkmans from one of Gupta's neighbors and linking one up with a jack to a decent amplifier, we began to listen through the tapes. I was anticipating aural wobble, but the sound was surprisingly sharp and clear. After listening to tapes of one male and one female interviewee, we inserted the *Switchboard* audio tape and pressed *play*.

The audio-collage component of *London Gay Switchboard* kicks off with a blast of punk music: an excerpt of around fifty seconds of Buzzcocks's "I Believe," taken from the middle of the song. The track provides a bracing blast of nihilism, vocalist Steve Shelley barking and repeating its single-note chorus/manifesto, "There is no love in this world anymore." This was, perhaps, a surprising choice for the start of an audiovisual work setting out to explore the politics and dynamics of a supportive and humanitarian NGO—an organization dedicated to providing care for the lost and lonely. According to Gupta, he chose the track because one of his interviewees, Cairns, was in a punk band. In retrospect, the opening lines of "I Believe" (which do not feature in *Switchboard*) echo Gupta's "structuralist and disruptive" plan for his tape-slide work: "In these times of contention, it's not my intention to make things plain / I'm looking through mirrors to catch the reflection that can't be mine." Although many of the elements of *Switchboard* operated in combination to provide a multifaceted map of the organization and the wider cultural and political context in which it operated at the time, Gupta's additional components (including this invigorating Buzzcocks excerpt) rendered that map somewhat opaque, hampering its legibility.

The first collage of voices lasts for nine minutes. It opens with a male voice describing the purpose of Switchboard: to give help and information to homosexual men and women, to provide details on the whereabouts of gay bars and clubs, to serve as someone to talk to when your lover of four years has just left you, and so on. The variety and volume of callers—160,000 every year—is identified. A second and a third male speaker enter the audio collage admixture. The founding of Switchboard in 1974 and its establishment of a working structure are mentioned. Skepticism is expressed about the ability of certain professionals, especially psychologists, to handle lesbian and gay concerns adequately. The third speaker spells out why he puts in the hours for Switchboard: "I do it out of a continuing sense of anger and frustration and sadness [about the] oppression of gay people." Val Bott, the only female voice included on the audio track, introduces the topic of gender by discussing whether a women-only version of Switchboard would be useful. Bott and one of the male voices put forward their views of the different pressures faced by women who call the helpline: "It's very much more difficult for women to escape from the prescribed heterosexual lifestyle," he says; "Women are very programmed to get married," Bott states.

A musical interlude follows: one minute and forty seconds of Bette Midler's high-camp disco belter "My Knight in Black Leather" (taken from her 1979 album

Thighs and Whispers). The song's intro, first verse, and chorus are included; a cut removes a verse and jumps to a repeat (with slight modification) of the chorus. "Knight" casts Midler as a cruising gay man: "I was just a pilgrim in the hot pursuit of love / Wandered from disco to disco, that's all my life was." The object of pursuit is a romantic ideal as well as a fetishized one: "Oh my knight in black leather / Hold me tight and love me forever / Rings on your fingers, love in your heart / Knight in black leather, we'll never part." The second collage of voices that follows this lasts for around seven minutes: appropriately, following the Midler track, the first voice talks about his "less rigid" ideas about gender and about gay male culture's investment in a performative masculinity. Bott's comments on gender continue: "It's easier for a man to be gay than it is for a woman to be gay." A male interviewee talks about Switchboard's staff needing to identify callers' differing needs: "What we have to spend a lot of time doing on the phone is sizing up the person on the phone . . . and refer them to the best place for them." Particular bars—The Coleherne, The Salisbury—are criticized by different speakers. It is suggested, by a male interviewee, that police should not be raiding public toilets where cottaging takes place; rather, the cottagers should be given advice on other places that they can go.

A bombastic burst of opera by Berlioz lasting two and a half minutes is followed by a twelve-minute collage of voices. This largely cohesive block concentrates on the workings of Switchboard: its structure and constitution; the nature of the shift work; its general meetings and the ways responsibilities are devolved to groups; how new volunteers are recruited and interviewed; what is required from a member of the Switchboard staff ("they should have a lot of gay zest, in other words they must feel positive about being homosexual"); different types of calls (the "information call" and the "chat call"). Judgments of other lesbian and gay organizations are made: the Gay Liberation Front is praised; the Campaign for Homosexual Equality is criticized for being "very middle class, very cliquey, cater[ing] to a very narrow area of personalities." An excerpt from Diana Ross's "Love Hangover" starts and runs for three minutes. A last minute of audio collage provides final statements or stories by individual speakers. A male interviewee talks about being sent to a psychiatrist by his family, but the medical professional refusing to believe homosexuality could be treated or cured; Bott argues that "just because we're gay doesn't mean we have things in common"; a male speaker states that "being gay is as much about the emotional life, about making friends, about honesty, truth and support." A gentle piano piece by Bach fades in, lasts for about three minutes, and marks the end of *Switchboard*'s audio track.

I outline the content of Switchboard's audio collage in detail here partly as a record for posterity but also to give a sense of its density. The fragmentation of the audio track is of a different nature from that of the slides. It is located partly in the DIY editing that results in distinct aural textures suddenly abutting each other; partly in the interruption of relatively formal accounts of an organization's mechanics by personal anecdotes and views ("What I hate most about England is the errant hypocrisies in life; it's not just homosexuality, it's sex period, it's feelings"); and partly in the affective rifts caused by the musical choices. Despite Gupta's attempts to provide some cohesive narrative to the piece through editing ("I basically cut them together so that they told this sort of story"), the disjunctions between opinions are marked—as evidenced, for example, by the final few voices and the variety of topics they cover. What cannot be known is how the images and sound—two assemblages of fragments—operated together in the completed work; in the absence of a written guide, only speculation is possible. Bette Midler may have sound-tracked the drag photographs; Donna Summer the Heaven series of images. But this is to presume that these groups of pictures were projected together in sequence, whereas they could have been dispersed across the full thirty-nine-minute run of the work. "I didn't even attempt to have matching sound and picture," Gupta told me. "I thought I would start off with matching—so the first time you heard the voice [of a particular speaker] you might be looking at the person, and thereafter I let the voices [mix]."

As identified, Gupta only staged *London Gay Switchboard* once, in 1980. He knew that he would need to show it to the volunteers at the organization, after working alongside them for several weeks and after a number of the staff had allowed him to interview them. "There was some pub night and I brought it with me. And they were quite startled. It wasn't what they were expecting. I think they were expecting a kind of feel-good NGO fundraising "this is their work" kind of thing. As it went on they were gasping." One female volunteer objected to having a male voice sound-tracking images of her at work. Gupta realized, "It couldn't go anywhere. It was killed before it got off the ground." At Farnham, he ran into further problems. At thirty-nine minutes, *Switchboard* was too long to be accommodated into a scheduled crit tutorial, usually about fifteen minutes in length. "It was way too long for the convention of the time, the way it was set up." In addition, he was hauled in front of the college administrators, who were concerned about his working on a gay-themed project. The age of consent for gay men in England was twenty-one at the time, and the average Farnham student was younger than this; the administration accused Gupta of proselytizing to the underage. After this negative experience, he chose in his final year to redirect his focus, attempting a project that ambitiously explored "why certain people are poor in India."

Despite the poor reception of *London Gay Switchboard* by the members of the organization—a reception that seems to have been partly responsible for the work's subsequent dissolution and neglect—Gupta did experiment for a second time with tape-slide as a format. After leaving Farnham, he moved on to the Royal College of Art for postgraduate study. Gupta discovered that the RCA "had a much posher version" of tape-slide, with twenty-four projectors linked to the audio track; he realized that "you could make an animated [work], like an actual movie." (The artist Nina Danino remembers that tape-slide "was available in the department of Environmental Media at the Royal College as an art medium alongside the Sony Portapak and a very well-equipped sound studio. The work in the department was cutting edge performance, projection, expanded sculpture, audio, and forms that were very experimental. Slide-tape there was part of this experimental avant-garde" [quoted in M. White 2018a: 24]). Gupta decided to make a shorter piece about Hampstead Heath, a large and notorious gay cruising ground in London. The work was anticipated to last for approximately twenty minutes. As he recalls, "the audio was a married guy who talks about why he goes there and what goes on. The visuals were the Heath in the daytime. I didn't go at night. I went to photograph the ground, the aftermath."

The slides for this work are in Gupta's archive; the whereabouts of the audio are unclear. Many of the images are devoid of human presence, featuring shrubs, details of trees and ferns, and close-ups of richly textured bark. The photographs were evidently taken during autumn months: fallen leaves, russet, ochre and yellow, silt the ground. Dry bracken, turning a golden hue, meshes messily with straw-like strands and angular twigs. Pockets of dead leaves lie in the hollows between twists of grey tree roots. A number of compositions concentrate on natural elements that are aesthetically striking: a tree branch damaged, split open, and beginning to rot, the split revealing the grain of the wood; an angular division in a trunk's growth, the bark a mottled pattern of light green and silver; a thin, solitary tree rooted in a tangle of dried grass. In one image (fig. 4), a leafy bush impinges on the left side of the frame; on the right, a tree trunk has been graffitied, in white, with a schoolboy-simple outline of a cock and balls and a shape that looks a little like a pair of angel wings but could equally be a spread ass. Knowing that this work is about Hampstead Heath, the viewer scans the images for evidence of cruising and public sex. Is the phallus graffiti a vandal's lark or a code, perhaps identifying the location as a rendezvous?

Indeed, a substantial number of the images that Gupta took for *Hampstead Heath* do feature people. There are documentary pictures that capture people using the park: families at play, groups of friends socializing, couples and solitary

Figure 4. Sunil Gupta, photograph from *Hampstead Heath*, ca. 1982. Image
courtesy the artist and Hales Gallery. © Sunil Gupta. All Rights Reserved.
DACS 2020.

figures strolling. Gupta asked two friends, a gay male couple, to do a bit of model-
ing for him and staged a number of images featuring them walking on paths and
framed in more static close-ups. One sequence, for instance, features several photographs of the couple's shoes, tan and dark brown loafers, and the bottoms of their
dark-blue boot-cut jeans against grass peppered with small brown leaves. Frame
by frame, the shoes move closer together, their physical proximity intimating what
is happening above the frame border. The intrusion of this staged component into
the Hampstead Heath photographs affects the others: images of solitary men or
of men in a couple or group who seem distracted, their gaze looking out-of-frame,
become records of cruising activity; shots of dense, dark undergrowth away from
the paths seem devoid of human life but perhaps feature furtive activity taking
place in their depths.

The *Hampstead Heath* tape-slide installation was never shown to Gupta's
tutors at the RCA and has never been publicly staged. As Gupta states, he went
searching for the "aftermath" of cruising: "I was looking for evidence, so [in some
of the pictures] on the ground there's some debris." As noted, some of his photographs of the Heath featured families with children of various ages. Gupta recognized a challenging juxtaposition: "There were these kids playing and there were
condoms, remains of sex, on the ground, in amongst the grass." Technicians at the

RCA saw elements of the work as it was developing and had negative reactions to the admixture of queer themes and practices and images of children. The piece's production was shut down. Once again, Gupta ran up against the age of consent and its impact on artistic practice: "I was so involved with being a gay man looking at autobiography; [I learned that] you can't look at childhood. All of our stories [at the time] start[ed] at 21. You can't have a kid in the picture."

In concept and shape, Gupta's *Hampstead Heath* was a more cohesive work than *London Gay Switchboard*, seemingly taking less advantage of the disruptive possibilities afforded by tape-slide. Indeed, had *Hampstead Heath* been exhibited, the use of the RCA's superior technology would have brought the work closer to cinema than *Switchboard*, edging it away from the queer potential of the quasi-ness of more rudimentary forms of tape-slide. *Switchboard*, in contrast, exploited the fragmentary nature of the medium, assembling together a fragile smorgasbord of visual and audio delights. Although I have attempted here to provide an account of the work's multiple textures and materials, the aim was never to enable a full reconstruction but rather—counterarchivally—to gesture toward and then cast asunder an imaginative process of reconstruction. There is the possibility that *Switchboard* could be fully rearticulated in the future (the images were all scanned in February and March 2020). However, I would suggest that to do so could limit its potential as a work composed of fragments, could fail to harness and exploit what Blanchot called the fragment's "energy of disappearing." For Blanchot, the fragment can be used to open a space for contemplating future forms of community. *Switchboard*'s vivid fragments—including images of a group of like-minded individuals forging a queer networked politics of support, bold political slogans about using art to confront the stifling forces of capitalism, perceptive audio snippets of provocative opinions about social and legal restrictions on queer life, and bursts of music that hymn anarchic visions of social life—fail to cohere. In isolation, in clumps, in sequences, in contrast, however, they record and throw into discordant conversation a variety of models of queer community being considered at the time of their making. The uncovering of queer archival fragments enables a registering of the tendency of much queer history and culture to be fragmented, to exist only in traces; it promotes a contentment with the partial and a skeptical attitude toward the attainment of a reconstituted lost whole; and it enables a reengagement with lost visions, however circumscribed, of how the queer future could be.

Note

Huge and heartfelt thanks to Sunil Gupta and Charan Singh; and to Laura Guy for her guidance and insights on the history of tape-slide. The research for this essay was conducted as part of the pan-European queer history project "Cruising the Seventies: Unearthing Pre-HIV/AIDS Queer Sexual Cultures," which was funded by HERA and the European Commission (www.crusev.ed.ac.uk).

1. All unattributed quotes by Gupta in this essay come from interviews with the artist conducted by the author on July 23, December 17, and December 18, 2019.

References

Altman, Dennis. (1971) 1993. *Homosexuality: Oppression and Liberation*. New York: New York University Press.

Archer, Michael. 2018. "Tx." In White 2018a, 5–9.

Baig-Clifford, Yasmeen, and Mo White. 2013. Slide/Tape: A Fresh Appraisal of an Abandoned Media Featuring Key Works in the UK since the 1970s. Exhibition program. www.vividprojects.org.uk/wp-content/uploads/2013/09/095.9.13-VP-Slide-Tape-Brochure-artwork.pdf.

Bissonauth, Natasha. 2019. "A Camping of Orientalism in Sunil Gupta's *Sun City*." *Art Journal* 78, no. 4: 98–117.

Blanchot, Maurice. 1986. *The Writing of the Disaster*, translated by Ann Smock. Lincoln: University of Nebraska Press.

Cott, Jonathan. 2014. *Susan Sontag: The Complete Rolling Stone Interview*. New Haven, CT: Yale University Press.

Dean, Tim. 2014. "Introduction: Pornography, Technology, Archive." In *Porn Archives*, edited by Tim Dean, Steven Ruszczycky, and David Squires, 1–26. Durham, NC: Duke University Press.

Deepwell, Katy. 2018. "Feminist Contributions to Slide/Tape." In White 2018a, 10–18.

Derrida, Jacques. 1996. *Archive Fever: A Freudian Impression*. Chicago: University of Chicago Press.

Dillon, Brian. 2018. *Essayism*. London: Fitzcarraldo.

Elias, Camelia. 2004. *The Fragment: Towards a History and Poetics of a Performative Genre*. Bern: Lang.

Gupta, Sunil. 1999. *Exiles*. London: Sunil Gupta.

Gupta, Sunil. 2011. *Queer*. Munich: Prestel.

Humm, Maggie. 1994. "Tropisms, Tape-Slide, and Theory." In *Changing Our Lives: Doing Women's Studies*, edited by Gabriele Griffin, 145–58. London: Pluto.

Laun, H. Charles. 1964. "Tape-Slide Programs." *American Biology Teacher* 26, no. 3: 173–77.

Roberts, John. 1998. *The Art of Interruption: Realism, Photography, and the Everyday.* Manchester, UK: Manchester University Press.

Sekula, Allan. 1978. "Dismantling Modernism, Reinventing Documentary (Notes on the Politics of Representation)." *Massachusetts Review* 19, no. 4: 859–83.

Steedman, Carolyn. 1998. "The Space of Memory: In an Archive." *History of the Human Sciences* 11, no. 4: 65–83.

Wallace, Jasmine. 2016. "The Fragments of the Disaster: Blanchot and Galeano on Decolonial Writing." *Journal of Speculative Philosophy* 30, no. 3: 292–302.

Wallace, Keith. 2011. "Me, Myself, and You." In Gupta 2011, 130–37.

White, Mo (Mary C.). 2007. "From Text to Practice: Rereading Laura Mulvey's "Visual Pleasure and Narrative Cinema" toward a Different History of the Feminist Avant-Garde." PhD diss., Loughborough University.

White, Mo. 2018a. *Slide/Tape.* Birmingham, UK: Vivid Projects.

White, Mo. 2018b. "Symposium Roundtable 1." In White 2018a, 19–25.

White, Patricia. 2008. "Lesbian Minor Cinema." *Screen* 49, no. 4: 410–25.

THE OTHER SIDES OF STONEWALL

Marcie Frank

One Dimensional Queer
Roderick A. Ferguson
Cambridge: Polity, 2019. v + 168 pp.

Buying Gay: How Physique Entrepreneurs Sparked a Movement
David K. Johnson
New York: Columbia University Press, 2019. xvi + 308 pp.

*Categorically Famous: Literary Celebrity and Sexual Liberation
in 1960s America*
Guy Davidson
Palo Alto, CA: Stanford University Press, 2019. xii + 227 pp.

New books by Roderick A. Ferguson, David K. Johnson, and Guy Davidson prompt
readers to reassess Stonewall as both a significant event and a pivotal concept
for queer scholarship. Ferguson aims to fit queer liberation into the vocabulary of
intersectional politics by emphasizing Stonewall's radical origins. Johnson reads
Stonewall's bourgeois preconditions in the contributions the physique entrepreneurs made to gay community networks by publishing magazines featuring nearly
naked men and running adjacent ads for businesses, including photography studios, mail-order catalogues, book clubs, and pen-pal services aimed at gay consumers. Despite their different politics, for both Ferguson and Johnson, Stonewall
remains a historical turning point, an event that organizes before-and-after narratives and infuses them with rhetorical, affective, and political energies.

  To rediscover aspects of Stonewall or unearth new details about it, both
Ferguson and Johnson assume its historicity. It remains a reference point for mea-

GLQ 27:1
DOI 10.1215/10642684-8776918
© 2021 by Duke University Press

suring the progress or regress of our own times for both, even though Johnson accesses its meanings by archival research and Ferguson by studying it as an intellectual and political inheritance whose "clarity greatly determines whether we can identify and compel an alternative future" (150). For Davidson, however, Stonewall is not just a historical event; it is also a permeable conceptual grid. Examining the liberatory impact of famous literary intellectuals James Baldwin, Susan Sontag, and Gore Vidal, none of whom consistently avowed their homosexual identities, Davidson's analysis passes through Stonewall, looping back to reconfigure our understanding not so much of the uprising itself as of its capacity to mediate queer identities, even those formed before it occurred.

Before-and-after Stonewall looks different thanks to Ferguson and Johnson. However, their work is not ideologically compatible: Ferguson emphasizes the radical roots of queerness in the Stonewall uprising to which he claims we should return, whereas Johnson portrays the political effects of the gay entrepreneurs' sponsorship of physique culture as culminating in, but also surviving, Stonewall into our own time. Their shared interest in the event reinforces its significance, though they depict its meanings in mutually exclusive ways. Davidson's treatment of the intersection of media and sexual identity in the case of his three celebrities nuances the political and cultural significances of sexual orientation itself by looking at the means by which it could be signaled before and after Stonewall. Compellingly, he connects before-and-after not in a linear way but in a self-consciously recursive fashion that makes past and present speak back and forth to each other and reminds us what queer theory can accomplish.

Ferguson wants us to see Stonewall differently and to apply its lessons to today. He returns to the 1960s rhetorically. He cites Sylvia Rivera's (2013) account of the Stonewall uprising not as the spontaneous outburst in defense of sexual freedom that it is sometimes taken to be but as the concerted action led by activists who trained with STAR (Street Transvestite Action Revolutionaries), the Gay Liberation Front, Third World Gay Revolution, and the Combahee River collective. Here, Ferguson finds inspiration for contemporary multidimensional intersectional politics. Queer liberation was not in 1969 the single-issue political cause that it has since become. Ferguson identifies its origins in antiracism, antipoverty, and anti-imperialist activisms to which, he asserts, we should now return.

Ferguson depicts the divorce of queer liberation from political struggles around race, poverty, capitalism, and colonialism as the consequence of the mainstreaming of gay rights and gay capital. To make Stonewall's lessons applicable, he accesses the legacy of 1960s radicalism by adopting not only the title, *One Dimensional Man* (1964), from Herbert Marcuse, but also his classic analysis of the conflation of state's and capital's needs with personal needs that serves to block from view any alternatives to capitalism. Ferguson argues that to be true to its own nature, queer politics should put aside economic interests that leave behind, when they do not exploit, people belonging to racial and ethnic minorities, trans folks, and many women. He presents Stonewall as a rallying cry because he believes current activists, who recall its multidimensional roots, can recreate its intersectional coalitions.

But the assumption, that a similar conjuncture of radical activism could be as effective now as it was in 1969, turns Stonewall into an ideal. In *One Dimensional Queer*, Stonewall is a flattering mirror that will reflect our moment if we can overcome the one-dimensionality of queer politics today. If, for Ferguson, Stonewall is a hortatory touchstone to be accessed from "both sides now," to borrow a line from Joni Mitchell, so that the politically rightward drift of the intervening decades can be overcome, for Johnson the similarities between before and after Stonewall normalize and make more continuous that which Ferguson depicts as a radical rupture.

In *Buying Gay*, Johnson discloses in the pre-Stonewall homophile networks of mid-century America the differences between radical and sexual politics whose divorce post-Stonewall Ferguson decries. Though "gay power" is now remembered as a slogan for queer liberation, two years before Stonewall, Johnson observes, it was the name of a column in *Vector*—a magazine published by San Francisco's Society for Individual Rights—that featured information about its advertisers (234). Before Stonewall, Johnson asserts, "gay power" was understood predominantly as gay economic power.

If it seems far-fetched to posit a single point of origin for the slogan "gay power," Johnson's research nonetheless supports Ferguson's argument that the desire to achieve a more equitable world through commercial interests helped to splinter the liberation movement politically. Observing that gay and lesbian ownership and management of more inclusive businesses were goals gay liberationists shared with the Black Nationalist, Black Power, and feminist movements (235), Johnson exposes to view, but from a different angle, the racial and class prejudices that Ferguson ascribes to the insufficiently anticapitalist, antiracist, and anticolonialist strands of queer liberation. He describes the peculiar reversal of fortune experienced by the physique entrepreneurs: before Stonewall, they had fostered gay community and leveraged political power in the face of government censorship and social discrimination; after Stonewall, they came to be depicted as the purveyors of exploitative sexual imagery that could foster gay self-hate.

As Johnson painstakingly points out, although the physique entrepreneurs were mainly white, the magazines' consumers were varied along racial as well as class lines. He documents among them Glenn Carrington, a Howard University graduate and Harlem-based physique fan who photographed his friends and fellow weight lifters in physique-inspired poses, and a lower-class white man named Michael Denneny from working-class Pawtucket, Rhode Island. Although some men of color complained about the lack of models of color in letters to the magazines, Johnson sees here evidence that they were already regular customers (16). The very first number of photographer Bob Mizer's *Physique Pictorial* (1951) featured black models. Johnson depicts Mizer's sensitivity to racial politics in the analogies he drew in editorials between the police persecution of physique photographers (for obscenity) and that of people of color (for anything); but Johnson also points out that the magazine's "All Negro Album" could be considered a segregation of sorts (15). In Johnson's account, physique culture could provide more racially integrated possibilities than did many gay bars of the 1950s, even if racial mixing occurred along virtual and imaginative rather than actual physical lines.

Ferguson and Johnson each see the relations among class, politics, and sexuality very differently: Ferguson would establish for *queer* an originary anti-capitalism, while Johnson traces the spark of the liberation movement to the gay communities sponsored by the bourgeois physique entrepreneurs. As their use of the terms *queer* and *gay* suggest, they treat different populations at different points in time and from different perspectives, yet both address the difficulties of achieving coherent political action within identity-based movements. Both move before-and-after Stonewall to harness its power to explain the changes it enabled. Johnson's historical account is linear and chronological; Ferguson reaches back over the intervening decades to reanimate in the present the energies he ascribes to Stonewall. Yet for both, Stonewall is a contained event whose preconditions and consequences can be adduced to enrich our understanding of what it was. For Davidson, by contrast, Stonewall leaves tangible marks on how we understand both the past and the present. In his title, *Categorically Famous*, *category* is not a noun but a modifier. It thereby acquires the flexibility to track the contributions Baldwin, Sontag, and Vidal made to the gay and lesbian liberation movement even though they did not "come out" in the current sense of the term.

If Baldwin, Sontag, and Vidal belonged to any single category, it was to that of the famous. With this perception, Davidson zeroes in on their status as exceptional. But each also used various strategies for a self-exceptionalizing that he brings sharply into focus through the lens of celebrity. Each was admired as a public figure and none of them was disqualified when his or her homosexuality came widely to be known. Even if they were each ambivalent, and differently so, about the public acknowledgment of their homosexuality, they each helped to shape the conception of homosexuals as an oppressed minority rather than as individuals with a psychological problem.

Rather than treat homosexuality as a subject in essays or autobiographical writing, Baldwin relegated it to novelistic representation. As Davidson explains, sexuality, for Baldwin, was a private matter, and the novel was the genre of private matters; moreover, positive gay self-affirmation and self-definition were to be accomplished alone or in a couple. The possibility of reading the white male lovers of *Giovanni's Room* (1956) as Baldwin's displaced sexual confession makes a transracial politics of sexuality imaginable, though Baldwin resisted seeing sexuality in collective, political terms. Nevertheless, Davidson reads the scene in Washington Square Park in *Another Country* (1962), in which Eric and Ellis walk by two "glittering, loud-talking fairies" (64), as a kind of recognition scene in which Baldwin registers the public emergence of gay collectivity as a potential liberated and liberatory force (63). Davidson thus grasps Baldwin's contributions to the conditions of possibility for gay liberation even though he never endorsed homosexuality as the grounds upon which to organize politically.

Sontag linked sexuality and liberty most famously in her celebration of the erotics of art in *Against Interpretation* (1966). But the impersonality of her writing, her understanding of style, and her style of stardom mitigate against seeing her as an advocate for gay and lesbian liberation in any simple way. She only publically acknowledged her own sexual preferences in 2000 and did so preemptively when the unauthorized biography by Carl Rollyson and Lisa Paddock was about to appear (76). Sontag both disavowed that she cultivated publicity and discussed her attachment to and admiration of others' stardom. In the dialectic of hiddenness and visibility in Sontag's work and self-presentation, Davidson discerns in her management of the constraints of gender and perverse sexuality the cues that allowed her to be recognized and embraced by her queer fans before 2000.

Observing Sontag's oscillating accounts of sexual pleasure as alternately political and apolitical, or quasi-aesthetic (121), Davidson explains that her contributions to the counterculture—camp and other styles of radical will—were less political than cultural. But he also sees that the cultural politics of the 1960s could energize political action, as "the widely promoted imperative to do one's own thing, culturally and sexually, helped to supercharge the gay liberationist impulse" (121). Indeed, Davidson shows that celebrity mediated the relations between politics and culture in all three of the figures he treats and helps us to see that it may well do so in general.

Sontag was the last of the old print-based New York intellectuals, whose home base was the *Partisan Review*, and the first of a new breed of intellectual celebrities who could discuss popular and underground culture alongside high theory in television-ready sound bites. Davidson locates his discussion of Sontag between those of Baldwin and Vidal, thereby attuning his argument about the proto-visibility of all three to the vicissitudes of publicity as it was being reshaped by new screen media and the new youth culture. Baldwin's lack of interest in sexuality as a collective basis for political organizing reflected not only his superordinate commitment to race but also, perhaps, a residual resistance to the culturalization of politics embodied by Sontag. Born one year later than Baldwin in 1925, Vidal exhibited a similar insistence on keeping politics separate from culture, though both men were equally willing to put cultural eloquence to political ends. Both traversed both realms, but culture and politics remained more distinct for them than they did for Sontag, who, born almost a decade later in 1933, was formed by, as much as she contributed to, their fuller hybridization.

Vidal may be more readily and publicly affiliated with gay liberation than the other two figures in Davidson's book, especially with the publication of *Myra Breckinridge* in 1968, the same year that William F. Buckley called him queer on national TV, but he also explicitly repudiated homosexuality as an identity. In the essays of *Sexually Speaking: Collected Sex Writings 1960–1998* (1999), Vidal repeatedly asserted the naturalness of same-sex desire and spelled out his position that homosexuality describes behavior rather than identity. Having published a gay novel, *The City and the Pillar*, in 1948 did not prevent him from running for political office twice, first as a Democratic candidate for Congress in New York State's 29th district in 1960 and then in the Democratic primary for Senate in California in 1982. As Davidson brings out, celebrity is critical to Vidal's navigation of the open secret of his homosexuality.

Vidal exploited being both an insider and an outsider, and it is hard not to see his homosexuality as offering him the leverage to play one off the other and to occupy both sides of this binary in turn. Born into a political family with elite privileges, Vidal joined the Navy instead of going to Harvard; he remained an autodidact who flashed his knowledge of the classical world alongside gossip about the Kennedys' Camelot and the Hollywood backlots. His celebrity derived from his capacity to glamorize this double status, and Davidson acutely tunes in to the undercurrent of embarrassment that runs beneath it.

In the Buckley episode, in particular, he discerns the importance of embarrassment, an affect often overlooked or considered to be minor in critical treatments of shame. Embarrassment assumes an audience, real or imagined; it thereby can toggle between openness and the closet before the transformation of shame into gay pride that Stonewall accomplished. Davidson sees in Vidal's public performances of the embarrassment of male homosexuality "part of the prehistory of the politics of gay pride, even if that prototypical pride was sometimes shot through with embarrassment" (173).

Davidson observes the striking contrast between the proto-visible homosexuality of Baldwin, Sontag, and Vidal and the mandatory visibility of all (first world) contemporary LGBTQ people that falls disproportionately hard on the shoulders of celebrities. This difference prompts him to reflect on the relationship between sexuality and "mediatization" within the politics of representation more generally. As he astutely observes, "sexuality cannot meaningfully be said to precede mediatization. Media helps make sexual identities public, meaningful, and political rather than simply appropriating them, distorting them, marketing them" (178), and this is as true for ordinary people as it is for celebrities. Liberation, like any political gain, does not lie beyond media in some utopian domain. Davidson is therefore unwilling either naively to celebrate the achievement of visibility as a goal in and of itself or to abandon the vibrant promise of sexual liberation linked to the project of coming out, of which Foucauldian-influenced queer theory and critical theory skeptical of surveillance have been wary. For Davidson, the achievements of gay and lesbian liberation and queer identities remain ongoing projects.

With his sophisticated treatment of the intersections of celebrity, media, and sexuality, Davidson underscores the differently networked mediascape in which we currently operate and marks out the value of history for political understanding without treating the archive as a transparent window onto what has happened. Just as Sharon Marcus (2019), in her analysis of the differences made by media to celebrity since the nineteenth century, holds constant the joint work of the celebrity, the fans, and the media, so Davidson maintains the persistence of sexual identity to highlight the new meanings of the production of outness in celebrity culture. Both scholars can vividly capture the shifting meanings and ranges of feeling associated with celebrity and sexual identity as structures because they do not assume their objects of study to be fully knowable or monolithically produced.

Davidson, like Ferguson and Johnson, recuperates Stonewall's goals, but unlike either of them, he does not assume that since Stonewall, we know what it might mean to achieve them. No historical event can predict the future even if it both shapes the present and reshapes the past. Disorienting Stonewall as both event and concept is required to revitalize the ongoing project of sexual liberation. In making us rethink what has happened both before and since Stonewall, Davidson prompts us to return with fresh eyes to Eve Kosofsky Sedgwick's analysis in *Epistemology of the Closet* (1990) of the co-constructed regimes of knowledge and sexuality. He asks us to consider what mediatization brings to what it is we think we know when we know someone else's or even our own sexual orientation.

References

Marcus, Sharon. 2019. *The Drama of Celebrity*. Princeton, NJ: Princeton University Press.

Rivera, Sylvia. 2013. "Queens in Exile: The Forgotten Ones." In *Street Transvestite Action Revolutionaries: Survival, Revolt, and Queer Antagonist Struggle*, 40–55. New York: Untorelli. untorellipress.noblogs.org/files/2011/12/STAR.pdf.

Sedgwick, Eve Kosofsky. 1990. *Epistemology of the Closet*. Durham, NC: Duke University Press.

Vidal, Gore. 1948. *The City and the Pillar*. New York: Dutton.

Vidal, Gore. 1999. *Sexually Speaking: Collected Sex Writings 1960–1998*. Pittsburgh, PA: Cleis.

"THAT IS NOT WHAT I MEANT AT ALL"

Andrew J. Counter

Someone: The Pragmatics of Misfit Sexualities, from Colette to Hervé Guibert
Michael Lucey
Chicago: University of Chicago Press, 2019. 344 pp.

Someone may be thought of as the third in a trilogy of books on sexuality in French literature by Michael Lucey, following *The Misfit of the Family: Balzac and the Social Forms of Sexuality* (2003) and *Never Say I: Sexuality in the First Person in Colette, Gide and Proust* (2006). One of the most distinguished scholars in sexuality studies and certainly the most interesting in French studies, Lucey has developed a set of conceptual preoccupations and a methodological approach that are at once idiosyncratic—to use one of his own key terms—and compelling. Methodologically, this has meant an approach to literature *as* sociological that is inseparable from a Bourdieusian sociological approach *to* literature, with a constant back-and-forth between the type of sociological thinking carried out in novels, on the one hand, and the external dynamics of the literary field, on the other. Conceptually, Lucey's work has been attentive to the "misfit," meaning at once the individual whose sense of self does not fit well with available categories, vocabularies, and representations, as well as the fact and typically uncomfortable experience of that lack of fit. In all three books, Lucey shows that "sexual identity" cannot be thought separately from social positioning, and vice versa, and the feeling of "misfit" often occurs at the intersection of the two. *Someone*'s productive innovation is to draw on the linguistic field of pragmatics, which studies the context-dependent, nonsemantic, nonexplicit functions of utterances. "Misfit sexualities," Lucey contends, "sometimes exist in language and culture without ever being *explicitly* talked about or *explicitly* laid claim to," but "leave other kinds of traces, more pragmatic than semantic ones" (9). Not so much loves that dare not speak their name as loves that have no name to speak, they are subject to an "ongoing denotational incapacity" (138); they are at their most visible in those moments when characters, narrators, or writers "try out" a bit of conventional sexual nomenclature yet feel—with anger, curiosity, or regret—that, in T. S. Eliot's words, "That is not what I meant at all. / That is not it, at all."

As a pioneering work of sexuality studies, *Someone* resonates with Eve Kosofsky Sedgwick's account (in *Epistemology of the Closet* and "Jane Austen and the Masturbating Girl") of the obscuring effect of the homo/hetero binarism on the "lush plurality of . . . sexual identities" that preceded its rise to dominance (Sedgwick 1994: 117). Lucey's book—though he would certainly not put it so conventionally—suggests that an equally consequential effect of the homo/hetero binarism is to eclipse the plurality of potential sexualities that exist contemporaneously with it—or better yet, *under* it, as one lives "under" a regime. In a disarmingly simple moment, indeed, Lucey explains that the point of his project is "simply to notice other sexualities that it is often all too easy to miss" (9). Intriguingly, these "other sexualities" often have something to do with a problematic bisexuality, though again, to put it like this is reductive in comparison to the subtlety of the social and sexual positionings Lucey brings to light. Nevertheless, in an early moment Lucey does note that "speech about bisexuality . . . often highlights the fact that there are forms of cultural knowledge about sexuality that cannot be done justice by taxonomies" (12), and in many chapters the deviation from a presumed or established monosexuality turns out to be more difficult to pull off, especially over time, than casual talk of "fluidity" would appear to suggest. Still, one of the most fascinating instances of a "misfit" studied here is when Hervé Guibert, a figure whose sexual identity most of us would consider straightforwardly nameable, says of the word *homosexuality*: "That's a word that for me has never felt like it had any relationship to me, which seems strange because obviously it does" (203). The clash between a way of feeling and an irrefragable but alien knowledge ("obviously") is symptomatic of the misfit's predicament, and Lucey's analysis of what Guibert means here supplies one of the most moving parts of the book.

For alongside its thought-provoking and finely sociological account of misfit sexualities in and around the literary field of twentieth-century France, *Someone* is also a finely crafted and aesthetically sensitive work of literary criticism. In chapters dealing with Colette, Jean Genet, Simone de Beauvoir, Marguerite Duras, Violette Leduc, Guibert, and Robert Pinget, Lucey combines brilliant exegetical close readings with rigorous contextualization and coaxingly reveals these often extraordinary works in all their unboundedness. Central to this effect is Lucey's own analytic voice, which has an unusually important role to play here. After all, Lucey is dealing with two corpuses that are, in their different ways, stylistically particular: on the one hand, his primary corpus, composed of works by broadly avant-garde French prose writers, some of whom are famous for their stylistic exquisiteness, and most of whom are in some way "difficult"; on the other, a secondary corpus drawn from sociology and pragmatics whose dominant idiom is jargon laden, even at times rebarbative. Between these two idioms, Lucey's own voice emerges as, in the best sense of the word, straightforward: unpretentious, patient, nuanced to be sure, but seeking nuance in clarity rather than convolution. The result is a book that requires attention, certainly, but rewards that attention so richly that the process of reading it feels like a working together, rather than a working against. I do not often find this in academic books; I do not believe many of us do. A book that creates that feeling is a precious thing indeed. *Someone* is one of those books.

Andrew J. Counter is associate professor of French at the University of Oxford.

References

Sedgwick, Eve Kosofsky. 1994. "Jane Austen and the Masturbating Girl." In *Tendencies*, 109–29. Durham, NC: Duke University Press.

DOI 10.1215/10642684-8776932

BAREBACKING'S LATE STYLE

Douglas Dowland

Raw: PrEP, Pedagogy, and the Politics of Barebacking
Ricky Varghese, ed.
Regina, Saskatchewan: University of Regina Press, 2019. xi + 302 pp.

It has been a decade since the publication of Tim Dean's *Unlimited Intimacy: Reflections on the Subculture of Barebacking* (2009). Much has changed: in the United States, same-sex marriage is now legal nationwide, and globally, the development of pre-exposure prophylaxis has made sex "safer"—at least for those who can afford it. Ricky Varghese's *Raw* tracks how the discourse of condomless anal intercourse has changed accordingly. What emerges from this well-edited collection is an awareness that barebacking is no longer scandalous, in either academic circles or public life. When once it was dangerous, now it is merely decadent. Today it theorizes as much as it titillates. Reading *Raw*, one cannot help but think that the discourse of barebacking has entered what critics such as Theodor Adorno would call a "late style," the moment when a discourse refuses a "harmonious synthesis" and productively resides between its culmination and its diminution (1937 [2002]: 567). Adorno described it as the "catching fire" that occurs when an artist nears the limit of their aesthetic (567). Thus, it is telling that Varghese organizes his collection's eleven essays into four categories of "limits": biopolitical, bodily, pornographic, and psychoanalytical and pedagogical. If there is something new about barebacking, it is that it is no longer new. Indeed, there's something about the concept that is just about to fall apart.

As Varghese notes in his introduction, "the writers of the various chapters can't agree on what barebacking is and what it is not" (xxi). To him, this disagreement shows the increasing elasticity of the term as much as it does a discursive uneasiness. We may not be able to define it, in part, because barebacking, much like other discourses of pleasure, "feels excised from the conversation as though it is either in excess of the conversation or a vestigial part of it" (xxv). Jonathan A. Allan's essay takes this issue up graphically, noting how contemporary medical discourse on circumcision plays on tropes of "primitivism and infection" to paradoxically assert that the removal of the foreskin is the health equivalent of a "natural condom" that will protect the circumcised from sexually transmitted diseases (5). Octavio R. González traces how the discourse of pre-exposure prophylaxis still relies on narratives of contagion: through the figure of the "Truvada whore," "we invoke a new villain, with a new name, but the song remains the same" (33). And Frank G. Karioris explores how barebacking is no longer exclusive to homosexual sex: examining tensions about condom use in heterosexual pornography, he notes that a binary of "virility/virality" encourages critics to ask "Who is risking what? Who takes on the risk?" (52–53). What we find in these essays is how the recycling of stock tropes and stories attempts to constrain a practice that has become unruly.

Raw's essays on bodily and pornographic limits engage with substances that are far from vestigial. Rinaldo Walcott explores the figure of "Black cum-joy" and reminds us that "Black sex is usually conceived as a dangerous kind of sexual activity" entrenched with "talk of death" (74–75). Elliot Evans, through the writing of Monique Wittig and Patrick Califia, outlines how blood is a "bridge between the self and other" that "can only be crossed in the structure of fantasy" (111). Evangelos Tziallas writes that with the rise of amateur and quasi-amateur pornography, both viewer expectation and demand has changed such that pornographic "narrative is seen as the purview of commercial safe sex productions, and a hindrance to the real" (123). Paul Morris and Susanna Paasonen explore how the pleasure depicted in bareback MSM pornography produces a queer optimism through an "unreasonable" politics (146). Yet the visual display of barebacking is certainly not as liberating as they suggest. The culmination of barebacking, the ejaculation of semen into the anal canal—what Gareth Longstaff in his essay calls the "splutter" of bareback porn—is more the attempt to "connect, implicate, and haunt the other . . . a queer attempt to renegotiate" what goes unseen (176). Ironically, Diego Semerene notes, "The excreting of the sperm, so often associated with breeding fantasies, functions as liquid evidence of the absence of breeding" (207). In these essays, we see how bodily substances, as metonyms of intimacy, can never fully capture the prolix meanings of barebacking, and if anything, conspire to limit it.

How these many limits connect to sex pedagogy is the focus of the book's final essays. Adam J. Greteman writes of how "Queer work in education cannot simply rely on the work of identity, despite the political salience and necessity of identity politics" (225). And Christien Garcia, examining sex education, notes that "the establishing of barebacking's significance as a queer foil to the restrictive confines of normative gay sex ultimately feeds the disciplinary production of sexual identity" (237). Tim Dean's lively afterword continues the discussion. He notes how "raw sex has come to occupy both sides of a basic conceptual opposition . . . that is, as sanitized, normative inside culture rather than an outlaw to it" (259). He continues to insist, as I noted in my review of *Unlimited Intimacy* in *GLQ* a decade ago, that barebacking is a subculture (Dean 2009: 209). Yet to see barebacking as a subculture today is to rely on a dangerous form of nostalgia for a different political, viral, and pharmacological order: only then could "raw" be radical, both utopian (unfettered connection) and dystopian (potential immolation) simultaneously. One worries, ultimately, that Dean's definition of barebacking is anchored in a rhetoric of authenticity that Varghese and his collection's contributors are right to avoid.

Yet Dean has a point. The discourse of barebacking has changed, and it can only look back on its younger days. As Varghese's collection commendably shows, though, that's the art of any late style, one that evades the critical rules and nostrums, challenges our theories, and eventually, whether we like it or not, goes on without us.

Douglas Dowland is associate professor of English at Ohio Northern University.

References

Adorno, Theodor. [1937] 2002. "Late Style in Beethoven." In *Essays on Music*, translated by Susan Gillespie, 564–68. Berkeley: University of California Press.

Dean, Tim. 2009. *Unlimited Intimacy: Reflections on the Subculture of Barebacking*. Chicago: University of Chicago Press.

Dowland, Douglas. 2009. "(Un)Limited Intimacy." *GLQ* 17, no. 1: 208–10.

DOI 10.1215/10642684-8776946

SEXUAL KNOWLEDGE AND THE FORMATION
OF CHINESE MODERNITY

Séagh Kehoe

After Eunuchs: Science, Medicine, and the Transformation
of Sex in Modern China
Howard Chiang
New York: Columbia University Press, 2018. xvii + 219 pp.

Across various epochs of Chinese history, eunuchs held considerable political power and control over the state. During the late Qing, however, at a time when China came to be regarded as the "sick man of Asia" and as a "castrated civilization," the figure of the eunuch became synonymous with ideas of backwardness, oppression, and national shame. While many studies of Chinese eunuchs have tended to center on questions of their political life and institutional power, *After Eunuchs*, written by Howard Chiang, takes a very different approach.

After Eunuchs provides a fascinating, persuasive analysis of the demise of castration in the late nineteenth and early twentieth centuries as a pivotal turning point in the production of sexual knowledge in modern China. Tracing the genealogical relationship between eunuchs in Imperial China and a famous case of the "first" Chinese transsexual in 1950s Taiwan, *After Eunuchs* examines the ways in which the translations of Western sexological texts, concepts, and methodologies provided the essential historical conditions under which new ideas about sex, sexuality, and the body as objects of empirical knowledge would emerge in China. Meticulously researched and drawing on an impressive range of sources across medical science, the popular press, and personal biographies, the book shows how Western biomedicine shaped and transformed sexual knowledge in China during the first half of the twentieth century, as well as how the rise of these new structures of knowledge and new regimes of conceptualization illuminate broader concerns about China's political and national sovereignty during this era.

Over the course of five convincingly argued chapters, Chiang identifies the visual realm, the subjectivity of human desire, and the malleability of the body as the three key coordinates in an "epistemic nexus" (13) around which new ideas about sex began to take shape during the Republican era. In chapter 1, "China

Castrated," he explores the historical production of knowledge about castration, revisiting the history of eunuchs through the prism of their bodily experiences. Chiang offers incisive analysis on the formation of a textual and visual archive by Western doctors, figures of the imperial court, and eunuchs themselves that documented the methods of castration in China and provides important reflections on how assumptions about masculinity, resulting from confusion over the nature and consequences of castration, have impacted the narration of the historical experience of eunuchs.

Chapter 2, "Vital Visions," investigates how new visual techniques of medical representation made it possible for sex to become an object of empirical knowledge. Here, Chiang explores how Republican-era biologists and popular science writers translated the epistemological authority of natural science through the production of anatomical, morphological, and chromosomal images of sexual difference. He also provides a detailed account of the role of the image in the gradual spread of the Western biological epistemology of sex from elite medical circles to vernacular popular culture.

Chapter 3, "Deciphering Desire," examines the emergence of sexuality. Centering on the intellectual journeys of Zhang Jingsheng and Pan Guangdan, two key figures in Republican-era Chinese sexology, Chiang analyzes the vibrant discussions about sexual desire that took place across scientific and popular literature, revealing how the concept of homosexuality emerged as a meaningful discursive point of referencing human difference and cultural identity in early twentieth-century China.

The next chapter, "Mercurial Matter," describes how Chinese sexologists came to embrace the plausibility of sex transformation and the related discourses of "sex change" that developed across mass circulation media from the 1920s to the 1940s. Taking as a case study the highly sensationalized media reportage of the story of Yao Jinping and his female-to-male transformation in mid-1930s Shanghai, Chiang shows how the 1940s represented a new era where people began to consider sex reassignment opportunities through the possibility of surgical intervention.

The final chapter focuses on the growing frequency of sex-change-related discussions in Chinese-speaking communities in the immediate post–WWII era. Detailing the media characterizations of an intersex soldier in Tainan named Xie Jianshun and the publicity that followed her transition, Chiang analyzes how the mass circulation press introduced Xie's story to readers across Taiwan. In doing so, he considers shifting understandings of transsexuality, as well as the role of medical science and its evolving relation to the popular press in mid-twentieth-century

Sinophone culture. Here, Chiang neatly locates these stories of corporeal variance within the convergence of culture and geopolitics in early Cold War Taiwan.

This book makes a rich and imaginative contribution to discussions about the psychobiological understandings of sex and sexuality that emerged in China in the nineteenth and twentieth centuries. By showing the significance of those decades between empire and communism as an important interlude in China's modern history, Chiang's work challenges the view that only after the economic reforms in the 1970s did China open up to the global circulation of ideas regarding sex, sexuality, and the body. Drawing attention to sexual knowledge as a significant element in the formulation of Chinese modernity, his book also provides an engaging, innovative analysis of the gradual displacement of colonial modernity by Sinophone articulations from the middle of the twentieth century onward. *After Eunuchs* will be of great interest and importance to scholars working on the history of science and medicine, sex and sexuality, and Chinese modernity.

Séagh Kehoe is postdoctoral research and teaching fellow at the Contemporary China Centre, University of Westminster.

DOI 10.1215/10642684-8776960

WHAT STICKS

Summer Kim Lee

Sticky Rice: A Politics of Intraracial Desire
Cynthia Wu
Philadelphia: Temple University Press, 2018. viii + 208 pp.

Sticky rice is a term for gay Asian American men who prefer sexual encounters with other gay Asian American men. In *Sticky Rice: A Politics of Intraracial Desire*, Cynthia Wu takes up the term to consider how intraracial same-sex desire between Asian-raced men in canonical Asian American literary texts become potential alternative sites for intraracial reconciliation, affiliation, and solidarity. Sticky rice speaks to a sticky politics—sticky in that one prefers "sticking with one's own" (23), but also sticky in that the intimacies with which Wu is preoccupied throughout the book are unwieldy and irreducible to modern gay male identity.

In each of the book's five chapters, Wu identifies dyads of male characters, and while some engage in sexual acts with one another, for others, sex acts are coded through figurative language. Wu reads against the grain of these texts, tracing unremarkable, elusive expressions of queer desire that reside in metaphor and innuendo, in what goes beyond plot or prose. These sticky encounters between Asian-raced men offer another means of confronting the irresolvable heterogeneity of an intraracial Asian American coalitional politics shaped by ethnic and class differences.

For instance, in the third chapter, on Philip Kan Gotanda's play *Yankee Dawg You Die* (1988), Wu addresses the friendship of its two main characters: Vincent Chang, an older, well-established closeted gay Chinese American actor, and Bradley Yamashita, a younger, emerging straight Japanese American actor. Each represents a different generation with clashing opinions on the political stakes of playing racist stereotypical roles. Meanwhile, the fourth chapter considers the relationships between working-class Chinese immigrant men in the bachelor societies of turn-of-the-century Chinatowns through H. T. Tsiang's novel *And China Has Hands* (1937). The novel follows Wong Wan-Lee, a Chinese immigrant laundry owner in 1930s New York, whose passing encounters with men become sites of intraracial class solidarity. In her readings, Wu locates queer desire and intimacy as alternative political horizons over and against assimilation, inclusion, and competition.

The first chapter on John Okada's novel *No-No Boy* (1957) considers the relationship of the protagonist Ichiro Yamada, released from prison for refusing WWII military service, and Kenji Kanno, a disabled veteran. Through Kenji and Ichiro, the tense relation between Japanese American draft resisters and veterans in the wake of Japanese American internment is given breathing room. Wu writes that these men's homoerotic relation hinges upon an "unanswerable question" Ichiro poses to Kenji: "Would you trade places with me?" (33). As Eve Kosofsky Sedgwick (1990: 61) has pointed out, queer desire renders such a question unanswerable; an identification *as* and *with* someone is nondistinguishable from the desire *for* someone. One cannot be separate from the other, unless a woman gets involved, which is what happens in *No-No Boy* and throughout the pages of *Sticky Rice*.

When Kenji begins a relationship with a Nisei woman named Emi, he asks Ichiro to have sex with her on his behalf because of his disability. However, Ichiro is not able to. Rather than interpret the stalled sex act as Ichiro's failure to align himself with heteromasculinity, Wu writes, "Ichiro and Kenji exhibit an attraction for each other that not only makes women irrelevant but also regards their very presence as a barrier to the intimacy they forge" (37). Wu recognizes that there is no corresponding same-sex desire for women in the text. The radical potential of queer desires, queer intimacies, and non-normative, racialized masculinities are contingent upon the irrelevance of women, wherein women can exist only in a heterosexual relation to men. As a "barrier," women must be excluded, left behind, and condemned to bring the boys together in solidarity.

One is led to ask, then, whether the relations Wu moves through are pairings or in fact, as Sedgwick (1985) has written, the triangulations of male homosocial desire upon which heteropatriarchy is built. Wu states that given how Asian-raced men have historically been excluded from white heteronormative mas-culinities, the relation between Asian-raced men must be approached differently, and instead might gesture toward the radical potentiality of intraracial male same-sex desire. But Wu's textual analysis throughout the book remains ambivalent about the radicality of such male same-sex desires. This ambivalence is the most striking, prescient part of the book. In the second and fifth chapters, Wu homes in on the significance of men's homoerotic relations with one another at the same time that she works to complicate and loosen such homosocial bonds as the sole site of Asian Americans' internal conflicts and divisions, thereby lending these texts to a queer *and* feminist critique.

The second chapter takes up Monique Truong's novel *The Book of Salt* (2003), narrated by Bình, a Vietnamese cook working for Gertrude Stein and Alice B. Toklas in Paris during the French Indochina regime. Unlike in *No-No Boy*, Bình acts on his intraracial desire with a mysterious man on a bridge, who is assumed to be a young Ho Chi Minh. Their desire is on the other side of "a chasm [that] divides Stein and Toklas's white, partnered, domestic, class-privileged lesbi-anism and Bình's economic and sexual transience" (54). Through a transhistorical understanding of the Vietnamese diaspora, Bình represents the South Vietnam-ese refugee displaced from his home while the man on the bridge represents the Socialist Republic of Vietnam. As such, their contact becomes a means of healing the split between the Vietnamese diaspora and the Vietnamese state.

The final, fifth chapter grapples with Lois-Ann Yamanaka's controversial novel *Blu's Hanging* (1997), which takes place in late-1960s and early 1970s Hawai'i and has been criticized for reinforcing Hawai'i's long-standing inequali-ties among East Asians, Filipinos, Native Hawaiians, and other Pacific Islanders. Unlike in other chapters, here Wu identifies the same-sex dyad as that of two East

Asian women, Big Sis and Sandi. Yet their relationship, coded as lesbian, valorizes East Asian middle-class domestic respectability over and against the irredeemable deviance of a working-class Filipino man named Paolo Reyes, whose portrayal as a rapist and child molester bars him from any sympathy or respectability.

What is interesting to note in this final chapter is Wu's observation that these two women's privileged "cozy domesticity" (145) mirrors that of Stein and Toklas in *The Book of Salt*. This brings up other questions. For why is it that lesbian desire is often conflated and therefore complicit with the comforts of middle-class respectability found in the home? Lesbianism gets confined to the gendered, classed, private realm of domesticity, becoming a place where scholars and writers base their critiques of middle-class respectability. In this context, what happens to the stickiness of lesbians' and, more broadly, queer women's desire?

Early in the book, Wu touches on queer and feminist Asian Americanist critiques of the heteropatriarchal forms of cultural nationalism in Asian American activism throughout the 1960s and '70s. She also cites art and scholarship on and by gay Asian men, whose pleasure decenters the desirability of gay white masculinity (Fung 1991; Nguyen 2014). But amid this crucial work remains an absence. As Gayatri Gopinath (2005) has written, the heteromasculinist, reproductive configurations of racial, ethnic, and national difference so often render the desire of the queer Asian diasporic woman an impossibility. Similarly, Vivian Huang (2018) has asked, "Whither Asian American lesbian feminism?"

Wu's attentive interventions within the canon of Asian American literature productively bring us to question the perceived political inefficacy and irrelevance of queer Asian American women and what passes between them. Throughout the book, queer Asian American women, their desires, and their shared social worlds hover, leading one to wonder what it is between men that sticks and what it is between women that does not.

Summer Kim Lee is assistant professor of English at University of California, Los Angeles.

References

Fung, Richard. 1991. "Looking For My Penis: The Eroticized Asian in Gay Video Porn." In *How Do I Look? Queer Film and Video*, edited by Bad Object-Choices, 145–68. Seattle: Bay Press.

Gopinath, Gayatri. 2005. *Impossible Desires: Queer Diasporas and South Asian Public Cultures*. Durham, NC: Duke University Press.

Huang, Vivian L. 2018. "Whither Asian American Lesbian Feminism?" Presented at the National Women's Studies Association Annual Conference, Atlanta, GA, November 9.

Nguyen, Tan Hoang. 2014. *View from the Bottom: Asian American Masculinity and Sexual Representation*. Durham, NC: Duke University Press.

Sedgwick, Eve Kosofsky. 1985. *Between Men: English Literature and Male Homosocial Desire*. New York: Columbia University Press.

Sedgwick, Eve Kosofsky. 1990. *Epistemology of the Closet*. Berkeley: University of California Press.

DOI 10.1215/10642684-8776974

SEXUAL INTIMACIES IN LITERATURES OF THE BLACK DIASPORA

Taiwo Adetunji Osinubi

Frottage: Frictions of Intimacy across the Black Diaspora
Keguro Macharia
New York: New York University Press, 2019. ix + 224 pp.

Keguro Macharia's book examines the centrality of sexuality to the elaborations of Black identities in the work of Frantz Fanon, Rene Maran, Jomo Kenyatta, and Claude McKay. Analyzing texts from the early to the mid-twentieth century, Macharia argues that these authors register, in their works, responses to colonial modernity's sexual antinomies in Africa and the Americas. Knitting together gender and sexuality studies, comparative literature, and postcolonial literary studies, he examines erotic constellations in contexts of slavery, ethnonationalism, colonialism, migration, and labor history. *Frottage* refers to both the method of artistic production and the sexual act; Macharia defines *frottage* as a "meeting place . . . between what Raymond Williams terms the residual and the emergent" (88). There is great potential in this definition: it captures the overlaps and productive interactions between historical and contemporary sexual practices and identities. Macharia's interpretations are imaginative, bold, and speculative. Frequently espousing a "yes, but . . . " position, he deploys contradictions productively.

Chapter 1 reads the dialogic relationship between Frantz Fanon and Audre Lorde as an example of frottage. For Macharia, despite Fanon's animosity toward queer subjects, his construction of desire as subjectivity remains a valuable analytic because his psychoanalytic language lends a force and a potency to desire that exceed his own purview. Macharia thus scrutinizes the conditions that facilitate or hinder desire's articulation and recognition in Fanon's writing. To reanimate Fanon, Macharia turns to Lorde's charge to make feelings and the erotic grounds for making history and knowledge. Some scholars have read Fanon and Lorde together (Whitney 2016; Thompson 2015), but Macharia's turn to the *erotic* explicitly—rather than, say, affect or phenomenology—crystallizes a valuable pedagogical insight. Where Fanon negates the erotic, Lorde embraces and redeploys it against the abnegation of blackness and queerness.

Next, Macharia interprets Rene Maran's ethnographic novel, *Batouala*, as a speculative work that imagines an "erotic diversity" disrupted by colonialism and insists that Maran captures the emergence of new sexual appetites (69). Maran, he concludes, articulates erotic freedoms and sex-gender instabilities that critics overlook. In reading *Batouala* against Edward Blyden's *African Life and Customs* (1908), Macharia compares two accounts of African sexuality written by men from the diaspora. Comparing an ethnographic novel to an ethnography seems right, but I daresay a novel by an African woman would offer more effective contrast and bring a woman's perspective to this study of "erotic diversity." As it stands, this book favors male authors.

Turning to Jomo Kenyatta's disavowal of Gikuyu homosexuality in *Facing Mount Kenya*, Macharia explains the document as a response to anthropological claims on African sexualities and to colonial regulations of African intimacy. Kenyatta, he argues, maps an unchanging sex-gender system that disregards women's agency and absents homosexuality from Gikuyu life in response to situated constraints. In repudiating homosexuality, Kenyatta mimics the gesture of his doctoral supervisor, Bronisław Malinowski, who disavows any local practice of homosexuality in his anthropology of the Trobriands (100). However, because Malinowski also ascribes homosexuality to cultural deracination, Kenyatta sought stability in Gikuyu ethnicity as a bulwark against his own deracination as a Europeanized African.

This historicization of Kenyatta's queer evacuation reveals Macharia's method at its best. It illustrates how discourses about sexuality in postcolonial contexts emerge from competitions to reestablish sex-gender constellations altered by colonialism. Kenyatta deemed homosexuality impossible because Gikuyu youth were already permitted sexual experimentation through the practice of *ngweko*, a form of supervised cuddling and frottage among unmarried adolescents that provided sexual instruction and release. The frottage in *ngweko* provides Macharia's conceptual metaphor. Misunderstood by missionaries and left behind with modernization, ngweko conveys the disruptions, displacements, and transformations to which African and Black diaspora sexuality studies responds.

Chapter 4 explores the connections between labor history and sexual antinomies in Claude McKay's *Banana Bottom* and his poetry collection *Constab Ballads*. Analyzing the poetry volume, Macharia argues that McKay formulates queer-feminist critiques of colonial sexual regimes in his early poems about life in the Jamaican constabulary force. McKay's elaborations of women's voices and "queer gender play" constitute a "reparative project" that expresses feminist sympathies while also depicting "the social and affective possibilities available in undesirable sociohistorical situations" (143, 149). Similarly, his vernacular aesthetics uses linguistic diversity to world antinomian sensibilities.

Macharia locates in *Banana Bottom* a "queer labor" that uses intimate life as the primary grounds for negotiating the pressures of class and community. Historically, subversions of colonial marriage practices constituted an antinomian practice in Jamaica. That history resonates in McKay's use of a transgressive marriage to ground a lineage of wayward subjects whose development and experiences question and confound sexual epistemologies espoused by different characters. The novel's sundry sexual epistemologies reflect the multiple knowledges naming Black sexualities. Thus, disagreeing with critics, Macharia insists that the marriage that ends the novel is not the conservative, generic gesture of the bildungsroman. Rather, it fortifies antinomian sensibilities and folds them into the marriage plot. Macharia's study of McKay will interest readers of the latter's recently discovered and now published manuscript, *Romance in Marseille* (2020), as it features the erotic sensibilities Macharia characterizes as frottage.

This book would achieve greater impact if Macharia's archive extended to contemporary narratives or covered existing iterations of intimacy studies and theorizations of friction as cultural contact. I also wish the author had engaged with women as writers and with extant studies of wayward genealogies such as Alys Weinbaum's *Wayward Reproductions* (2004). Macharia says he does not write back to a predominantly white queer studies, but engagements with it would fortify his interventions. Having said that, I realize he writes as an independent scholar in Nairobi and his African positioning suggests a critical orientation. Macharia's innovative concept metaphor for infinite contact zone erotics will influence studies of sexuality in contemporary transnational African writing and African diaspora literature generally.

Frottage is invested with a generative retrospective sensibility that sutures twenty-first-century debates about intimacy and sexuality to its early twentieth-century archive. Macharia implicitly asks readers to consider how the fluidity and plurality of sexual figurations created within colonial modernity are being rearticulated now. His attention to African languages and Caribbean vernacular traditions point to the dangers of erotic or sexual monolingualism; his deployments of frottage enrich Black diaspora studies and Africanist scholarship. *Frottage* creates possibilities for conceptual rethinking and cultural analyses that attend to the unpredictable productivities of all forms of intimacy in literatures of the African diaspora. I recommend it to scholars of queer and gender studies, comparative literature, African literatures, and diaspora studies.

Taiwo Adetunji Osinubi is associate professor of English studies at Western University, Canada.

References

McKay, Claude. 2020. *Romance in Marseille*. New York: Penguin.

Thompson, Vanessa Eileen. 2015. "'The Master's Tools Will Never Dismantle the Master's House': Frantz Fanon on Whiteness in Hegemonic Social Philosophy." In *On Whiteness*, edited by Nicky Falkof and Oliver Cashman-Brown, 285–92. Oxford: Inter-Disciplinary Press.

Weinbaum, Alys Eve. 2004. *Wayward Reproductions: Genealogies of Race and Nation in Transatlantic Modern Thought*. Durham, NC: Duke University Press.

Whitney, Shiloh. 2016. "Affective Indigestion: Lorde, Fanon, and Gutierrez-Rodriguez on Race and Affective Labor." *Journal of Speculative Philosophy* 30, no. 3: 278–91.

DOI 10.1215/10642684-8776988

BRIDGES OF LIGHT

Roberto Strongman

Ezili's Mirrors: Imagining Black Queer Genders
Omise'eke Natasha Tinsley
Durham, NC: Duke University Press, 2018. xi + 264 pp.

> Written in a language of gaps, fissures, and queer assemblage,
> *Ezili's Mirrors* is a difficult text. And while black women are often
> discouraged from claiming our right to be difficult, I'm asking you to
> wade through this recalcitrant disjointedness to bear witness to the
> difficulty of piecing together divinity from fragments of queer life.
> (23–24)

Ezili's Mirrors signals the firm establishment of a new collective critical voice in Africana religions' scholarship whose plurivocality and etherealness invoke and harness the power of trance, thus contesting received notions of objectivity in the long view of Caribbean ethnography. Tinsley's newest offering is indeed difficult, in the most productive sense of the term. Its structural complexity will frustrate readers who cannot easily surrender positivistic expectations. Those who trust her will be rewarded as she guides us through an intricate maze of snapshots and soundbites that cohere in a colorful, artistic pastiche of queer black spiritualities.

The introduction presents us with the most Vodou content in its commentaries on the aesthetic possibilities of Ezili, the goddess whose avatars represent various aspects of archetypal Haitian femininity: Freda, the sensual; Dantò, the mother; and Jewouj, the fierce. Liminally, Tinsley travels between Haiti and Louisiana to reclaim the queerness of Marie Laveau, the Vodou Queen of New Orleans. Chapter 1 has New York City as a backdrop for a discussion of the Haitian Vodou diaspora and a most important discussion of Janet Collins, the first black prima ballerina of a major US dance company. Chapter 2 interprets the 2002 queer Vodou documentary film *Des hommes et des dieux / Of Men and Gods* by Anne Lescot and Laurence Magloire in counterpoint to the 1980s New York City ballroom culture. Chapter 3 is devoted to BDSM. The way in which black women's power fosters the construction of the paradigmatic black dominatrix leads to a close reading of Mary Ellen Pleasant, a black entrepreneur, originally from New Orleans, who in the nineteenth century used her fortune to fund the abolitionist movement in California. Chapter 4 is a bacchanalia of contemporary black female singers and femme identity through the figure of the sacred mermaid Lasirenn. What goes up must come down, hence the acknowledgment of drugs and recovery in this chapter. The conclusion is the after-party of the book, where its fullest revelation comes into view: as Tinsley discloses and honors her Cherokee and Geeche family origins as well as her black female academic mentors through a kind of "theoretical polyamory" (187), we come to understand the book as what I would term a *queer kunstlerroman*, a portrait of the artist as a young femme.

Each of the four chapters, the introduction, and the conclusion are connected by "bridges": six short personal interludes, often in a stream-of-consciousness rhetorical style that reflect and project upon the material of the larger chapters. In this sense, these interludes are luminous iterations of the mirrors invoked in the title. Structurally, the bridges suture and cushion Tinsley's sequined textual quilt as a Vodou *drapò*, demanding some critical distance to perceive the brightly lit patterns that might be invisible to the uninitiated who frustratingly search for meaning in minutia. Further, the rhizomic structure of the bridges displays the archipelagic and therefore meta-Caribbean aspect of the work, making visible links with Tinsley's previous work on West-Indian female same-sex desire, *Thiefing Sugar: Eroticism between Women in Caribbean Literature* (2010).

The fragmentation of the narrative into three different fonts is dizzying, evoking the transpersonal experience of possession that so distinguishes Haitian Vodou. Each of the fonts articulates different voices that the author employs to talk to academic, spiritual, and ancestral personae. *Ezili's Mirrors* creates a thin space in which the metaphysical cannot be disassociated from the physical, for the mystical multiplicity of Being is already inscripted into the living plurivocalic fabric of the text.

The work is deeply postmodern, without needing to cite Lyotard, Barthes, Jameson, and Co., for the work is postmodern in the way in which Afro-diasporic cultural practices such as jazz, in spite of the difficulties it brought Adorno, have always been postmodern. The first lines of the acknowledgments, as well as those of the first and last bridges, tell us to "read this book like song" (ix, 1, 169). And musical it is! The author makes us relive many of her youthful revelries, introducing us to her "party girls" (133) and various music stars: Alicia Keys, Whitney Houston, Rihanna, and Prince. Beyoncé figures prominently here and in her next book: *Beyoncé in Formation: Remixing Black Feminism* (2018). In the recycling of song lyrics, the text evidences a strong element of *sampling*, whereby the author virtuously and iconoclastically blurs the lines between writer and DJ. The postmodernism achieved in the redeployment of the musical quote also has a visual counterpoint: the labyrinthine design of the book relies on the filmic technique of cross-cutting or parallel editing, in which the writer-as-cineaste switches back and forth between two or more scenes, often creating a sense of disorientation or parallel action. Furthering the visual richness of the text and muddling the distinctions between the personal and the public, we are introduced to her relatives through photos, giving the academic treatise the quality of a family album. Tinsley's book is not so much about centers as it is about making connections. It is neither a quest nor a linear thread; it is the song that animates ideas.

Ezili's Mirrors is part and parcel of a body of contemporary scholarship that makes visible the non-heteronormative potential of Afro-diasporic religions: Randy Conner and David Sparks' *Queering Creole Spiritual Traditions* (2004), J. Lorand Matory's *Black Atlantic Religion* (2005), Aisha M. Beliso-De Jesús's *Electric Santería* (2015), Elizabeth Pérez's *Religion in the Kitchen* (2016), and Solimar Otero's *Archives of Conjure* (2020), as well as my own *Queering Black Atlantic Religions* (2019). Tinsley's *Ezili's Mirrors* makes an original contribution to the development of the field of queer black religion and to the ways in which this scholarship has a wider, public impact in the representation and self-understanding of queer-of-color spiritual communities whose members experience lives of constant fragmentation and recomposition daily, globally.

Roberto Strongman is associate professor in the Department of Black Studies at the University of California, Santa Barbara.

References

Beliso-De Jesús, Aisha M. 2015. *Electric Santería: Racial and Sexual Assemblages of Transnational Religion.* New York: Columbia University Press.

Conner, Randy, and David Sparks. 2004. *Queering Creole Spiritual Traditions: Lesbian, Gay, Bisexual, and Transgender Participation in African-Inspired Traditions in the Americas.* New York: Harrington Park Press.

Lescot, Anne, and Laurence Magloire. 2002. *Des hommes et des dieux / Of Men and Gods.* Paris: Collectif 2004 Images.

Matory, J. Lorand. 2005. *Black Atlantic Religion: Tradition, Transnationalism, and Matriarchy in the Afro-Brazilian Candomble.* Princeton, NJ: Princeton University Press.

Otero, Solimar. 2020. *Archives of Conjure: Stories of the Dead in Afrolatinx Cultures.* New York: Columbia University Press.

Pérez, Elizabeth. 2016. *Religion in the Kitchen: Cooking, Talking, and the Making of Black Atlantic Traditions.* New York: New York University Press.

Strongman, Roberto. 2019. *Queering Black Atlantic Religions: Transcorporeality in Candomblé, Santería and Vodou.* Durham, NC: Duke University Press.

Tinsley, Omise'eke Natasha. 2010. *Thiefing Sugar: Eroticism between Women in Caribbean Literature.* Durham, NC: Duke University Press.

Tinsley, Omise'eke Natasha. 2018. *Beyoncé in Formation: Remixing Black Feminism.* Austin: University of Texas Press.

DOI 10.1215/10642684-8777002

About the Contributors

Ashon T. Crawley is associate professor of religious studies and African American studies at the University of Virginia and author of *Blackpentecostal Breath: The Aesthetics of Possibility* (2019), winner of the 2019 Judy Tsou Critical Race Studies Award from the American Musicological Society, and *The Lonely Letters* (2020). He is currently working on a cultural studies, gender, and sexuality history of the Hammond organ and its use in black sacred contexts, a project titled "Made Instrument: Polyphonic Intention." All his work is about alternatives to normative function and form, the practice of otherwise possibility.

Glyn Davis is a reader in screen studies at the University of Edinburgh. His forthcoming publications include "Imagining Queer Europe," a special issue of *Third Text* coedited with Fiona Anderson and Nat Raha; *Queer Print in Europe* (2021), coedited with Laura Guy; *The Richard Dyer Reader* (2021), coedited with Jaap Kooijman; and *The Living End* (A Queer Film Classic) (forthcoming 2022).

Marcie Frank is professor of English at Concordia University in Montreal. She has previously published on Susan Sontag and Gore Vidal. Her most recent book, *The Novel Stage: Narrative Form from the Restoration to Jane Austen*, was published in February 2020.

Shilpa Menon is a PhD student in anthropology at the University of Illinois at Chicago. She works on mobilizations around transgender identity in Kerala, India.

Seth Palmer is an assistant professor of anthropology at Christopher Newport University. His historical-ethnographic scholarship engages religious publics, human-spirit relationalities, transnational rights regimes, and emergent political imaginaries in Madagascar and the broader Western Indian Ocean world. Seth is currently completing a book manuscript that considers the multiscalar entanglements between queer social worldings and spirit mediumship networks both within and beyond the Malagasy northwest.

Vaibhav Saria is an assistant professor at the Department of Gender, Sexuality, and Women's Studies at Simon Fraser University. Their book, *Hijras, Lovers, Brothers: Surviving Sex and Poverty in Rural India*, is forthcoming from Fordham University Press in spring 2021.

David K. Seitz is a critical geographer based in Los Angeles. His research investigates the cultural, political, and affective dimensions of geographic processes including gentrification, immigration, and queer community formation. He is assistant professor of cultural geography in the Department of Humanities, Social Sciences, and the Arts at Harvey Mudd College in Claremont, California, and extended faculty in the Cultural Studies Department at Claremont Graduate University. He is the author of *A House of Prayer for All People: Contesting Citizenship in a Queer Church* (2017) and recent articles in *Antipode* and *Social and Cultural Geography*.

Liza Tom is a PhD candidate in media studies at McGill University. Her research focuses on the role of nongovernmental organizations in the lives of transfeminine communities in Bangalore, India.

Ricky Varghese is a psychotherapist and art writer based in Toronto. He is a candidate in training to become a psychoanalyst at the Toronto Institute of Psychoanalysis and is the inaugural Tanis Doe Postdoctoral Fellow in Gender, Disability, and Social Justice at Ryerson University (2020–22). He is currently working on two monographs, one about suicidality, the ethics of risk/risk-taking, and the death drive, and another about sexual difference and bodily comportment as represented in the socialist realist cinema of Kerala. He is also compiling an edited collection tentatively titled "Sex and the Pandemic."

Alexa Winstanley-Smith is a graduate student in the Department for the Study of Religion at the University of Toronto.

Fan Wu works at the intersection of performance, poetry, and criticism. You can find his writing online at *Baest Journal, Aisle 4,* and *MICE Magazine*.

DOI 10.1215/10642684-8777016

Keep up to date on new scholarship

Issue alerts are a great way to stay current on all the cutting-edge scholarship from your favorite Duke University Press journals. This free service delivers tables of contents directly to your inbox, informing you of the latest groundbreaking work as soon as it is published.

To sign up for issue alerts:

1. Visit **dukeu.press/register** and register for an account. You do not need to provide a customer number.

2. After registering, visit **dukeu.press/alerts**.

3. Go to "Latest Issue Alerts" and click on "Add Alerts."

4. Select as many publications as you would like from the pop-up window and click "Add Alerts."

read.dukeupress.edu/journals

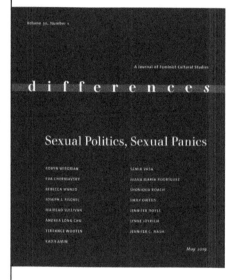

Printed and bound by CPI Group (UK) Ltd, Croydon, CR0 4YY

13/04/2025

14656484-0001